Deliver Us

NORTHWESTERN WORLD CLASSICS

*Northwestern World Classics brings readers
the world's greatest literature. The series features
essential new editions of well-known works,
lesser-known books that merit reconsideration,
and lost classics of fiction, drama, and poetry.
Insightful commentary and compelling new translations
help readers discover the joy of outstanding writing
from all regions of the world.*

Luigi Meneghello

Deliver Us

Translated from the Italian and with
an introduction by Frederika Randall

Northwestern University Press ✦ *Evanston, Illinois*

Northwestern University Press
www.nupress.northwestern.edu

English translation and introduction copyright © 2011 by Frederika Randall. Published 2011 by Northwestern University Press. First published in Italian in 1963 under the title *Libera nos a malo*. Copyright © 1975 by RCS Libri S.p.A.–Milano. All rights reserved.

Printed in the United States of America

10 9 8 7 6 5 4 3 2 1

Library of Congress Cataloging-in-Publication Data

Meneghello, Luigi.
    [Libera nos a malo. English]
    Deliver us / Luigi Meneghello ; translated from the Italian and with an introduction by Frederika Randall.
        p. cm. — (Northwestern world classics)
    "First published in Italian in 1963 under the title Libera nos a malo. Copyright © 1975 by RCS Libri S.p.A.–Milano."
    Includes bibliographical references.
    ISBN 978-0-8101-2742-5 (pbk.)
    1. Meneghello, Luigi—Childhood and youth. 2. Malo (Italy)—Social life and customs. I. Randall, Frederika. II. Title. III. Series: Northwestern world classics.
PQ4873.E4744L513 2011
853.914—dc22

                                                                2011009134

CONTENTS

Translator's Introduction: The Dispatriate   *vii*

Deliver Us   *1*

On Vicentino Usage (Author's Note)   *337*

Appendix A: Important Types of Death   *339*

Appendix B: Matters of Malo   *343*

Appendix C: Toward a Dedication   *345*

Translator's Notes   *347*

TRANSLATOR'S INTRODUCTION:
THE DISPATRIATE

There is no good way to reproduce the sparkling sense/nonsense of *Libera nos a malo,* the title of Luigi Meneghello's first[1] and best-loved book. *"Deliver us from evil":* the well-known phrase, in Latin, comes from the Paternoster, of course, but it also evokes pure childish fun, for Malo is the name of the country town near Vicenza in northeast Italy where Meneghello was born and raised. That *malo* pronounced during the mass set off a chain of associations for a native, not only because it bizarrely summoned up a real place on the local map, but because the vernacular *male* means not just evil but also pain, suffering, illness, and harm, practically the sum total of everything terrible. "Deliver us from *luàme,*" the children prayed: from the dung heap, "the dark splatter of death, the lion's jaws, the bottomless pit." And yet the little town of Malo—the name is a lopped off version of its medieval place name Maladum—was not, we quickly learn, a place synonymous with misery, suffering, or sorrow. There certainly was all that, yes, but also much to laugh about. It seemed that even a place on a map could be impertinent, irreverent.

By turns sharp, amused, ironic, light-handed, and sometimes vigorously rude, Meneghello's memoir is a recollection of childhood in a time and place—rural Italy of the 1920s and 1930s—that was already disappearing when it was published in 1963. Although the events in his story take place less than a century ago, Meneghello describes a world in some ways closer to the peasant Italy of the Middle Ages than to the twenty-first-century urban sprawl that characterizes the region today. Here as elsewhere in Italy in the 1920s, most people still lived in the countryside and worked as farmers or tradesmen. Much of the Veneto countryside was backward and unlettered; most people had probably never even seen a train.[2] All but a few spoke a dialect as their first language, painfully mastering the awkward cadences of standard Italian only when they began to go to school. Malnutrition was still widespread; death was not so far away that children didn't think about it. In a playful appendix, the author lists the real and imagined causes of death for sixty-four types of human beings, animals, and insects as the children understood them.

> Rabbit: Sharp blow.
> War dead: War.

As Meneghello liked to remind people, he was born in a portentous year: 1922, the year of Mussolini's March on Rome. His mother Pia was a schoolteacher; his father Cleto, an auto mechanic who ran a small family hauling and transportation business with his brothers. The shop was across the courtyard from the house, as were the drying sheds for tobacco and the rooms where silkworms fattened on mulberry leaves. Ball bearings and inner tube rubber from the mechanic's shop were the raw materials of Luigi's (or Gigi, as he was known throughout his life) childhood toys and games. The creek, the woods, the water hole, the vine rows and the sorghum fields, the manure pit, the garden with its moles and rabbits, its pumpkins, its grasshoppers and its may bugs, were his territory.

It was a territory ruled by hard work, the Church, and Il Duce. Here, as in many other parts of Italy, the Catholic Church exerted a powerful hold on morals and on the popular imagination. The newest element in this universe was Fascism, and it was during the 1920s that the Fascist regime with its noisy propaganda and its promises of virile modernity came to dominate Italian political life, society, and expression. Questioning authority, whether that of the Church, the state, or the family, was not encouraged by anyone. And yet the people of

Malo constituted their own part-archaic, part-modern society, through which the laws and language of the priest and the prefect trickled down only partially and imperfectly. In some ways the town was fiercely controlled from on high; in other ways, it was strangely free.

When Giorgio Bassani, Meneghello's editor at Feltrinelli, decided to publish *Libera nos a malo* in 1963, the book was termed a *romanzo,* a story, or a novel. In part, perhaps, that label served the same function as the familiar disclaimer: "any resemblance to real persons, living or dead . . ." It's worthwhile, however, keeping in mind that Italians do not divide their literature by the same fiction–nonfiction dichotomy that we have in English, but rather by a distinction between *romanzo,* a story, and *saggio,* an essay. A *romanzo* may be fictive, but it is not always so. And as Meneghello's most perceptive readers have observed, this is not a work of fiction.[3] It's a work of memory that implicitly acknowledges the pitfalls of memory—lapses, anachronisms, exaggerations, mistakes—but it is told with the utmost respect for the truth. When the author recounts how he and his oldest friends return to Malo as adults and meet up to repeat, revise, and embellish the tales of their childhood adventures, he's letting us know that, yes, he may have altered a name or polished a story, but not in any way that would make it untrue. Often, he consulted his friends and family to confront his memory of an event with that of the others. For this was not just a personal memoir but a collective one, an account of his people and their world told in an original mix of linguistics, folklore, and ethnographic speculation.

Yet certainly this is also a *romanzo*—if not a novel. The literary invention lies in the shaping and the telling: the wit, the pitch-perfect tone, the effortless shifts from elevated language to small-town wisecracking, the pared-down brevity of his tales, the deft portraits of people sketched in just a few words, the dizzyingly rapid juxtapositions, the way, in the end, his narrative traces the arc of a human life. As a writer, "I enjoyed myself defying the conventions of the *romanzo* current in Italy at the time," Meneghello said. He wanted to achieve both "the spell cast by a story" and "the bite of an unconventional essay."[4] His "motley" themes ranged from the world of childhood to that of the adults, from the precepts of religion to those of the secular society, from poverty and misery to eros, love, and its variations. Closest of all to his heart were reflections on language and the experience of using multiple languages: one spoken, one written, and one only vaguely apprehended in church during the mass.

In the beginning there was Vicentino, the dialect of Vicenza, or more specifically, of "upper Vicenza province," Meneghello's native tongue and the vernacular of Malo. Then came standard Italian, the language that children learned to read and write and eventually to speak in elementary school, including that strained and bellicose variation that was the language of the Fascist regime. And finally there was Latin, the Church Latin of Paternoster and of *i sequèri*, as Aunt Lena called the prayers she muttered in order to recover lost thimbles and needles. (*Liceo*-educated Italians like Meneghello himself were of course fluent in Latin by age eighteen.) Unlike other writers in the distinguished current of twentieth-century Italian dialect literature—Carlo Emilio Gadda, Pier Paolo Pasolini—Meneghello doesn't so much shape characters and sentiments out of dialect as use dialect expressions to illustrate the mindsets and thought processes of his native environment. And although his experiences are very particular to his time and place, the theme Meneghello draws from them is universal: the ways that childhood's words, places, things, and people shape the very contours of thought itself.

"Languages," he later wrote, "become extinct more slowly than things do, and so there is a lapse of time in which things that have disappeared are still accessible as ghosts that linger in the language."[5] Old words for old things: shards of a genuinely different world that had been superseded, and which Meneghello made it his business to try to reconstruct. Words could be eloquent archeological remains in other ways too. Some friends of his kept a mynah bird in their house in Montecchio, not far from Malo. This bird had a way of calling for Renzo, one of the sons in the family, "he would say Rènsooo . . . with that particular cadence they had in the Agno valley." Over the years, the people of Montecchio had long ceased to say "Renzo" that way, but "the mynah bird had registered those tones and reproduced them to perfection—and even a little more than perfectly." And so, Meneghello wrote, "peasant civilization, so rapidly laid to rest in this vigorous little town, lives on in this Vicentinophone bird."[6]

"I'd like to think," he wrote elsewhere, "that languages are fastened together by links, at least in terms of their comprehensibility." If all the generations of the Meneghello forebears ("about sixty back to the Romans . . . several thousands back to pithecanthropus") were brought together, they'd make up a town about the size of Malo, he reckoned. "And thus we could each plausibly say something to the person next to us and watch as it passed on to the next person until finally, down at the end of the line, the ape Meneghello laughed—or we shook a fist at him."[7]

Libera nos a malo begins with the clatter of rain falling on a roof, a sound that conjures up the beginning of consciousness itself in the aural space of childhood, a town so small that God himself has his place in the sky just above the rooftops. Next, tiny Gigi is bouncing on his parents' bed, singing Fascist songs whose bloodthirsty, macho imagery he doesn't quite understand but rather likes. We soon learn about the more immediate violence in Malo, the diseases and epidemics that kill his classmates. We learn about their sexual education too, and how they confess their misdeeds to the priest so as not to be saddled with too many Hail Marys. Everyone was a believer; a man who did not believe in God did not belong to the realm of "normal" people. The priest, however, might be mocked in secret, especially if he drank too much or otherwise transgressed. Yet no adult he knew in Malo ever opposed the Fascists, Meneghello observed; no child of his acquaintance ever missed one of the parades organized by the party. "I never heard a single political criticism of those rallies, not even a crude one, although there were other criticisms, of the type 'all these parades sure are a pain in the backside . . .'" "Not only were there no anti-Fascist leaders in town, there was not even one educated person who opposed Fascism."[8] Like just about every other boy of his time Gigi was a member of the Fascist youth organization, a *balilla*. His father and his uncles had been Mussolini enthusiasts right after the Great War, and growing up inside the Fascist system, Gigi was schooled in the logic and the rhetoric of the regime. In 1940, when he was eighteen years old, he won a national prize in the government-sponsored Littoriali della Cultura e dell'Arte in the category of "Fascist Doctrine,"[9] a fact that, later, can't have been very easy for him to mention publicly, as he does in *Libera nos a malo*. Subsequently, he was one of relatively few Italians to ponder and write about his education under Fascism, in his book *Fiori Italiani*.[10]

In January 1943 Meneghello was called up and served with the Alpine troops until the armistice in September of that year, although he was never sent into combat. When the army was disbanded without orders on September 8, he and his fellow soldiers walked and hitched across Italy from Tarquinia on the Tyrhennian coast to his home in the northeast. On his return, he met up with an anti-Fascist friend and political mentor he had known in two years of study at the University of Padua, and joined a band of partisans hiding in the hills north of Vicenza, soon becoming commander of a detachment of the anti-Fascist Partito d'Azione. In *I piccoli maestri* (translated in English in a substantially revised version as *The Outlaws* and made into a 1998 film directed by Daniele Luchetti)[11] he gives a vivid, moving, antiheroic account of those eighteen months "up in the hills" fighting the Germans and the Fascists. In his introduction to the English edition, he wrote that the book grew out of "the moral shock . . . of coming to understand what Fascism was after having been brought up a Fascist, and the feeling during the civil war that it would be unpardonable to survive it."[12]

In 1947 he applied for and got a scholarship from the British Council to carry out a year's research at the University of Reading. He stayed on, founding the Department of Italian Studies and remaining as a professor until he retired in 1980. "At a certain moment, I felt Italy didn't want me anymore," he told Marco Paolini and Carlo Mazzacurati in the documentary film they made about him in 2006.[13] The Partito d'Azione, the progressive political party he was deeply involved with, had failed miserably to gain popular consensus after the war.[14] In 1948, already at home in his new home in Reading, Meneghello married Katia Bleier, a Hungarian-speaking Jew from the Yugoslav region of Vojvodina who had been interned in Auschwitz in 1944 and had survived the 1945 death march to Germany and Bergen Belsen. She would be his lifelong companion.

Katia, when the German camp was liberated in April 1945, had made her way back to Zagreb, where her family had lived for a time before the war. There was no one left (her parents and other relatives had been selected for death on arrival at Auschwitz), and so she decided to join her sister who had survived the war in Malo (having had the relative good fortune to be deported by the Italians, not the Germans). Unable to get a visa, Katia simply stole across the Yugoslav-Italian border.[15] Meneghello tells the story of their first meeting in the summer of 1946, among a group of friends in Malo. At the end of the evening, he walked her home, and they stood and looked up at the starry sky.

"Miss Bleier, do you believe in God?" he asked her.

"No," she replied.

"I'm going to marry this one," Gigi said to himself.[16]

The previous year, when the twenty-five-year-old Meneghello had gone for his interview with the representatives of the British Council, his command of English was more theoretical than practical. "I will can" was his phrase for the future tense of "to be able," although he was proud of the fact that "at the same time I was able to make a meticulous distinction between I will can and I shall can."[17] The late Cambridge don and literary critic Frank Kermode taught at Reading in those early days, when for a year, Katia was in a sanatorium being treated for tuberculosis. Gigi, left to look after the household, "wasn't cut out for domestic life," said Kermode, who recalled the "daredevil and disastrous meals" Meneghello prepared for his friends.[18] His grandiose-sounding research project, an "investigation of contemporary British culture" was the object of mirth on the part of his more practical-minded British colleagues, and after a while he abandoned it. His "encounter with the culture of the English, and the shock of their language," not only shaped his thought and his writing, but also his adult interests.

And there is no doubt that Meneghello's ear for the humorous tonality and pithy precision of Malo dialect, for the comical and wretched sides of Veneto rural life, was sharpened by his exposure to another language and another culture. In time, he would translate passages of *Hamlet* and *Macbeth* into Vicentino, convinced that the vigorous orality of Elizabethan English had more in common with his childhood dialect than with stiff, written Italian. Meneghello would spend most of his life in England, living, after retirement, a stone's throw from the British Museum in London and visiting Italy frequently. In the very last years of his life he returned to live in Thiene, a small town near where he was born. He died in 2007.

Libera nos a malo is not an easy book to translate, particularly into a language like English, which has no real counterpart to the Vicentino dialect that is such an important element in Meneghello's portrait of his native place. Together with Venetian, Paduan, Veronese, and so forth, Vicentino (the dialect of Vicenza) belongs to the Venetan idiom, that spoken in the Veneto region. Venetan is one of the twelve or so main idioms spoken in Italy (Romance languages all, they include Lombard, Piedmontese, Neapolitan, Sardinian, and Sicilian, among others). All are distinct from literary Italian, which is based on Tuscan, the language in which Dante wrote *La Divina Commedia* in the early fourteenth century, thus effectively setting the future standard for written Italian. Although these regional dialects are all derived from Latin, they are different enough as to be partly unintelligible across linguistic borders. In his several works devoted to the vernacular, Meneghello explains in some detail how even Vicentino itself varied from town to town, so that the farmers who lived in the countryside outside Malo used quite a different lexicon and even different syntax from the townsfolk, although they might live within miles of one another.

The problem for a translator is not so much to render the meaning of dialect expressions, which are usually made clear by the author, as to convey the experience of having two different kinds of languages at one's disposal: an exclusively oral, richly expressive local idiom, and a more learned, less flexible, standard national language. For better or worse, today's English does not discriminate all that much between the spoken and the written registers, and when new vernacular expressions arise they are often quickly absorbed into the written language. "People ought to be warned," writes Meneghello in *Libera nos a malo*, "that Italian is not a spoken language." But fifty years later, the Italian language has evolved so radically in the age of mass media that it has become for all intents and purposes a national spoken language, even though sizeable numbers of Italians also speak a dialect in the family. And in parts of twenty-first-century Italy, as among various minorities around Europe, the use of the local dialect has lately become a heated matter of pride and identity—and sometimes a rationale for poisonous intolerance of the others—in ways that Meneghello, when he recorded Malo speech in 1963, did not anticipate.

Today, *Libera nos a malo* is considered one of the classics of twentieth-century Italian literature. Perhaps one reason it has not been translated into English previously was that Meneghello always stood to one side of the postwar Italian literary mainstream, and not only because he lived abroad. His tone was ironic, his language chiseled; working every day in contact with the English language, he also seemed to absorb some of its concrete, empirical, antitheoretical philosophical underpinnings. For that matter, he said, he had always felt "quite at odds with the false profundity and the fake, artificial obscurity of a part, unfortunately dominant, among [Italian] writers and critics." Neither a Christian Democrat nor a Communist, he did not belong to either of postwar Italy's "two Churches." Neither a neorealist nor an avant-gardist, he did not fit the Italian literary canon of the 1960s either.

He had become, as he termed himself in a 1993 book, a "dispatriate." Not an expatriate, nor an exile longing for his native ways and language. Not an emigrant driven by economic forces, or a refugee fleeing political chaos. But someone who had taken a good, hard look at his mother culture even as he was adopting a second one. Someone who had moved abroad not only physically, but psychologically and intellectually, who had "taken apart and remade his cultural and national identity," as fellow writer Domenico Starnone said of him.[19] Dispatriation: it was an experience that is probably even more pertinent and more eloquent today than it was when Meneghello first used the term, in this era when so many of us are now crossing and recrossing the borders of our globe.

✦

I would like to thank the PEN Translation Fund for making this project possible. Heartfelt thanks also to Professor Giulio Lepschy for his generous assistance with various matters of translation. All errors are exclusively my own.

Notes

1. *Libera nos a malo* was followed by eighteen other works of narrative and nonfiction.

2. Luigi Meneghello, *Maredè, maredè* (Milan: RCS Rizzoli, 1991), 205.

3. Far from fictionalizing, Meneghello was loath to put down anything that was not "demonstrably true," writes Domenico Starnone, "Il nocciolo solare dell'esperienza," in *Luigi Meneghello: Opere scelte*, selected works edited and with an introduction by Giulio Lepschy (Milan: Mondadori-I Meridiani, 2006), xxx.

4. Luigi Meneghello, *La materia di Reading* (Milan: RCS Libri, 1997), 64.

5. Luigi Meneghello, *Jura* (Milan: RCS Libri, 2003), 203.

6. Meneghello, *Maredè, maredè*, 213.

7. Luigi Meneghello, *Pomo pero* (Milan: Rizzoli, 1974–2006), 12.

8. Ibid., 35–36.

9. Between 1934 and 1940, the Fascists held competitions among promising young intellectuals and artists, called the Littoriali della Cultura e dell'Arte.

10. Luigi Meneghello, *Fiori Italiani* (Milan: Rizzoli, 1976).

11. Luigi Meneghello, *I piccoli maestri* (Milan: Feltrinelli, 1964). Translated by Raleigh Trevelyan as *The Outlaws* (London: Michael Joseph, 1967).

12. *Luigi Meneghello, Opere scelte*, 1670. The "civil war" refers to the period 1943–45, when partisans battled against the Fascists and Nazi occupiers.

13. Marco Paolini and Carlo Mazzacurati, *Ritratti: Luigi Meneghello*, documentary film with text (Rome: Fandango Libri, 2006).

14. See Luigi Meneghello, *Bau-sète* (Milan: Rizzoli, 1988), for an account of his growing disillusion with postwar Italian politics.

15. Francesca Caputo, "Cronologia," in *Luigi Meneghello, Opere scelte,* cxxiii.

16. Ibid., cxxiv.

17. Luigi Meneghello, *Il dispatrio* (Milan: Rizzoli, 1993), 9–10.

18. Franco Marcoaldi, "Così è finita la mia Inghilterra," *La Repubblica,* December 29, 2009.

19. Starnone, "Il nocciolo solare dell'esperienza," xxv.

Deliver Us

Chapter 1

IN THE BEGINNING there was a thunderstorm.

We arrived last night and as always, they gave us the big room to sleep in, the room where I was born. When the thunder started booming and the rain began to clatter down, I felt I was home once again. The rain came in scrolls, in waves that drew back with a hissing noise: these were well-known sounds, village sounds. Everything here is animated, alive, perhaps because the distances are small and fixed, as in a theater. The clatter was in the courtyards nearby, the thunder up there above the roofs, and I could tell just by listening that a bit higher up was the usual God who made the thunderstorms when we were children—he, too, a personage of the town. Sounds and sensations are heightened here: it must be a question of scale, of internal proportions. The shape of the sounds and of these thoughts (but they are really the same thing) for a moment seem more real than life itself, yet there's no way to bring them back with words.

✦

The surface is bouncy, it's impossible to stay upright so you try to keep your balance by hopping around. You sink and come up with your legs wide. It's fun! They're laughing and I laugh too, and trying to keep my balance, I sing: *Alarmi siàn fas-*

sisti, abasso i cumunisti! Beware, we are Fascists; down with the Communists!

What a good time we're having! Falling down, standing up—they're almost the same thing. The world is golden this morning. *E noi del fassio siàn i conponenti.* And we of the Fascio, we are the Members. Good words, these. Who knows what they're supposed to mean?

Years will go by before I'm able to separate the morning dance on Papà and Mamma's high bed from the laughing and the words. And yet even then I did understand the intoxicating promise:

> *La lota sosterén fina la morte*
> *e pugneremo sempre forte forte*
> *finché ci resti un po' di sangue in core.*

> We'll keep on battling unto death
> we'll run them through, we'll run them through,
> so long as blood flows through our veins.

I pictured that "run them through" as stabbing blows delivered from on high.

There were songs full of tormenting thoughts, with delicious dangers lurking behind:

> *Mama non piangere se c'è l'avansata*
> *tuo figlio è forte e vincere sapràn*
> *assiuga il pianto dela fidansata*
> *perché lassalto si vince o si muor.*

> Mother, don't cry when we attack
> your son is strong and we must win
> so dry the tears of his beloved
> up there we either win—or die.

And then there were the instructions for the Arditi, the shock troops:

Scavalca i monti, divora il piano
Pugnal frài denti, le bonbe a mano.

Mount the hills, devour the plain
dagger in your teeth, grenade in hand.

I loved the terrifying syntax of the last two lines, my childish mind racing ahead, hearing the way the words were compressed: *With a dagger between your teeth and a hand grenade in hand.* The Arditi were like that, they were mounters of hills charging with a high hurdler's lift, they were devourers of the plain, the *piano.* The piano looked black and shiny to me, lit up by two table lamps, it too supplied with a sparkling mouthful of keys. The Ardito in his gray-green uniform and black beret would first mount it on the run, then whirl around and begin to gnaw on it.

Vibralani! Mane al petto!
Si defonda di vertù:
Freni Italia al gagliardetto
e nei freni ti sei tu.

Vibralani! Hands on heart!
For valor is at hand:
Should Italy brake before the flag,
That bridle be you too.

"That bridle be you too" didn't confuse us, nor those "hands on heart." The order was to bring them up to the chest horizontally, in an unknown, austere form of salute. It was a signal used among the *Vibralani,* to whom, as we sang, we felt that in some way we too belonged as honorary members.

The brakes that were bridling Italy were, according to Bruno, those of our Fiat Tipo-Due automobile, external brakes on the right-hand running board behind the staff for the triangle-shaped pennant. That was where Italy, with her turreted crown and her long white dressing gown, stood.

✦

Here in town, when I was a child, there was a God who lived in church, in the great space above the high altar where as a matter of fact you could see his stirring portrait among the rays of gilded wood, way up high. He was old but pretty spry—certainly not as old as Saint Joseph—and very stern. He was incredibly shrewd, and so they called him omniscient, and in fact he knew everything, and what was worse, he saw everything. He was also omnipotent, but not absolutely, otherwise he would have gone around with a pair of scissors cutting the willies off all the boys who did bad things. The little willy-wielders were his mortal enemies, and if he could have, he would have punished them like that, but thank God he couldn't.

✦

"I'll take Norma, you take Carla."

And I would take Carla, but in secret I would long for Norma. Oh, the paleness of Norma! That white, white skin on the inside of her thighs. Carla was a nice-looking little girl, curly-haired and well made, dark skinned and warm hearted, but Norma was a soft snare into which I yearned to tumble.

However, I would take Carla, because the idea of contradicting Piareto never even crossed my mind. I was the youngest (and Norma, who was all of, maybe, six, the eldest), and it wasn't up to me to choose. And anyway I wouldn't have liked to offend Carla, who was so nice and willing.

And so, in the thickness of the vines halfway down the garden, in a shadowy underwater-green place, having put down our wooden swords between the rows, we did bad things with our women squatting in the dirt.

With Norma, however, I spent an hour of heavenly rapture in the big room above the cellar, behind an object of which I remember only the basic outlines—a nest, a screen, a roof—of what was probably the stump of a car body. There were leather-upholstered surfaces and little silk curtains mounted with a spring mechanism and a pull to draw them down over the glassless windows. It was one of the many bizarre pieces of junk up there: we had shoved it up on top of the drums and sawhorses, way up high at the level of a window that looked out over the fields. It was like being in a drawing room without any wall behind, but nicely sheltered from the world.

We would climb up there to play, Norma and I, and without any preliminaries, without a word spoken, I was admitted for a brief time to the communion of the waxen skin, to the sweet junction where it grew ever paler.

Impueracts! For the First Communion, which we made in church when we were seven, they dressed us up like little sailors, and the little girls in white. When my turn came and I had to go and confess for the first time, I knew very well that I must also confess all the bad things, years and years, a whole lifetime's worth of bad things. But how, in what words? It was Norma who taught me. She had made her Communion a few years before, and for a while she had stayed away from the forbidden games, engaging in them only rarely and with reluctance.

One day when I was peeing against the wall of the manure pit, Norma came by with her wire basket on her way to the vegetable garden to pick some salad. I turned toward her and began to urge her over with a festive wave of what I was holding in my little hand. But Norma was indignant.

"Away from me, you *mas'cio,* you pig!" she said. "Don't forget that soon you'll be taking Communion!"

Later we were down in the courtyard (night was falling) and walking up and down, Norma confided in me the formula to use for confession. I learned it off by heart and when the time came I repeated it to the priest: *Impueracts*. Adults and priests knew all about the game we thought of as so secret—and this was how they called it.

✦

Every father confessor had his own style and his own preferences, and so you would try to select one or the other according to the sins of the week. The main practical issue was penance, for the sanctions could vary rather widely. The older ones among us would advise the less expert: "This time you're better off with Bocaléti, but in the evening, however." Bocaléti was Don Emanuele, and in the evening he was more benevolent.

Don Antonio was lean and mild, he had a tremulous voice and wore an air of such innocence and modesty that we truly hated having to go and bother him with our wickedness. Yet when you did go to him confession turned out to be pretty easy.

You would talk about your disobediences, your tardy arrivals at mass, your fights, your swearwords; you would expand on certain generic sins like envy and vanity to gain time, always thinking about that crucial matter. Finally Don Antonio would pose the Question, which he alone in Malo asked in this particular way.

"Have you transgressed . . . against Holy Modesty?"

This was his personal expression for *impueracts,* and his delicate formula made possible equally delicate replies. And so between gentlemen, without the least need for improper language, as neatly as if filling out a questionnaire ("How many times?" "Nine." "Alone or with others?" "With others." "With others meaning boys, or with others meaning girls?" "With girls.") you would find you had finished confession and were absolved with just three *hailmarys* to say. And then off you went to enjoy a couple of hours of complete innocence, with the delicious certainty that you would have, should it happen tonight, a good death and join the chorus of angels.

✦

Anzoléti, little angels, that's how we called our tiny fellow townsfolk who had lived too short a time not to be promoted angels at the very moment they breathed their last breath on earth.

"Who's the bell for?"

"Didn't you hear? It's an *anzoléto.*"

Every other day the bell rang for them. They were dying like flies, and in the cruelest months, in the great days of summer, we lived in a cloud of little angels on their way to heaven, so thick that it blocked out the sun.

Roberto, the first Roberto of my Aunt Lena (from whom the other one, of today, takes his name) died at the age of four from gastroenteritis. When I understood that he was dying I went through a few hours of utter agony. The nursemaid had taken me to my grandmother's house, and there, in the entry hall among the green plants by the window, the idea that Roberto was going to die hit me in waves. I was all cut up, it was hell; but I felt neither terror nor loss. What was happening simply seemed intolerable: there was me, and soon there would be this thing, and I didn't believe the two could coexist. I was seven years old, and these existential agonies were among the worst I can ever remember.

Now the thing had arrived, Roberto was dead, an object the color of wax that looked like Roberto was lying on the divan in my aunt's dining room. It was already easier for me to bear, in this padded air of mourning that stifled all sounds. It was as if the death of dearly beloved persons produced, along with all the rest, a sliver of comfort. The big door at the front entrance was closed, and in our house and in that of my aunt, to one side of the entrance and the other, all was silent. Even Bruno and our cousin Mamo, who were the same age as Roberto, weren't making noise. They were in the entryway, peeking through the keyhole into my aunt's dining room. There, they took each other by the hands and on tiptoe, danced a little dance of joy. Raising their eyebrows as if they couldn't believe their good fortune, they whispered a joyful incantation in a low voice, "Dead! Dead!"

The day they buried him, a high-backed armchair decorated with brass tacks was carried out into the garden, and the good women took Aunt Lena out there. From our garden you could hear the tolling of the church bells, there was a big pine at the bottom, it was August. Aunt Lena dressed in black had fallen back in the preposterous armchair that stood between the dahlia beds and the vegetable patch. The good women were muttering.

It was that moment that funeral ceremonies are designed to set apart very distinctly, that irrational moment of anguish, in which anguish no longer has any meaning and seems to be just a midsummer reverie accompanied by the comments of hens and beetles, in an eddy of space between here and the hills, translucent, punctured by the *gong* of the bells.

✦

When the epidemics came the courtyard was invaded by a team of wily, nasty little men wearing hoods and red cloaks, who tossed out splashes of infected mortar. The mortar caused a case of ringworm that would lead to death within minutes, and this was the epidemic. The courtyard was crowded with little coffins made of pinewood, in the process of being built. When they were full they were piled up at the end against Aunt Lena's wall. In order to be saved you had to reach the pump, that is, the water spigot on the outside wall of Aunt Lena's kitchen, and immediately hose down the infected parts. And so why did we ever move away from the pump? Why did we run around among the little men continually risking our lives between the piles of coffins? We always did so, every two or three months when the epidemic came. When it came I used to dream about it at night, and in fact I don't remember it directly but only through those dreams every two or three months.

A little angel flew away from a courtyard up in Capovilla, above where we lived. It was an earthen courtyard, not like ours with its stones. There was a clay pit: a stunned-looking donkey that walked around and around a dark little hole in the ground, inside which long steel blades sliced through the clay. Keep away from the machine with the knives, children! However, if a rubber ball should spin inside, it was natural to go have a look, to reach out a hand. The little pieces of angel each had its own pair of wings, transparent like dragonfly wings, and each flew up on its own.

✦

We were taught that it was best to begin our confession with the biggest sins. It's like the case of the farmer who has to send a chick, a hen, a dog, a goat, a pig, and a cow through a thorny hedgerow. If he begins with the smallest of them, the difficulty and the scratches happen again and again each time an animal goes through. But if he sends the cow through first so that it makes a big hole in the hedgerow, the others can pass through easily.

The cow was almost always the same, the usual Binda of bad things (Binda was a popular name for cows among our farmers). But we didn't always have the courage to send her through first. And sometimes one of us would appear in church with another cow altogether. One Saturday Mino showed up with an enormous beast, pulling her behind him all embarrassed. She wouldn't budge, she seemed to have decided she absolutely wouldn't go in, but by pulling and jerking, Mino, all red in the face, managed to drag her to the confessional. But get her to go first, no—that he was unable to do. And so he confessed all his other sins, one by one; he dug around in his distant past, he accused himself of merely hypothetical transgressions, he discussed his most marginal misdeeds with great punctiliousness. He was praised for his zeal and urged not to err on the side of *scruples*. And now there was nothing left but this cow, Bisa.

The priest had by now long ceased to ask, "And then?" and when Mino fell silent he began to recite the words of the absolution. Mino, seized by panic, pushed Bisa forward.

"I also have another sin, a big sin. I said bad things about priests."

His distraught tone alarmed his father confessor who wanted to know exactly what he had said about priests, but Mino held back. "Oh, you know . . . bad things." But in the end he had to report the actual words. He had said that priests were *bai da tabacco*, tobacco weevils.

Instead of being outraged when Bisa appeared, the priest was seized by a violent attack of hilarity, and Mino, now unnerved and dismayed, had to wait several minutes to receive the absolution.

None of us ever succeeded in repeating the feat my father had achieved at about age ten or twelve, up in the church of Santa Libera, in Castello. The church was empty and my father had wanted to see what it was like to sit inside the confessional. It was just fine in there, but unfortunately a pious lady appeared, and seeing the curtains were drawn, she decided to take advantage of the opportunity. My terrified father took her confession, struggling to put on a big voice, and at the end of it he gave her absolution. But he would never give us any more details, because, you know, what passes through the confessional must remain a secret.

✦

Imperfect contrition, it seemed, was not difficult to achieve because you only had to feel, not "contrition" in the usual sense of the word, but "displeasure in having offended God for fear of divine punishment, for example the pains of hell."

So, would I go to hell with these sins? There was no doubt about that. And would I mind going to hell? Obviously, yes. Therefore, I had imperfect contrition, and because that was sufficient for a confession, that should have been the end of that. But my misfortune was that this reasoning—which had been validated many times in my cautious appeals to the authorities—didn't fully convince me. To get off so lightly seemed to me wrong: I mean, who *wouldn't* mind going to hell? Why would the need for imperfect contrition be spelled out if it really consisted in something that was already implied?

The most radical solution would be to get hold of that other kind of contrition, which was called perfect because in fact it offered an absolute guarantee; but that was a hard and uncertain endeavor. And so I arrived at a compromise: I could tolerate imperfect contrition, but not when it came as a privilege. It would have to be something I felt deeply about. That meant imagining the consequences of sin as vividly as possible, as if I had already been judged and found wanting. I must put myself in the shoes of my unlucky double who had been sent off without absolution. I knew very well how things would go in that first quarter of an hour: I would find myself barefoot, in a nightshirt, in a place lit up by unpleasant flickers of light, waiting. How would that feel, hmmm?

In deep concentration on the kneeler, my face pressed at length on the palms of my hands, I waited patiently for that volatile imperfect contrition. Distracted by the church bells, the bustling of the sacristan, the whispers of the others who were waiting, "Hey, take it easy, or you're going to become a saint!" But I persevered, and when Contrition briefly fluttered its wings within the reddish geometry that my hands stamped on my eyelids, my heart leapt up the way it does in a hunter, and I hit the mark.

Now I could hand myself something like a certificate of proven contrition. To indulge in any further doubt would be to abandon myself to scruples.

Perfect contrition was another thing altogether. Normally the surrogate was enough for me, but at times, pangs of uncertainty struck.

To begin with, there was a practical consideration: if, when you confessed your sins regularly, imperfect contrition was enough, it was all too obvious that if you didn't go to confession, imperfect contrition was worth nothing at all. To have it or not have it was exactly the same thing: you sank like a stone. Week to week you went to confession, it was true. But when the need arose, how could you be certain you would have the good luck to die on Sunday, or at the worst by Monday morning? Because obviously, you spent the rest of the week in mortal sin. And it would be terrible indeed to find yourself on the verge of death, with that (all things considered) ever-so-generous offer of total pardon in exchange for a little, tiny act of perfect contrition—and not be able to produce that damned little, tiny act. *Madosca viola!* Madonna! To feel yourself slipping slowly toward death, distracted by the women weeping around you, by the mirror they have put in front of your lips to see if it still clouds up, and no perfect contrition! Wouldn't it be a good idea to practice, to train?

And beyond that there was an even more elusive concern. It seemed to me that in confession, the very act of accepting an easy pardon instead of at least trying to attain the difficult one (that is, if you didn't suffer about having offended God) constituted in and of itself a new sin that was not included in the confession pact. It was something I would need to talk to my father confessor about even at the risk of hearing him tell me that these were merely scruples. Oh, the despicable greed with which certain sinful boys and girls took advantage of that loophole, scruples! "*Scruples,* the priest said so, you're not supposed to have scruples, it's a sin." But I knew they were not scruples. It was like saying to God, "You asked for it. So there."

And so I tortured myself to inflict, if only just for a second, perfect contrition. The technique was complex and difficult; the path was long; the results unreliable. But I persisted, and a few times I actually made it. Exhausted, happy, I would get up, my head spinning. On those few occasions, for a few hours at least, I was absolutely worthy of heaven. But most of the time I had to give up and just hope for the best.

✦

Who knows if Ampelio, that time he confessed to Don Emanuele, had perfect contrition?

You could confess on your own, like the adults, beyond the high altar in the confessionals reserved for the various priests—Don Tarcisio, Baéti (Don Antonio), the senior priest, Battilana. In fact it was preferable to hide behind the screen, even though they knew us right away by our voices. But often, we children had to confess all together, in a group.

"Hey, have you children over there confessed? Okay, step up."

And we stepped up and then knelt all in a row on a riser behind the altar. A few yards away the priest, seated in front of a prie-dieu, listened to one little penitent at a time. Ampelio was on his knees, the church was silent. All of a sudden you could hear the booming voice of Don Emanuele, taken by surprise.

"Oh, no! You *mas'cio!*"

Ampelio's ears were flaming red.

◆

The few times that we went with Mamma to the evening service, I would always say that the best of the litanies was the one that came after the *Jànua-coeli* because right after that the prayers ended and we could leave the church—but this wasn't true. In fact, I liked the litany that followed the *Jànua* because of the soaring beauty of its syllables, which took flight in Mamma's enchanting voice.

My mother sang and I waited anxiously for the *Jànua,* and then came that luminous image, *stella matutina,* morning star. And then we left the church.

◆

We did our best to achieve merit. For one whole year Guido and I competed for most devout. We would attend the *fioretti di maggio,* the May devotions, and every evening there was a brief sermon by Don Bernardo, who was still with us then. We made a rule that the proof of devotion depended on how close you were to the pulpit—the closer, the more devout. We would go early to get a seat in the front row (in fact it was a side row, on the side of the pulpit) and then, moving our seats at the right moment, we would get in front of everyone. Then when the sermon began we would start shifting the seats rapidly, me first, then Guido, then me, then Guido, until we had moved right up under the pulpit. But this way we always ended up equal, and so we had to find another measure of devotion. In the end we decided to count the number of times Don Bernardo's spit hit us on the face. We would listen to the sermon, paying attention to the tiny sparks that flew from the pulpit;

Don Bernardo would get fired up and he let a lot of spit fly, and we would tally up in a whisper the targets hit: "Seventeen, eighteen, nineteen . . ." "Eighteen, nineteen, twenty . . ." It was against the rules to dry yourself off, because your adversary had to be able to inspect you when you went outside. I don't remember whether at the end of the month I was ahead or Guido, but whoever won it was a close contest. We were both very devout at that time.

Chapter 2

A DAY SPENT IN THE ATTIC. There, packed in three or four boxes and scattered over the floor, lies our family history, especially that of us children: a storm of exercise books, accounts, letters, and volumes shedding their pages. Textbook bindings and multicolored notebook covers bob up, as familiar, as startling, as faces in a dream. There are picture postcards that Mamma sent to Papà when they were courting; First Communion cards, magazines from the twenties that were already ancient when we paged through them looking for women with their skirts up over their knees; diaries, sketches, middle school compositions, *liceo* essays, university papers, letters from friends, letters from girls.

None of this has anything like the potency of the little exercise book headed up, in an unsteady hand, with the title Notes, inside which Thoughts were interposed between Equations and Dictation, all spelled out in the wobbly cadences of dialect and the country script of the child I was in my second year.

"My teacher is called Prospera Moretti. My school is located on Via Borgo and is nice and spacious."

I can't bring myself to return to that nice and spacious school today, an old house in the middle of town now inhabited by people I don't know. Three classes met in the same upstairs room. It was a "private" school, a curiosity left over from another world. It permitted the better-off families to send their children to school before the statutory age of six. Then after the third year, there was an exam—the first of our lives—in order to enter the town school.

✦

"I never kicked my teacher like Bruno Erminietto did."

I don't remember what started it. When the brief drama unfolded, Maestra Prospera had already lost her patience. She was standing at the edge of the block of seats; she had grabbed Bruno Erminietto by an arm and was pulling. He was clutching onto a desk, she was scolding loudly, confused blows were raining down. Now the guilty one was detached from his desk, at the mercy of his adult foe.

Flutter of skirts and underskirts, shrieks. Bruno Erminietto was biting and kicking, aiming at the invisible shins behind the skirts. Ah, now he's found the shins and is pounding them with hard kicks, his back bent.

Then he's overwhelmed and dragged off, his feet sliding over the tile floor.

In the morning we stood in line in the hallway, waiting to go up to class. Faustino was fooling around, showing off the nail of his little finger, which he had allowed to grow very long. He was showing off, and I was trying to stop him.

"That nail is going to turn ingrown if you don't cut it," I said, "it's going to become an Incarnate Nail."

"What's an Incarnate Nail?"

I told him; it had all been explained to me very thoroughly.

"A nail that gets this long, half a meter, even more, and curves back at the top."

"Great," said Faustino. "That way I can scratch you from far away."

First, second, and third fitted into each other like pieces of a puzzle: the first in parallel rows like a beach in front of the teacher; the dunes and rocky coast of the second under the windows, spreading out into the middle rows of desks; in the back, the foothills of the third. Just under the blackboard was a sandy strip of preemies, the little ones not yet old enough for the first year, "observers" who observed with what looked like fear.

My brother Bruno, admitted to this little sandy strip at about age four, watched Maestra Prospera's first lesson with growing unease. She was explaining how to take the Pen in hand, holding her thumb, index, and middle finger in the air just in front of Bruno's nose. The index and middle finger must be parallel; underneath is the thumb, which when the Pen is then introduced, pushes it up and holds it in place. This is the old way to hold the Pen, the only suitable way to make those exercises we traced before we wrote our letters. I believe that we, Maestra Prospera's pupils, were the last ones in town to have learned it.

The teacher's three fingers descending from on high—large, tense, forked—looked like a terrible trap to Bruno. He knew there was a plan afoot to make him do the same thing with thumb, index, and middle finger, and he was certain he would never succeed. The three fingers coming down at him looked gigantic and deformed as they approached his nose. He knew he was in clear and present danger, and he began to shout: take away those Pens and give him some Mints!

The way we saw her, Maestra Prospera was not a woman but a fact of nature, like the bell tower. We sensed however, from her old-fashioned hair style or perhaps from her diction, that there was something antiquated about her. And in fact she was an old-fashioned woman, who awarded colored mints as prizes and meted out punishment by rapping on our knuckles. Sometimes she made us kneel behind the blackboard on tiny, sharp sorghum grains, and she often sent us down to the ground floor for punishment. She kept to herself, and when she left school she was scarcely ever seen.

She died after the war when I was still in town, and it was my generation of alumni who took her to be buried: Mino, Faustino, and Guido and myself. We were unsettled, saddened, and found ourselves repeating phrases we realized we all knew by heart.

"This morning I opened the shutters and saw the sun. Then I washed my face, my ears, and my neck. I dressed and combed my hair. After drinking my *caffelatte,* I went to school. My school is located on Via Borgo and is nice and spacious. My teacher is named Prospera Moretti."

"But there *is* a but . . ." Of course there was a but, although not the one that Maestra Prospera was thinking about when she summed up her report to Mamma and Papà, always with the same phrase. "He would really be doing rather well, as I say . . . But there *is* a but." For her these were ritual words alluding to the fact that the child—any child—was "lively." Her *but* was impersonal, it was a generic quality of childhood, and when she mentioned it, she seemed to be coyly pretending to be more severe than she was.

Meanwhile there really was a *but,* there had been for a while. The *but* of the vegetable garden, the *but* of nursery school. At school this was mainly embodied by that little fetish that the teacher herself had suggested we call the Baby Doll, and also by Mino's blonde cousin, with whom he was authorized (while I was not) to get up from his desk and play while the teacher was otherwise occupied. There was a *but,* but you had to look out when adults were listening, because they didn't understand these things, or pretended not to.

"In my school, which is located on Via Borgo, bad children are sent downstairs to the ground-floor toilet for punishment."

Complications could arise because at times the bad child, made to exit quickly, took the key and locked his schoolmate in the toilet, or the assistant who was called Elsa, or even Maestra Prospera. This toilet was itself spacious, a tiled space with a frameless window looking out on a small courtyard. For me it was a source of fantasy every time Antonia was given permission to go there. Antonia was a plump young lady with red hair, all of eight years old. My designs on her focused on the thoughts provoked by a word used by the big girls in the third year, of whom Antonia was the most conspicuous. The word was *cesto,* basket, and it was the frank, open, female metaphor for backside.

The tiled surfaces of the toilet, the window, Antonia—they all made a sweet halo of images, and in the middle Antonia's *cesto* shimmered like the ostensorium at the mass. I dreamed of it vividly, but without desire, rather with a feeling close to disinterested pleasure, like that attributed to the contemplation of beauty. Antonia's pale, soft *cesto:* what did I want to do with it? Contemplate it, perhaps from the window; weigh it, although it seemed to flutter in the air: in short, play.

My relations with Giulietta were another thing all together. She was a girl passing through, daughter of one of the doctors who had come to Malo for a few months: dark, modern, exciting. She had been put in with the second year in the row in front of mine, and, bending down and twisting around after a pencil I'd let drop, I tried to get a look at her legs. I saw a thigh and it was like being struck by lightning. It was pale above the rubber band that held up her black sock, pale with bluish highlights, flesh that made your innards weak.

✦

I went to and from school with my cousin Este, who was one of the big girls, not as important as Pozzàn, but only a little less so. Pozzàn would stop in front of the Caffè Nazionale, the big girls all around her. We'd stand in a circle on the sidewalk.

"Okay, so we're mad at Mantiero," Pozzàn would say.

"At Mantiero," the big girls would say, "mad at Mantiero." Then we'd all go home to have lunch. Because I alone among the big girls was small and male, I had nothing to say and nothing special to do, I just had to remain mad at Mantiero. I put my heart and soul into it, even though no one was checking.

There were nine big girls, eight of them mad at Mantiero, and Mantiero herself. In truth they didn't pay much attention to me; I laughed when they laughed; when they put on a stern face, so did I, sometimes even a bit too stern. "What's the matter with him? He's got a pain?" they would say to Este. They never spoke directly to me but only via the Este proxy. I would quickly smooth out my face, and they would go back to chattering. When they had something that was truly a secret they would tell Este to send me away, and then they would natter among themselves while I stood to one side.

I stayed mad at Mantiero for many days, and when she passed by alone on the opposite sidewalk, her little black shawl tied around her shoulders and a sorrowful, dignified expression on her face, I felt a pleasant sense of complicity with the big girls, and tried to catch the eye of my cousin Este or Pozzàn to show off my intransigence. They gave no hint of their feelings. One day Mantiero came out with all the others, and we all went down the street together. I felt terribly tense, all the more so because those formidable big girls really knew how to hide their true feelings. They talked about this and that, and Mantiero took part in the conversation and the jokes. "Now they're going to tear her to pieces," I thought to myself; instead, when we got to the piazza everyone said good-bye and went off on her own. As soon as I could I asked Este,

"Este, we're mad at Mantiero, aren't we?"

And Este said to me: "Be quiet, big mouth, you don't understand anything."

I realized that I had been left all alone to be mad at Mantiero; the big girls had betrayed their own cause with almost unbelievable frivolity. And that wasn't the only time the big girls made a fool of me. We were on our way down to the piazza, Flora, Este, and me, when Signora Ramira came out on the sidewalk in front of us, red-haired, slender, and presumptuous. My cousins were bad-mouthing the little figure before us, criticizing the way she swung her hips. "Her ass is heaving," they whispered.

I was walking in the middle of them, and I too wanted to participate in the conversation, make a contribution. I thought about it, and I said, "Her twat is heaving." This comment, although not based on any empirical observation, nevertheless seemed to me quite worthy, but my cousins acted scandalized and threatened to denounce me to Aunt Nina. So that was it: you could gossip about the ass, but not about the twat.

Maestra Prospera taught us the alphabet and numbers and the use of certain words, such as "spacious," "grains," "shutters," and other such refinements of the written language. One time we also came across "precipices," and the teacher made Elsa look it up in a big black book that contained, she said, all the words there are.

But she got angry when, in the second year, I wrote an essay at home in which I said that Easter is "one of the most important ecclesiastical celebrations." She told me I couldn't know what ecclesiastical meant, and I tried to bluff and said I did.

"And what does it mean?" she asked. I had to improvise; I said it was the most important *solenità dell'ano,* meaning "ceremony of the year," in dialect but in Italian, ceremony "of the anus." It was a fairly ingenious try, but it didn't pass muster.

The written word, the Italian language, had a strange effect on us, who spoke dialect. My mother had a pupil just about my age named Mansueto, a cheerful, gangly, asymmetrical, appealing boy. On his way home after a lesson involving who knows what "aromatic" substance, Mansueto stopped under the column in Contrà Muzana and tossed a rubber ball into the air, reciting, as if he were singing a canticle,

> The ball is air-o-
> matic! Aromatic
> ball. Air-o-matic!

There's a word I believe I myself introduced one afternoon in Malo. Quite a few of us had gathered in my grandmother's courtyard, there was a big pile of sand, and we were building fanciful constructions, castles and towers, in a state of great elation. All of a sudden I saw that one of these constructions was about to fall and I said: "It's *disintegrating*." That magic word, which I had heard somewhere and which, although unknown to all the others, was immediately understood, spread like wildfire. They were all muttering "It's disintegrating, it's disintegrating," and milling around while our monument crumbled. The new word itself was the event.

I had been having run-ins with words as far back as nursery school, where my arrival was somewhat bitterly marked by a linguistic, not to mention social, discovery. It was when I naively suggested I wanted to do *pissìn*, pee-pee, the only such pertinent word I knew, and was loudly derided as if I were a little girl by those hardened men of the people between the ages of two and five who said *pissare*, piss.

Chapter 3

THERE HAD ALSO BEEN an inaugural trauma at nursery school, the admissions ceremony, when each child in his or her blue-and-white checked smock came forward in the gravel-covered courtyard outside the front door to kiss Sister Eulalia's *panaro,* her polenta board. We already knew that life held such hazards: when we drove down to Vicenza in the car with Papà, we hid under the seats as we went past the toll post so that when the old lady in the guard booth offered her *panaro* we wouldn't have to kiss it.

I didn't have anything against Sister Eulalia (who was old and good-natured and who wore a pince-nez), and I wasn't much worried about having to kiss her *panaro* with the others. But when my turn came and I found myself faced with the *panaro* on that gray October morning, I felt uneasy. It was huge, saffron-colored, and riven with flaccid vertical, parallel lines. I found it frankly repellent, and the whole thing, traumatic.

I woke from this unpleasant dream covered with sweat the night before starting nursery school. But in the morning, the reports I'd heard about the admission procedures proved completely untrue.

✦

From the outside it looked like a doll's world, with colored paper stars and little candles. The anteroom of paradise, on a little mound at the bottom of the courtyard had an acacia tree on top, and there, gathered around it, we would pray: *Beauteous Virgin, send rain* when it was dry, and *Beauteous Virgin, send sun,* when it was damp. Among those dripping branches, imagining them laden with candles and little loaves of *pan d'oro,* you could see what paradise looked like, the light shining in your face.

Ignorant of confession, barely out of the Creator's hand, *artless infant souls* contemplated their return on high, thumbs in their mouths. Those tiny souls were nourished with rice and milk on the even days and noodles in broth on the odd ones, and they lived in our little hearts.

Hearts were subject to two ailments, both mortal: they could be lost (out of unrestrained desire for a toy, for example, or for mints), or they could break, as a result of misfortune or disappointment. Loss of the heart brought on a sweeter, drowsier end, while heartbreak was abrupt and more painful. Various things could bring on heartbreak: being shut up under the stairs, Mamma's departure—and, at least in that year when Mamma wasn't there—those little blue flowers called *occhietti della Madonna,* Virgin's eyes, that when you looked at them close up lying on the ground, you felt your heart grow larger and larger and you waited impatiently to see if it would break.

> *Careghete, Dòne!*
> *che porta le Madòne*
> *che porta i Andoléti*
> *Schiti! Schiti! Schiti!*

> Chairs for you Ladies!
> chairs to carry the Virgins
> chairs for the Little Angels
> Chickenshit, chickenshit, chickenshit!

These chairs had a square seat, and you made them with your own arms, weaving together four wrists and four fists. You sang out your wares to a hypothetical public of Ladies standing at their doorways along the street, wiping their hands on their aprons. But the chairs were not for sale; they were the vehicles of a procession, they bore the curly-haired Virgins and the sweaty little angels in suitable glory. The little faces registered no amazement before paradise, but a quiver of hilarity would run through the assembled when the chair collapsed as a warmish hail of chicken droppings fell to earth. The Virgins and the angels, stricken by the celestial hens, laughed and kicked their skirts up, and you could see all the way to Venice.

Under the surface, however, our nursery school days were not without problems.

The Sister called me in, closed the door, and asked me, in confidence, to help resolve a mystery. Imelda's green woolen beret had been missing for two days, and no one had been able to find it. Was I perhaps such a good boy that I might be able to do so?

I didn't make much of an effort, above all because I had other things on my mind. In the first place, an amorous disappointment, and as a matter of fact, to do with Imelda herself, and it was no mere crush but a true passion, largely unrequited. And second, I was in trouble at home on account of—hard to believe, but true—a green woolen beret.

Two days before there had been a terrible scene. I had a black leather coat lined with pile, a very elegant coat with pockets on the diagonal. When I got home and they took off my coat they saw the lump. "What have you got there?" They pulled out the green beret. "Who does this belong to?" They seemed worried and I, naturally, said nothing. They said they were going to make me talk, and they tried. First I was standing up, then I was on the floor near the shapely leg of the kitchen table;

there were high, shrill voices; there were Mamma's copper-colored boots laced up with many little eyelets right over the ankle. I had never really been hit before, and more than anything else I was fascinated by it all.

I didn't talk, but here's what had happened: the Sister had told us all about the seventh commandment, joining her little finger and her index finger in that rotatory gesture that signifies stealing. At that point I was at a dead end in my relationship with Imelda.

In those days I was allowed to return home for lunch, a special privilege on account of the rice and milk, and so every day I had to go through the cloakroom where we hung up our coats and hats. I stopped to look at Imelda's green beret and felt a blind rush of love that was indistinguishable from the desire to steal. *Steal*, not just walk off with.

I tried for quite a while to steal the green beret from the hook by rotating my fingers. Impossible; in the end I had to pull it down with the other hand, put it on the floor, and *steal* it from there.

The Sister had no more need for my help, however. After a while Imelda showed up in the green beret—how, I didn't bother to find out. It was enough for me that I never said anything to anybody. These are not things you can discuss, they wouldn't have understood at all.

✦

Who was Olmo?

His head, like a huge beetroot, was shaved, and his clothes were rougher than mine. A farm boy, probably. He must have then emigrated somewhere, for he disappeared from town just after nursery school, leaving behind no more than the name, Olmo. I used to watch him rest his head on his arm and his arm on the bench with his fist closed, and then his hand would unclench and a red rubber band would fall from it. I, too, had my head resting on my arm and had been ordered to sleep, but I was peeking. It was then, for the first time, that I thought about what a strange thing it is to sleep. Olmo was not there anymore; there was only a dim, disabled beetroot, and between the beetroot and my eyes, a lifeless, half-opened hand in the stuffy summer afternoon.

Sleep still interests me. Now I know that certain areas of the brain are permanently asleep and that sleep is not sharply distinct from wakefulness. We are always sleeping a little: we sleep on our feet, and, as every motorcyclist knows, while driving a motorcycle, and in other circumstances. Each slice of the brain, maybe every tiny piece of it, sleeps in turn; while we're on watch, a little wedge of cells naps, sinking into deep slumber. In my imagination, sleep circulates at random, it jumps around like little lights that flick on over here, and off over there. A part of us is always sleeping, but all parts never sleep. Something is wakeful when we lie asleep, something that produces that sow as tall as a calf, long and thin like some sort of huge pink dog, that I believed we had bought and was thinking about. *Orca-miseria,* when that thing is fattened up it will be a ten-ton pachyderm, it will eat too much and be disgusting.

✦

Behind the scenes on the nursery school's little stage, waiting to go on, Zaira showed me her *broda,* her impetigo. She pulled her dress up over her knees and further up, and then, Good Lord, even further, and I saw it. It was about the size of a big coin and even had the same copper color. In town we called it *brosa,* but Zaira came from the countryside. She let me touch it with my finger and it felt a bit rough and neither hot nor cold. It was certainly an interesting *broda,* but the prankish, silly way it was shown off left me too confused to appreciate it as much as it deserved.

At nursery school they had us sing songs full of worthy sentiments, but other songs came to us from the world outside.

Ramona
Co na palanca se va in mona.

Ramona
Just ten cents, and you can give her a poke.

I thought of it as a nice song, a little gloomy with that reference to the derisory poverty of those who possess no more than a single coin: not a very original idea but a nice song. I thought Mamma would like it too, but instead she didn't like it at all.

Mamma herself and Jovanka, who came from Slav lands across the border, sometimes sang a refrain that I liked both for the music and the words. It said:

Creola
dalla bruna rèola

Creole girl
of the brown au-reole

There were other nice words, but those were enough. Creoles wore lavender-colored ribbons around their brows, they had dark skin, wore veils, and underneath you could catch a glimpse of the brown, brown au-reole. You could just barely catch the smell of Creolin disinfectant.

"Come and I'll learn you the song of the blackcaps," said Jovanka the Slav, and she would launch into it: "Passionate kisses . . ." And they must have truly been passionate, for she put real enthusiasm into the song.

She also learned me to draw a man. First you did the profile, bit by bit, from the high, intelligent brow down to where the neck attached to the chin, and then you closed this profile with the skullcap of the head, taking care to make it proportionate. There was also the problem of the arms. I made them one on one side, and one on the other, the usual little sticks that finished in four or five little rays. "I'll learn you to make arms," said Jovanka, and she went so far as to make me draw the sleeves of a jacket in two dimensions. It all came out a bit overlong, crooked, and unattractive. I could see that myself. But it seemed to me that the roughness of the figures was more than compensated by the grown-up ambitions of the whole, and so when Maestra Prospera, one day just before a holiday, said, in a lighthearted moment: "And now who wants to come and draw a man on the blackboard?" looking at me and Faustino sitting among the big children, I made the foolish mistake of allowing myself to be chosen.

I began with the usual profile, and probably the excitement accentuated my errors, and I began to erase and redraw, but no—it just got worse. The whole class had been enthusiastic about the teacher's proposal, and when I'd been chosen—me, not Faustino—it had seemed to me that the majority wanted me. But as my drawing progressed, a hush fell where there had been excited whispers, then an embarrassed silence. And as I began to work on the complicated convolutions of the ear, the first hostile comments began.

It was an utter disaster. I'd made a stiff, sour-faced moron, his left arm swollen and twisted around like an elephant's trunk so as not to touch the sidewalk with his hand. Now the crowd was loudly calling for Faustino, and that Barabbas was bouncing in his seat, keen to go up to the blackboard. He came up and, with a big smile, drew a circle, and putting three dots inside made a perfect head. He then drew a square little body, vibrant and alive looking, sketched in a pair of short pants, and with a few other simple, lighthearted strokes made a very cheerful and energetic little man on the blackboard.

Everyone was applauding, and when Faustino, just for good measure, made a beret with two more strokes and perched it on the head, the crowd went wild.

The teacher tried to set things right. "You see," she said, "this is a smiling little imp, and this is a serious fellow on his way to work."

Serious fellow! He was a nitwit, a blockhead on two legs, pompous, disagreeable, ugly as sin. The sort of fellow who slapped people in the face. Darkly, deeply, I understood what art is: something light-handed, something *simple*—fine technique isn't the point. Faustino held out his hand, and I even had to congratulate him.

Chapter 4

AT THE SOLARIUM WE WERE all equal, as equal as anywhere. I heard one of the women who helped dress the little ones say so. "See? As soon as you put on their clothes in the evening, they go back to being either poor folk or gentlemen, but in the daytime they're all the same."

You had to know how to look after yourself at the Solarium: it was a small green jungle populated by little desperadoes like the one whose nickname was Pessàta—that was what they called him in his own family, but woe to you if you called him that to his face. During a match once, I accused him of cheating, I said *busiàro,* liar, and he grabbed me with his left hand and with the right applied his knuckles until I retracted. I had to make a formal statement attesting he was not a liar. Afterward, I moved some distance away and putting on an amiable voice, said: "But you do tell *pessàte.*" Now *pessàte* are little fish in the creek, but here at the Solarium, they sounded like great big lies. There was enough ground between us so that I was able to take shelter before he got his hands on me, otherwise I wouldn't be here to tell the tale.

✦

There was a gentleman at the Solarium who we never saw in person, but his presence filled the air every afternoon: he was an aristocrat, he was Milanese, and he had scandalous habits.

We would line up after our refreshments, grab the hem of our undershorts, and pull them up the backs of our thighs to show off our behinds as much as possible, and march along reciting:

El Conte da Milàn
co le braghe in man
col capèl de paja
Conte canàja!

The Count from Milan
his shorts in hand
his hat of straw
Count Canaille!

At this point, after a sly silence, the column would begin to chant loudly, in a derisive, denunciatory tone:

Prete mas'cio! Prete mas'cio!

The Priest's a pig! The Priest's a pig!

Was the Priest maybe a relative of the Count? Or perhaps the Count himself dressed up as the Priest, or the Priest trying in vain to pass for the Count—and all this to cover with phony eloquence our desire to show off our backsides? Who knows; what is certain is that you will also find *canaille* among the nobility and the clergy, and it's always a pleasure to unmask them.

✦

Here is how things worked: there was the universe of Italian, of conventions, of the Arditi, of the Creoles, of well-bred, respectable *Perbenito* Mussolini, of the palpitating Vibralani— and there was the universe of dialect, of practical reality, of natural functions, of vulgar things. In the first world flags flew and Ramona sparkled with gold like the sun: it was a sort of pageant, both believed and not. The other world was real, and you merely had to put the two side by side and someone would start laughing. We'd laugh with the servant girls:

> *Bianco rosso e verde*
> *color delle tre merde*
> *color dei panezèi*
> *la caca dei putèi.*

> White, red and green
> the color of the three turds
> diaper-color, like
> baby shit.

This wasn't meant as a criticism of the tricolored national flag, not at all. The flag was run up on Aunt Lena's balcony, it was described in "Thoughts" at school. The three turds were lined up in the garden under the Count's wall, as shiny as paint, big flies buzzing around them, and Colomba came and tossed a wet diaper over them and mixed the colors together into a yellowish mess.

White, red, and green was just a phrase in Italian; all the rest was its counterpart in dialect. But there was a polemical side to all of this: we sensed that dialect gave immediate, almost automatic access to a sphere of reality that for some reason adults wanted to contain and control. We sensed, too, that adults were playing games about this, and we admired that young, anonymous man of the people—inimitable, alas—who protested so radically as to attack the very fundamentals of our society, Family and Religion.

He had endured, fuming, the various rules imposed by his parents. But when the ecclesiastical authorities gratuitously interfered, he was driven to fury. He left the following brief, laconic document:

Me pare me mare
Me manda cagare
El prete me vede
Mi taco scorède

My pater, my mater
Said go to hell, boy
The priest was watching
So I laid a fart.

He was angry, no doubt about it, yet even in the telling of his tale, this premature rebel without a cause seems to have had to suppress a smile.

✦

We sensed that there were equivocal, darkly dishonorable pacts linking adults, the conventions of respectable life, and the Italian language. This make-believe of theirs annoyed us.

When a gaggle of relatives trapped us in their midst, and demanded at all costs that we say something (something nice, something in Italian) to Signora Lea, a lady of great importance encountered on the street, and we had nothing to say to Signora Lea, and those troublemakers insisted, how were we to behave so as not to lose all self-respect?

"Shitandfarts," Bruno Erminietto blurted out to Signora Lea, and turned and darted off.

✦

In general, you could smell adult deficiencies in the air. We laughed among ourselves when we heard that Giuliano had been put in prison because he had *nicked something*. But we were left in some doubt, because Giuliano was a knife grinder, and putting the blade to the whetstone, and sometimes nick-ing it, was part of his job, and so why had they put him in prison?

I put this together with some other fragmentary information at my disposal to draw up a theory that I quickly aired. "I know why Giuliano's in prison, he's in prison because he nicked something," I said to a group of adults. When I picked up signals they were embarrassed, I added very casually, "He nicked his willy."

The result was spectacular. They thought they were clever, that they could pull the wool over my eyes, hide the fact that one of them, a silly respectable adult, had committed the comical, perfectly illegal, eccentricity of honing on his grindstone not knives and scissors—but a willy!

Chapter 5

MY MOTHER USED TO TELL me that when I was small and she took me around in her arms (I was the first, born after three years of marriage), people would fondle me and murmur, "*Povaretto,* poor little thing, so handsome!" My mother, who didn't come from around Malo, was taken aback, and when they then said, "Oh, poor little thing, what beautiful eyes," she was positively despondent.

Our wet nurses came from a faraway town called Arquà, much smaller and poorer than ours, where there lived a cat named Petrarch to whom they had even built a monument. Ernestina was my nursemaid, and she is among the first things in the world that I remember. And a very nice thing it was, too.

Out in the barn, Ernestina and I inspected the broken toys, and there was a beautiful sunset, and I felt happy.

"I had a really nice day," I told Ernestina. She rejoiced with me about the really nice day.

"I want this day again tomorrow," I said. Ernestina smiled and said that tomorrow would also be a nice day. I became suspicious and said coldly:

"I want this *same* day again tomorrow."

"This day is already over," said Ernestina, "there will be another day tomorrow."

I began to thrash around like a madman, sensing that there was some kind of intolerable rule here; it wasn't Ernestina's fault, but I was scratching her and howling, "I want this day to come back! *This* day! I want it back!"

No luck.

The personality of the servant girls was colored by what they had been charged with doing and preparing for us while Mamma was out. The *caffelatte* that Sansòn made for us in the morning was deeply, poisonously blue. We sat at the table facing each other, and when Sansòn looked the other way, my brother Bruno, whose hands were sweet and plump, would thrust them into his bowl and wash them thoroughly.

In those days Bruno was blond and curly-haired and obstinate; when he grew older he was someone you had to watch out for, even a bit *carogna*, a scoundrel. *Carogna*—"carrion"—was what our grandmother called him, after I staged a little show with props (wood, a hatchet) in an act of retaliation, convincing her that he really had hurt me. Grandmother Esterina reproached *carogne* and doted on *vìssare*, "viscera," sweethearts, you might say. We were aware this was archaic diction, used only by the old. And strangely, when we were with our grandmother—and when we were good—we were a bit grandparents ourselves. It was odd to feel oneself viscera, and odd to feel a grandparent. (The word *Nòno*, grandfather, is a term of endearment just slightly below *vìssare*.)

Under our day garments we wore cloth corsets buttoned up the back, and everything else was attached to this, including the garters that hung down to hold up our woolen socks with more buttons. For many years Bruno lived in fear he might come to shame because of the corset. The servant girls dressed us, but he had tried many times to button up his corset by himself, in vain. He knew he would never be able to do it; he also knew that when you are called up for military service you are not allowed to take a servant girl along. And so, when the time came for those born in 1925 to be called up, how was he going to dress himself in the barracks? What would happen to his undershorts and his socks when they had to march out or leap into the trenches, when they had other things to do with their hands?

The first poem I composed in Italian was brief and went like this:

> *Ultima sera d'agosto*
> *Sotto le brache c'è un mostro.*

> It's the last night of August
> Inside your shorts there's a monster.

I taught it to Bruno, and as the end of August neared and the crickets chirped ever louder, we used to sing it in the courtyard, hunkered down by the Professor's wall because at night the privy was thought to be too far away for us children. Later I decided we should begin with a preview in the last week of July, on the quiet nights when the first loud cries of the crickets began to be heard. We would stop at the end of July, and then resume in the last days of August. There was great excitement and satisfaction on the night of the thirty-first, when the words exactly matched events, as if the year was following our plan and the crickets had gone wild. In a few hours it would be September; this moment wouldn't come back for another year, and there was no way you could do anything about it.

After our pause under the Professor's wall, we leapt across the courtyard like frogs, singing my end-of-summer lament.

One night when we were out there, Dino arrived. He had rented out the Cinque and was putting it back in the *garàs*, and when he came down into the yard he heard us and wanted to know what we were singing. He really liked the second line and laughed very amiably as if to say: Aren't my nephews clever! I was flattered and pleased: it's a pleasure to make up funny things that really make people laugh. But while we were wiping our behinds, it occurred to me that maybe he had understood one monster, while I had another in mind.

✦

Hail storms are one of those things that will always belong to Montale. *Infuria sale o grandine? Fa strage/di campanule, svelle la cedrina./Un rintocco subacqueo s'avvicina* . . . "Is that salt or hail raging? Slaughtering/the bluebells, uprooting the verbena./A watery tolling comes near . . ." The poet's lines are perfect, but they are much too polite for Malo.

It was dry salt, and sulfur. You could feel God's litigiousness in the fierce, blind fits of rage, in the bullying big carts he deployed around the rim of the heavens above town, in order to dump their contents on us. The loads of salt fanned out in the air, striking the roofs and courtyards in great veils. You could see the extra blows raining down with every gust of wind; you could make out perfectly the bigger spheres, transparent eggs driving down between one cartload and another and bouncing like steel balls on the ground. They were coming at us, but with no particular aim. Yellowish cows, looking poisoned, stood steaming under the walls.

We didn't see the flowers die, but the vines were mutilated, and the sorghum ripped from the ground. Before the storm the air was black and mirrored; the magic world engraved in quartz, sullied, and there were curtains of lye-colored spray and gushes of sulfur; no "watery tolling" but a malign crackling on dented surfaces, the twang of shots going this way and that. There was no real light in the storm, nothing shining, just a claustrophobic glimmer, a squall of opaque rays that collided and turned to dust. Everything shot past everything, contradicting, annulling all.

It was like being in a trap, with the devils downstairs that came to peer into the vents that were suddenly dark, while we watched from behind the shutters, now looking down in the courtyard, now toward the great gusts that closed us off from the town of Schio.

And then it was all over, a deafening silence fell, the sky cleared, the sun made its return and seeped into the wreckage, revealing the green heart of the grain.

✦

In May the garden is full of bees, hornets, shoots, buds, tender leaves, and everywhere *bai:* in the air, in the soil, on the leaves. See this *bao?* It's a big *bao,* all the world is made of *bai:* earth-worm-*bai,* snail-*bai,* mouse-*bai,* dog-*bai,* man-*bai,* angel-*bai* that fly like this *bao.* Fly away *Bao!*

In the buzz of industrious bees there was a clue to that thing that darts in and out of time, and I felt myself leaving our *man-locked set,* and infinite time and infinite space were little drops of sound in midair, at just about the height of the walls of the garden, and they floated through the air without falling to earth.

We knew they were only *ave,* bees. *Ava:* a buzzing jujube fruit; a tiny, striped witch; a worm that wasn't a worm; a secret that can't be unlocked because it doesn't speak; a yellow drop that can sting.

> *Ava aveta, do lo ghètu 'l basavéjo?*
> *Ava: sa te me bèchi te lo incatéjo.*

> Little bee, you, where's your stinger?
> Bee, if you sting me I'll tie you up.

Don't play with the *Ava.* It comes from the world of the numinous. It's not *bao.* It's *Ava.*

✦

A man's personality is made of two strata: on top, lie the superficial wounds in Italian, French, Latin, or whatever; down below, the older wounds that, healing, made scars of the words in dialect. Touch one and it sets off a chain reaction, very difficult to explain to someone who has no dialect. There's an indestructible core of material that has been apprehended, picked up with the prehensile shoots of the senses. The dialect word is eternally pegged to reality because the word is the thing itself, perceived even before we begin to reason, and its power doesn't diminish with time, given that we've been taught to reason in another language. This is true above all for the names of things.

But this core of primordial material (both in the nouns and in every other word) also contains uncontrollable forces precisely because it belongs to a prelogical sphere, where associations are free and fundamentally manic. And so dialect is in some ways reality, and in some ways nonsense.

It is with something like physical pain that I touch those deep nerves connected to *basavéjo* and *barbastrìjo, ava* and *anguàna,* even just *rùa* and *pùa.* They sizzle like a flash of lightning; you feel the last knot of what we call life, that lump of matter that cannot be crushed, the bedrock of existence.

I don't mean to say that this *is* dialect—but there is this in dialect. Of course it is not merely in dialect that you find it, there's even more of it in that other dialect of the eyes and the other sense organs, in those moments when chance or certain emotional states put the world of words out of phase with the world of things.

I tried to talk about this ineffable thing when it came upon me a few years back in the town of Strigno in the Valsugana hills, where my brother Gaetano was in the Alpine artillery and my cousin Roberto had been gun master in the same unit. I went up there with Papà and Katia. Gaetano took us to visit the barracks, the mess hall, the empty grounds (I think it was a holiday), and then to where the weapons were mounted. The four guns were lined up along the edge of a small clearing, humble, almost as if they had been abandoned.

I felt the ineffable thing come near, and while Gaetano was showing me Roberto's cannon, I was seized by panic. I can't say just what it was: it felt like grief and fear. The guns were mute, chilling objects, and it seemed unbearable that a creature that speaks should coexist with things, matter. I felt as if I could *see* what life looked like at its rock bottom. I looked away, clenching my eyes and teeth. Enough, no more!

Chapter 6

I RECENTLY REREAD A DIARY written by Don Tarcisio, the priest who was my teacher in fourth and fifth, titled *Malo in the War Years* and covering the period from 1914 to 1920. From these modest pages emerges, at least for me, a fairly vivid picture of the town to which my mother, a refugee from Udine in the far northeast, came in 1917. There's all the atmosphere of war with the explosions and the gunfire lighting up the overhang of mountains all around, and the comings and goings of the soldiers, the deaths at the front, the refugees, the knife fights in the inns, the social welfare committees, the death notices, the religious services, the mass Communion rites (up to six thousand of the faithful in a single day). There's a passing reference to the so-called boarding school that was situated for a time in my grandfather's house in Contrada Grisa, an institute "serving soldiers exclusively." Don Tarcisio's Malo was a very old-fashioned place, far more conscious than today of the distinction between the "notables"—those who had titles, were wealthy, or educated—and the others, with an atmosphere that today would seem both patriarchal and cheerfully good-natured.

Don Tarcisio was already in service back then, theoretically in the "school" that is today the town hall, but which in those days was often used to billet soldiers.

When we went to take the exam for elementary school, Don Tarcisio offered some suggestions before he gave us the dictation, using among other things the word "accustomed," which we had never heard before, but so gracefully that we were able to understand.

Polished, round, cultivated, and courteous, Don Tarcisio smoothed and combed his hair, no longer thick but still dark, with great care. He was no country priest, but a man of urbanized, even somewhat refined civilization. He enjoyed his well-being in an uncomplicated way, had a respectable love of good food, cigars, and travel, and a polite but natural way of speaking. There is a diary of his travels to Palestine titled *Jerusalem!* and quite an accomplished sketch of the pregnant Virgin that hangs on the walls in the church in Castello. You sensed in him a vein of good-natured, tolerant, cultivated, peacefully modernized Catholicism. In summer he went to the beach on the Tuscan coast; in town, he sometimes visited the Count along with the seraphic Don Antonio, he, too, a teacher.

He taught us many things; the first that come to mind were certain *obiter dicta,* such as that sexual reproduction was perfectly normal in nature, and that it was no transgression against the fast if on Friday we ate a salad with little strips of lard in it, because lard strips were a condiment and did not constitute meat. He read us stories, and I remember that when he got to the end of de Amicis's "Dagli Appennini alle Ande" he had tears in his eyes. He also read us stories in dialect about Fric Froc and Santuciarèla, and they too were irresistible.

In time we learned to write and even to speak in Italian, with the help of our books. "In *balilla* Vittorio's home, there was no one utterly idle." That meant the house was completely empty, because "utterly idle" was the elegant way to say "absolutely." It was fun to use the expression in everyday life.

"Have you been to mass?"

"Yes, Auntie."

"Really?"

"Utterly idle."

Aunts, who were a bit old-fashioned, didn't approve.

Mino and I, who sat in the same row, kept our arms crossed over our chests. We also blew saliva bubbles; Mino's were beautiful, mine a bit less. Don Tarcisio saw us and said, "You're disgusting," and I stopped altogether while Mino went on making little ones on the sly, sucking them in rapidly when the teacher looked our way.

We were in the central row of desks, about halfway down the row, and it was like being right in the middle of our little society. Behind us were the ox drovers, stationers, and carpenters; in front, painters, orphans, and tobacco curers. All social conditions were represented, all the districts and the villages.

A child's odor would vary by class and place of origin, just as certain habits and styles of dress would vary. Girls smelled different from boys; if the students were out of the room you could still tell if the class was mixed, and how many girls were in it.

On the way out of school Toni skipped down the stairs pushing and being pushed, he stopped a moment to play, resting his hand on the wall where "Long live the Levy of 1907" was written in fading script, and began to cough and spit up blood. He must have spit up no more than a small saucepan's worth, but there on the sidewalk it looked like a great lake of blood, and the color was bright red. The rest of us stopped playing and just stood there, somewhat embarrassed.

When Toni had finished he wiped his mouth on his sleeve and joined his playmates. Toni's brother had died of consumption the year before; he had been at the school where my mother taught, and when he died they sent us back a little book we'd lent to him in the last weeks. Mamma put it out in the sun to dry, page by page, because sunlight kills the consumption bacillus, and books were expensive.

Consumption was an insidious disease that the teachers had been ordered to tell us was not hereditary, but everybody knew it ran in families. And you could also catch it if a Consumptive

Person, either just casually or with malice aforethought (because sometimes the disease made people nasty), went "fffff" in front of your mouth. It came in various versions: there was the Tubercular Consumptive who might live for a long time, although always very thin and tired; there was the Rank Consumptive who spat up blood and would be dead within the year. These were the normal forms of consumption, but there was also Galloping Consumption (the name describes its nature) in which the bacilli grew very large and instead of crawling over the lungs and grazing on them, would begin to gallop inside your chest. The sick person would heave up and down with the rise and fall of the little hooves, and in just a few hours would be a goner.

After Toni spit blood I was somewhat scandalized by his relative calm about the whole matter, not to mention that of the other children. I thought I was the only one to really understand that he was practically on the verge of death—and even today I'm always a little surprised when I run into him, with his three or four children, over near Valdagno where he works in a factory.

✦

Sometimes it's the words that emerge first from people's memories; sometimes the things. *Sgànbare* they say over in San Bernardino; *sgàlmare,* they say in town: the word is still used today, but the memory of the thing itself has faded. Some of my old companions from town who today have refrigerators and bathrooms in their houses, find it incredible to think that we once wore *sgàmbare—our* term—and they tell me that only the farmhands wore them. But in fact, we, too, wore clogs. Those cheerful wooden soles clacked on the sidewalk, and there was a metal tip held in place with two nails. The high-class ones had a brass tip and the refinement of a piece of rubber soling, so you walked as if you were on a carpet, although you couldn't slide on them.

The child comes home from school, with his cloth book bag slung across his chest (the sophisticated shoulder straps would only come later), long socks, short trousers just over the knee. Whistling happily, his little clogs ringing on the paving stones of the portico. The others are already at table in the kitchen, and the mother smiles and says, "My dear little fourth-grader." The boy eats his soup, happy to be in the fourth and proud of his new clogs. They give vent to his feet.

The shorts made by our tailor-barbers were a nuisance. We wanted them short and roomy, which was to say, modern and elegant, and they, encouraged by the mothers and the aunties, made them long and tight fitting. Peeved, we called them "hose pipes." They didn't go below the knee, of course, because that was one of the few distinguishing marks of class: the barefoot masses wore their breeches halfway down the calf. But ours came close, unfortunately: just an inch above the knee. Today very short trousers are only to be found in the countryside and up in the hills, while in town, exotic "English-style" shorts are in fashion, I'm told. Up in Feo I saw some young kids from the hills dressed up for a festival with their bottoms hanging out. Anything goes.

✦

In the school playground we had games that were partly spontaneous, partly organized by figures like Capotta, who was the son of the new tax collector. He came from somewhere else, and at home they spoke only Italian; with us he immediately adopted our dialect, although he was unable to distinguish between the polished idiom of the town and the rough way the country and hill folk talked. He had a hoarse, metallic voice like a bugle call, and was boisterous, cheerful, and extravagant.

Capotta, always happy when he could make a lot of noise, went around enlisting people to his cause, tyrannizing everyone with his shouting. He could do the singsong part of our playground rhymes perfectly, but he had the awkward pronunciation of the mountain dwellers.

Chi-è che du-ga? Chi-è che du-ga?

Who wants to play? Who wants to play?

We smiled at this foreigner who couldn't say c*hi ze,* but we admired him too. And we played.

The gentle fricatives of town speech became rough stops in the hills. In Malo, to play was *zugare;* in Feo, it was *dugare.*

Il dì dei dughi era dòbia. The day for play was Thursday. When Mother put salt in the milk and the children stayed home from school.

Dugare sounded harsh and rough; did the little girls in Feo also "play"? Those little girls with their rag dolls, so polite and bashful?

Capotta disappeared from town during the war but reappeared after it was over, now a young man. He was part of a traveling theater company, and we all went to see the play with great curiosity. "What role do you think Capotta's going to play?"

It was one of those popular standbys of provincial theater, *The Scream,* anchored around that chilling scream backstage that always terrifies the audience. Capotta did not appear onstage; instead he did the scream, and he did it magnificently. It was obvious that unlike us, he had continued to play.

What did we play at? *Dàrsela,* "you're it," obviously, which I later heard called *Muffa,* by the pretentious city children of Vicenza. There was also *Deliberarsi,* "home free," which the snobs also called S*chiavi-libri,* "slaves free" and *Bandiera-Vecchia,* "old-flag" and *Bandiera-Nuova,* "new-flag."

Bando bandìa
polenta rostìa
chi che la ga
se la tegnarà.

Bando bandìa
polenta rostìa
the one who's got it
has to keep it.

What you're threatened with having to keep here is ringworm. To disinfect yourself you had to recite the verse three times, then pass your arm under your knee and suck your index finger (not your thumb, that won't disinfect anything!) three times, three very distinct times, while hopping along.

The fundamental weapon in these games was the *schinca,* "the dodge," something like swerving back and forth in a ball game, but purer.

The *schinca* is a divine gift. It's not speed, it's not agility, it's not stealth. You can't learn it, and you can't acquire it; it's one of the most mysterious forms of skill I know. Aldo's masterful *schinca,* or Bìcego's darting one, are for me unforgettable models. Bìcego, who was a famous soccer player, now works in town. Aldo emigrated as a young man and now works, in the same business, in Detroit.

Ata patanda—luca fanda
tèlo mèlo—luca tèlo
tème ale—fóra ti.

Fóra ti: "You're out." The rest is nonsense rhyme.

Serenity, timelessness, a peaceful world that runs right down to this very courtyard where we are playing, an orderly world protected by the eaves and the great big canvas of the sky. The flow of life, the polished stone floor of the courtyard outside the cellar windows. Afternoon air, silence, Sunday.

Aliolèche tamozèche
taprofita lusinghè
tulilàn blen blu
tulilàn blen blu.

Blu, blu—it was an adventure in shades of blue. Strange places under a pallid, frail sun; gold buttons, melancholy in the middle of the morning. All the other rhymes seemed to me insipid, or affected, even when they weren't. There was *L'ora-lòjo de l'arziprete* ("The priest's pocket-watch"), *La mia gata vuol morir* ("My cat's going to die"), *Soto la pergola nasse l'uva* ("The grapes hang down from the arbor"). And there was the wonderful *Unci dunci trinci/ Squarsquarinci / Mirimirinci / Un-fran-ghè*, a nonsense rhyme that ended up with the king's daughter being expelled.

But to me they seemed fussy and pretentious. Instead, there was the beautiful:

An pan
Fiol d'un Can
Fiol d'un Béco
Muri Séco
Cole Gambe Disti-rà.

An Pan
Son of a Dog
Son of a Louse
Ended Up a Stiff
With Your Legs Stuck Out.

I was fascinated by the rapid demise of the unlucky An Pan, and the heraldic rigidity of his legs.

✦

There's a string of names, of games. *S'ciopascóndare:* hide and seek in little places among the trash bins and heaps of sticks, in narrow, musty crevices among the spiderwebs, deep inside the bastion of schoolbags, inside the mountains of silk cocoons, while time stops, sound ceases, and you feel you have left this world and are just eavesdropping on it. You wait, hunkered down among the rubbish, upside down in a padded lair; you slither through the forbidden tunnels of the drying rooms.

What there was of the inexpressible in these childish rites, the underlying mystery, the panic of the children hiding and of those searching, can only be hinted at by that other game, *Cucò,* "Coo-coo." It was play as metaphysics, in places and times deserted by man: the woodpile, the hayloft, the cellar, the barn. Play as allusion.

While *Borèla* was all rabble and strife, an excuse for brawling under the crude light of the dirt courtyards, down at the feet of polite humanity. *All hits pay* for me in this hardscrabble universe; *no hits pay* in the next session when we are just even rivals, and when I score, I own the right to all the marbles that you, with your imperfect aim, have failed to knock out. The law of the land came into force as fast as we spoke it, and when the moment of legalized larceny arrived we would yell with triumph and snatch up the whole row of colored marbles. The Law was ours.

On the edge of our world there was *Kan-Pa-Nón,* like hopscotch, the reign of the girls, with its unwarlike geometry. In the land of the scratched lines, the young ladies moved as if in a dream, and the skipping stone made no sound.

Don't disturb this peace, my little lads, my rude guests, take care, may Santa Libera protect you from losing your turn.

Chapter 7

THE GIRLS AT SCHOOL and women in general we called *cavre,* goats. It wasn't really an insult, but a half-affectionate nickname, a rustic compliment.

Two of these little goats courted me openly in the fifth. They would walk up and down in front of our house, wrapped in their little shawls, and as they went by they would peer into the courtyard where we were playing ball. For one of them, who was dark and petite, I felt a sentiment that was new to me. In the newspaper I had seen a photograph of a "student" who was walking arm in arm with "a pretty classmate" during some festivity. I wanted to do the same with my admirer, take the wanton little goat away on my arm, and see what happened.

✦

Our attitude toward females was to change, and we began to experience small, sentimental infatuations. Norma's skirts now fell modestly below the knee, but all of a sudden there were Marcella's eyes.

Marcella's hour was early afternoon, her season high summer, and the light that belonged to her was that dazzling one that throbs over the white stones of the creek. We played on the shingle; I was the director of great works of hydraulic engineering, with troops of workmen to help redirect the stream.

Marcella would sing "Màila, love's first dream," and I, just by chance while I was moving stones, would find myself near her, and standing up, would look into her eyes. Oh, Madonna! Those eyes were right in front of mine, and they were laughing: large, damasked, astonishing, they attracted the light as she laughed and drew it in, like antique mirrors. They drew me in too, like magnetic objects in whose field you find yourself, and feel you are losing your balance somewhat. (I've seen that same unreal brilliance and felt the same magnetic pull looking at the bright planets that a telescope can draw down from the sky on a starry night.)

Marcella had stopped singing, and we looked at each other. I had a big stone in my hand, and she had a daisy, from which she was slowly plucking the petals. Then she moved off smiling and began to sing again, and I put the stone down where it belonged in the dam we were building.

✦

When Bruno Erminietto was in love with Adriana, she sometimes came to his house to visit with her parents. They sat her on the divan, as blonde and fluffy as a doll, and Bruno would get up beside her and do the pear tree.

You do the pear tree by putting your head down and your legs in the air. Thus, upside down with his face all red, Bruno Erminietto courted his love by imitating a tree.

We all loved Adriana, as we did Marcella: some of us in secret; some blushing furiously and making savage gestures of hostility. But no woman in town was loved so much and by so many, and with such fulminatory effect, as pale Sidonia.

In those days I had a little soccer team of which I was both boss and captain because the ball belonged to me. Sidonia first came to town on a Saturday; on Sunday Uncle Dino, coming home from the last mass, asked me who we were playing against that day. I told him I had cancelled the game because half of the team was in love. "And with the same woman," I told him gravely.

"*Ostia,*" said Dino, "and who would this vampire be?"

I told him; she came from Vicenza, and had just arrived—and Dino had the politesse to ask no more.

I loved Sidonia as one had to love her: immediately and unconditionally, as a creature come from the big city of Vicenza to Malo to show us what a miracle was. Others courted her more vulgarly. Savaio would steal the place beside her on the sidewalk and sing: "Sidonia / I want to go with you to Patagonia."

Insufferable show-off: to Patagonia! No sooner had Savaio sung one verse than he'd thought up another. There he went again: "The Italian doesn't think twice / he takes her by the hand / he carries her far away / under a tree, so nice."

And then what does the Italian do? Well, he had better sit down on a stone (there must be stones over there where it is so nice) because his legs certainly won't hold him—and just try to endure the luminous rush that comes off this woman's face.

Sidonia had come to stay for a while with her aunt in town, and she took part in several events with us in her *piccola italiana* uniform. She looked good in a uniform, and she looked even more elegant with her long straight brown hair caught up in the black silk net that the girls wore on their heads.

We were in the reception room of the Hotel Roma, we males of the *balilla* sitting this way, and the *piccole italiane* that way, at right angles. Sidonia was in the second row. It must have been early January, because they made us practice a hymn to the Fascist Befana. The first days of the year: an eminently poetic and amorous period, with the unreal atmosphere of the holidays and the curious sharpness and brightness that the cold, the winter sun, and the many confessions and communions lend to the sentiments.

La Befana Fascista nel sole
ha una luce di fede e d'amor.

Under the sun the Fascist Befana
emits a glow of faith and love.

I have to say that the Befana, in the guise of a Fascist woman, her ugly face raised to the sky trying to smile and be transformed, left me with a touch of nausea, which however enhanced my vague, light-headed feelings of love. Those active, concrete words won out, and the *sun*, the abstract sun of January, and the *glow* of the lamps of the Hotel Roma, triumphed, and above them that shining face.

Chapter 8

COMBAT! With Flora and Este, Aunt Lena's daughters, both of them taller than me, I had fierce but bloodless wrestling matches, pure sport. The ring was a block of pink stone that divided the portico from the courtyard. We would fold our arms around each other (mine were a bit lower) and stand there *dans d'immenses efforts* without anything happening.

Sometimes my cousins tried to use girl fighting techniques on me, pulling my hair hard, but it was easy for me to hit back by grabbing their long hair. Those two Amazons were quite a bit stronger than I, and standing there practically unable to breathe inside their big, strong arms, I had to struggle not to be crushed.

Luckily females don't really know how to fight, or we'd be in trouble. Nature itself takes care of counterbalancing its monsters. Woe to us if the *lìpara* weren't blind, if the *sioramàndola* weren't deaf as a doorknob. The viper, the salamander.

✦

Real matches take place between men.

You grab your opponent by the collar. This doesn't constitute an act of aggression.

"Go."

The grabbed party grabs in turn, also by the collar, if there is a collar, otherwise by the shirt.

"You go."

Each side exhorts the other to attack, but holds back from attacking himself. The contest now proceeds to intimidation.

"My uncle's been to Rome."

"My cousin went to America."

America trumps. The fighters let go of each others' collars and walk off grumbling.

The only time Mino and I had a match *da-bon,* a serious battle, rather than a match *da-mato* (for fun, for sport), we started on the slope of Monte Piàn, fairly high up.

We started fighting for some trivial reason that I no longer recall. The slope was steep, with patches of woods and pastures that flowed down toward town. We were on the ground with our arms wrapped around each other, and we began to roll down the hill biting and scratching. At a certain point as we rolled under and over each other, I saw Mino's twisted face framed between sky and mountain just a few inches away from mine, and I felt a sharp desire to bite him to death.

Fortunately the outburst of fury itself exhausted us, and when we had rolled all the way down the hill and lay at the bottom dirty and tired of war, we let each other go without any more fighting and immediately opened peace talks.

✦

Combat is an affair for two, but only one of the two can "scrap" the other, that is, reduce him to impotence and impose a punishment (like that conferred on the boy in fifth who was scrapped in the school playground and made to open his mouth so the winner could spit in it).

The punishment was held to be unfair and exaggerated because the winner was a Rank Consumptive.

Bruno claims he once scrapped the trashman's son Giovanni Martin, and that may be, but as I recall it, it was a fight without winner or losers. It also went on for a long time, more like a state of affairs than an event.

It happened right in front of our house after school. It began with schoolbag blows but quickly progressed to the classic formula, rolling on the street. Papà was in the doorway, and he decided not to interfere. At first we all took an interest, but after a while we wandered away.

"Are they still there on the sidewalk?"

"No, now they're in the ditch."

"Who's winning?"

"No one."

"Hand me the 22 wrench."

The two were by now indistinguishable in the mud, which meant you could say Bruno was still a contender. A battle like this not only can't have winners but in a certain sense cannot even come to an end, and in fact it didn't completely end even when the night, as in chivalric legends, parted them. Back in their own homes, the two soiled heroes kept up a tired battle with their distant opponents while their mothers washed them.

✦

"Cheat! Cheater!" I yelled. I'd seen the bee on the back side of the coin as it fell. At least I thought I'd seen it, in the instant between the downward spin of the copper coin and Bicego's lightning grab, but maybe it was only my imagination. Now, though, there was no more time for doubts.

"Cheater!" I said again. "It was tails."

"You're the cheater," said Bicego. "It was heads and it's mine."

Careful now. This guy was strong—not strong like the dark, dark Squala, who was a hard carbonized stump, a terrible monster of might—but very, very strong. He could throw a stone twice as far as me with his left hand. He was a lefty, full of mysterious skills like the *shinche* he deployed in the school playground. He came from Cantarane, from a more dangerous race than ours.

Barefoot, dark, lean, and wild, Bicego resembled a machine to smash adversaries: to do battle with him would not be to exchange blows and roll on the ground, but to engage in a brief, sinister, and nasty adventure. What if he jumped and bit, or raised his naked foot and slyly heaved it at you, or made some unknown move that shattered your bones? I was scared shitless, but it was too late to pull back.

"You're a swindler," I said, "A cheat and a swindler."

There was a silence deep as a hole in the ground. Mino was looking at me with a dumb expression, his mouth half-open. Marcella's eyes widened, and Cicana, who was scratching his arm, stopped.

There we were. Bicego stood motionless, his eyes half-closed, his lips drawn, no expression whatsoever on his face. I knew what was about to happen, or at least I knew what it was called. This was Combat with Bicego: it felt like a dream, but it wasn't. There he was, beginning to walk, now slowly coming toward me, as if far away and deep in homicidal thoughts.

Pa-fiò-san-sìa. Fathasonanolyghost.

The rest has been canceled by the mind's dark censor.

It seems I was quick to call people thieves, because one time Aunt Lena, who was very partial to her children, came out of the laundry toward me with Flora behind her sobbing, and said to me in a fighting tone:

"For what motive"—she said it just like that except that instead of "for," my aunt said "by"—"did you call her a thief?"

Right there and then, I was speechless. Okay, if we go and look at motives, for what motive indeed had I said that? Motive, motive: a word like that had the power to set my mind wandering about the curious relationship between ends and causes, about how words could cause confusion, and how it was illusory to think you could resolve the problem by working back from words to facts.

My aunt dug in, tilting her head slightly to the side, the veins of her neck swelling.

"For what motive? What did she steal from you?"

An idea came to me, and abandoning abstract speculation, I lunged for it shamelessly. I said she had stolen my peace, and for a moment it was my aunt who was speechless.

The fact is that words that pertain to larceny are compelling by themselves, for no further reason. The word *pande* had this charm.

"*Pande.*" The news spread out in murmurs, rustling, causing consternation.

"*Pande,* Jesus Lord, *pande.*"

It reached the hamlet of Barbè, at the Two Swords it split into two streams, one going downhill toward Listón, the other up toward San Bernardino. At our house it came through Aunt Lena's dining room and into Uncle Checco's workshop where he was filing a piece of iron in the vise, and stopped, looking over the tops of his glasses. It went past Colomba who was at the washtub, showing the tops of her titties which were lily white. Colomba, her sleeves rolled up, came to tell her sister Dosolina, who looked after us, and I learned it from Dosolina.

"Right, *pande,*" I said to my friends, shaking my head.

Just how the activity of *pandere,* the infinitive form, worked was not at all clear to me, but I understood immediately that *pandere* was something doleful, a token of fallen humanity, a shackle of woe.

I ruminated over the name of the man caught in the act of this very thing, a man with a name as gloomy as the night, Còpano. He was in the hospital torn up by a flash of lightning that had exploded in the dark while he was engaged in a risky and solitary enterprise.

He seems to have *panto*, past tense of *pandere*, for three days, and then the order arrived to send a vehicle to take him to prison. Uncle Ernesto went down with the dark blue Venti and I went with Colomba to watch. There was a circle of young men and girls around the Venti. My uncle got out and opened the door in front of the hospital, and we all stood there watching. My heart was pounding. Two carabinieri came out, and there he was! A male nurse had loaded him over his shoulder, gripping his arms. He looked like an old peasant, his head shaved, a beaky nose, a bushy moustache, but I immediately recognized him as the knight of nocturnal prey, the hero deposed. I prayed silently while the nurses and carabinieri inserted him into the Venti, belly down.

"Do not *pandere* any more, if you can, and if you can't help it, go ahead, *pandi*, I understand."

Nobody uses this verb anymore, at least not in town. Down in somebody's garden in Contrada Chiesa near the creek, the chicken thief got riddled in the back with birdshot.

Chapter 9

IN PRÀ ("THE COMMONS") under the ravine below Castello that we called *il giarón,* we played bocce with stones from the creek and games of soccer in a trapezoid-shaped pitch between high plane trees in double file. Sometimes they brought in a merry-go-round, and from time to time a circus.

The most memorable was the circus with Fanny. She was one of Uncle Dino's fiancées, and to my mind he was a man exceptionally well provided with fiancées; in fact there were times when he seemed to be the actual or potential fiancé of all attractive women. As a child viewing Fanny from below while she balanced herself on the wire, bare-legged, powdered up, and all sparkling beneath her yellow parasol, I felt she was an enchanting creature. She was not, however, the most important attraction in the circus.

There was the Strongman, a gentleman bared to the waist who broke chains and other objects and who announced he wanted an automobile to drive over his chest. My uncle Checco went to get the OM with the 13 VI plates, a six-seater with an open top, drove up onto a little platform, and pretending to hesitate, loudly declining all responsibility, came down with the left front tire on the bare chest of the Strongman who was lying on the ground, and remained in that position for quite a while. The gentleman under the wheel now began to converse with Uncle Checco behind the wheel, and then Checco, who had gotten into the spirit of the thing, produced a last gush of amazement, sounding the horn and setting off a huge applause, before getting off the Strongman's chest. The Strongman wanted to try again with the back wheel, after loading up the OM with the heaviest members of the audience and the chief carabiniere, but the chief himself said no, much to the dismay of all.

But the real hero of the circus was Ferruccio, the jumper, a creature not of this world but of that intermediate zone between the circus lights and the tops of the plane trees. He worked with two instruments, a sack of hay to receive him during the brief moments he touched earth, and a springboard. We knew about these wooden springboards, because they were often used for jumping, but Ferruccio's was the latest thing in a springboard. Used for the most amazing jump in the grand finale of the show, it was majestic, as tall as a house. The approach was situated at the bottom of the Castello ravine, so as to take advantage of the downhill path to work up speed. Few things are more attractive than a Gypsy at the moment he turns and gets ready to jump: that hint of laziness and untidiness about him vanishes and you see his concise elegance. Ferruccio would come running down the trembling ramp, stamp his feet as if in magnificent scorn, and fly up between heaven and earth. The supreme jump was executed without frills, it was pure epic. It was, of course, a *salto a pesce*, a "fish dive": jumps can be divided into "ordinary," that is, up to a certain height, and *a pesce*.

The world of jumping is complex: Jump-the-Bar, the Somersault, the Plunge, and more. The jump is a catalyst of personality. Who are you? What will you jump down from? From the window of the storeroom, from the Castello aqueduct? What can you jump over? How many rows of benches at the nursery school; how many big benches? In *The Mark of Zorro*, Duglà—Douglas Fairbanks—jumped down from towers and leaped over two carriages.

In theory, the plunge has no limits; in practice, if you land hunkered down, the limit is the impact of bottom on soil, which is a function of the ground's pliancy index.

The jump in all its forms was considered a spectacle, and spectacles fascinated us.

✦

Children tend to be flexible and double-jointed. Flora and Este remained exceptionally flexible even as young women: they could raise a foot and touch their necks with ease, ignoring the principle that it's best not to show off your underpants, whether they be white or powder blue. But small children are incomparably more flexible and double-jointed. When we held our own circus in the garage, employing the toddlers Annamaria and Gaetano, we tied them in knots, we made parcels out of them, balls that we could roll onstage.

The theater was in the storeroom over the cellar. I don't know why we wanted our stage up so high. An irregular plane held up by boxes and sawhorses, it was in fact very elevated. You could easily stand underneath it; there was less room when you stood on top of it. To go onstage you went up a little iron stairway that had once led to the upper deck of a bus. There were splits and gaps between the planks, from which the actors sometimes had to be rescued. The whole trembled and wobbled, and the brief performances always had a certain vibrating quality to them. At the back of the room stood the family dungeon, which we covered with a heavy rubber sheet during the performances.

A space for the audience was carved out by pushing the capon and rabbit cages against the wall. The tile floor was swept and washed with care. Both spectators and actors were crawling with that ferocious parasite known as the chicken louse. Along with dramatic performances, we had acrobatic intervals with contortions, splits, and pear trees. The actors, some speaking, some mute, scratched themselves, and the spectators in all the classes of seats also scratched themselves: in the normal seats, which cost five cents; in special, which cost ten; and in the stall seats, which cost fifty cents and were made of car seats complete with their side doors. When a seat in the stalls was sold, the theater season opened. The spectator in question was led to his place and closed into it.

Often the stage would become unbalanced, and at a particularly dramatic moment in the action would collapse to one side. The public would help us right it, but if any of the actors was seriously hurt, the show was suspended, and there was haggling about partial reimbursements of the ticket price.

When the performance was over, we would uncover the dungeon and put it back in service. As a rule there was no need to capture our prisoners by force. The victim would be enticed into the storeroom with a specious excuse; we'd climb up on the mountains of old debris down at the end of the room, leaping from a piece of tin roof to a tower of old oil drums, along interlaced supporting members, over airborne planks. There was a trap made of a tall pile of worn-out rubber tires, with an innocent flap of canvas on top that looked like a ledge. The victim was encouraged to step on it, and fell into a well of rubber. After a certain period of time contact was resumed, and the jailbird was treated to a harsh but not inhumane prison regimen while he waited for the ransom to be paid.

✦

The black horn was in the middle, a twisted automobile horn missing the rubber bulb. The glossy painted metal curves ended in a bare brass mouthpiece with a thin copper reed inside. We would sound it from time to time, blowing into it to call our clients, and then the horn was put back in the place of honor, next to ticket number 101. The clients came, some with five cents (two tries) and some with ten, and they often got close to the horn; there were many hits on ticket 100 (old postcards) and 102, with a sign that said "Thanxs."

Flora would take the money, Este held out the shoebox with the little scrolls of numbers in it, I stood by with my left hand in my pocket, and in my left fist, the slip that said 101.

Here was how you did the lucky dip. The prizes were laid out on a wash table over stools in the doorway of the dining room. There were a few broken toys, ball bearings of steel, glass stoppers, stretchy pieces of "Innertube," a car battery for the fools. Sometimes, to attract clients, I'd mount my bicycle atop two chairs behind the table, next to a card marked with a name rather than a number. The dippers knew that there was no scroll with "Girastenco" or "Guera" on it in the box, but the bicycle still worked to bring them in. There was no need to confess this trick, because omission of the absurd could not be considered a mortal sin of omission, but for other objects that we protected using the same trick, like the black car horn, it was considered prudent to make confession in church. And so once the lucky dip was over and we had spent our earnings, one of us went to the priest. (The sin was far less grave if the number was honestly deposited in the box at least for an hour or two before we closed, to give the last clients a chance and when our economic goals had already been met. If someone did in extremis draw the protected prize, the dip was shut down and the win was extinguished.)

The black horn figured in a lucky dip that went on for three days, when it was decided to introduce number 101 the last afternoon. For two days we had been inveigling well-off Malo youth and extracting resources from them. But on the morning of the third day, Moro-Balào showed up.

He was a beggar by profession, and in his free time, a student in the fifth. A person of experience and interests far beyond our own, he nevertheless liked the black horn very much. He tried the lucky dip a couple of times, staring at us, gave us back the postcards, and said:

"How much do you want for that horn there?"

Flora made up a crazy price, one franc. Moro-Balào said, "I'll be back this evening."

He did come too, and counted out the franc in five-cent coins, with one or two ten-cent pieces. I thought he was awesome: dusty, all alone in the world, practical, able to make a franc a day. There was a moment of tenderness, almost bewilderment as he took the horn; I could see his hands were trembling. Then he went off hooting it and we closed up the draw and got our celebrations underway quickly.

A few days later Moro-Balào grabbed onto the rear end of a truck as it slowed down (he often moved around that way, hanging his bread sack on the hook under the sign No Hitching a Ride). Hooting religiously at all the curves, he neglected however to get off at a safe spot, and when he jumped down horn in hand, he was flattened by the vehicle behind him.

Balài, who was Moro-Balào's aunt and the mother of the boy who was actually named Balào, was a washerwoman. She also came to us to do our washing too, a small, bony woman galvanized by hard work. She worked ferociously at the washtub in the courtyard or down at the laundry; her hands were swollen and disfigured and in the winter were one solid chilblain, not just on her fingers but everywhere, and in the water these chilblains turned lurid colors and cracked open.

The Lord had the bright idea of sending this poor woman a cancer, and in a few months she was dead. One afternoon I came in the kitchen and saw her: a bizarre, terrified creature who was standing by the door talking in a whisper to my mother. She had run away from the hospital and had only a few days to live. I think she wanted to speak about her son and say goodbye to someone beyond just the nuns at the hospital.

One time the real Balào came to our kitchen with his mother. We had an unheard-of luxury at home, a metal box full of biscuits, and they offered one to the little boy who took it hesitantly and said thank you in a cross tone of voice. He didn't eat it, however. They thought he didn't dare to and tried to encourage him: "Why don't you eat it, you little bonehead, it's good, you know." But the real Balào wanted bread, and now that he had the biscuit, he offered to barter it for a half a small loaf. The whole thing made a deep impression on me.

He came to the Solario with me, and when we sang patriotic songs he grew visibly elated.

> *Arma la prora marinaio*
> *metti la Giuba di Batàlia*

> Arm the prow, seaman,
> put on your Battle Dress.

Arm-the-prow: obscure words of war, like saying to the seaman, "On guard, mate!" The word "seaman" set off a series of reactions in a boy who'd never seen the sea, but the lyric heart of the matter was the Battle Dress, which was certainly blue, and in which little Balào saw himself transfigured on the deck of the ship as it headed across the Adriatic toward Dalmàssia, the salty wind in his face and his stomach miraculously stuffed with bread.

"You see how it works?" I explained to Bruno. "First we take Yugoslavia, this plum colored one on the right, and then we move to the other side and take France. You see this liver-colored one? That's France. Okay. We take it."

Bruno would get excited. "Are we really going to take France too?" he asked. And then he'd start to sing, not very appropriately:

> *Andiamo la guera*
> *co la s'ciopéta nera*

> *co la s'ciopéta bianca*
> *Viva la Francia!*

> We're going a-war
> with the black shotgun
> with the white shotgun
> Hurrah for France!

Perhaps he meant to sing the praises of a France that was already ours, but that "Hurrah" sounded slightly premature, a bit out of place. I therefore composed an anti-French hymn, a very poisonous, somewhat personal Frog-hating jingle that began "And the French are Chickens," in which the best part was the long-winded opening yell "A-n-n-n-n-d," which sounded a note of war.

We also sang the other military hymn, which was quite well known in town and which seemed to us both martial and realistic.

> *Andiamo la guera*
> *col s'ciopo inpartèra*
> *col s'ciopo inparmàn*
> *pin! pun! pan!*
> *Dame na ciopa de pan.*
> *An! an! an!*

> We're going a-war
> a-war with guns
> with guns in hand
> ka-pow! ka-bang!
> Gimme a piece of bread.
> Yum! Yum! Yum!

The man with the gun gets the bread. Bruno and I, hunched over the map of Europe, did not then realize how close we were to the spirit and the methods of the military and political conflicts that we would later witness. Underneath we thought—never confessing it to ourselves—that we were playing. But in fact, that's effectively how you took France and Croatia, Greece and Poland.

Chapter 10

WE LEARNED ABOUT NATURE by observing how the country folk behaved, exploring the territory behind Castello and along the creek and on the screen of the Cinema San Gaetano. There was also the Radium, which didn't belong to the priest and where you could see scandalous movies, but then they closed it and the scandalous movies were only to be seen over in Schio.

What was it all about, that film called *The Gaucho* (pronounced *Gau-ko*)? What it certainly was about was the leper with his head stuck in a wooden plank at the end of a pole that people used to keep him at a distance. The leper is standing in the middle of a circle of people, and the Gaucho says to him:

"Go into the heart of the forest and do away with yourself."

Do-away-with-yourself was an exotic way of speaking; it had a dreamy quality to it. Our expression *cópete*, "kill," reflexive, could never mean *do-away-with-yourself*. So how did one say *do-away-with-yourself*? You didn't say it; there was the expression *sbàrete*, "shoot yourself," but you'd already have to have the shotgun in hand. You can say *cópete sètu?* You want to kill yourself? But that meant: Look out, be careful not to harm yourself.

Then the Gaucho leaned back against a window, in a sort of mezzanine or on a landing, and spoke to the girl. He had his hands behind his back and very slyly the leper appeared behind the window and bit his hand, and really dug in, while the Gaucho cursed him and tried to get away.

El ghe la ga petà, the audience exclaimed like a tragic Chorus. "He's infected him."

Even *petare,* to give it to him, to infect, was rich with significance—fleas, ringworm, consumption—and now this stupendous disease called leprosy.

At this point the leper could turn to the Gaucho and say: "Go into the heart of the forest and do away with yourself."

In the heart of the forest, not just *in* the forest, but in the *heart,* a concept as bold as "the pearl of the Adriatic." The heart of the forest was infested with ruthless and treacherous creatures; luckily they were often crippled and deficient, as men are.

> *Se la lìpara ghe vedesse e la sioramàndola ghe sentisse, no ghe saria pi òmini al mondo che vivesse.*

> If the viper could see us and the salamander could hear us, there would be no more human race alive on this earth.

The *lìpara* doesn't see us, she finds her way by smell, and when she jumps (and she can jump six or seven meters) if another odor distracts her she'll mistake her aim and snap the air with her jaws.

When the *lìpara* chases a man, as is her habit, she follows his smell. It's useless therefore to run in a straight line because the *lìpara* is extremely fast and can easily catch up not only with a man but with a dog or a horse. Faced with a *lìpara,* you must escape by running zigzag, so that the smell moves back and forth in waves through the air and the *lìpara,* too, begins to zigzag and breaks her backbone.

At that point you can turn back and observe (but not touch!) the triangular-shaped head and the dead eye of the blind creature.

The *sioramàndola* is much rarer. She lives in damp places, near springs in the woods, eats mainly air and kills out of sheer cruelty, using her tongue.

I saw a *sioramàndola* just once, at the Fontanella, the spring behind Castello. Piareto and I were chattering away unawares under the leafy branches of the beech trees, leaning over the crystal spring water to drink. There, on a stone lapped by the little rivulet, sat the *sioramàndola*. She was green like the light all around, with spots of yellow and brown like the dry leaves. She was sitting there with her back to us.

I stopped Piareto just as he was about to throw a stone at her (but the stone bounced and made the little monster furious), and we tiptoed away before the *sioramàndola* turned her head.

✦

The green grasshopper is a large oblong-shaped insect, not very strong. Under its wings, so fragile they look vegetal, it wears underclothes of transparent, yellowish silk, The brown grass-hopper is thickset and muscular, especially its saw-toothed legs, which it can use like a tiny slingshot. When it shoots you see its scarlet underpants flash.

Green grasshoppers don't eat brown grasshoppers. For the brown grasshoppers, however, we would provide a diet of green grasshoppers neatly chopped up: skinny, flabby thighs at noon, then a mixture of eyes and antennae; for supper, a delicacy— breasts. Many of them put on a kind of hunger strike, refusing to eat and turning their heads from side to side, so that it was necessary to force feed them. What can you do: there's always a certain degree of force in the relationship between a large creature and a small one.

We kept them in large stalls made out of paper boxes, at-tached to long white or black leashes. We would take them out for walks to distract them, with these leashes tied to our fingers, They tended to die by drowning during the big swimming meets in the pool over at Castello, or were torn apart during the training sessions when we tried to teach them a new style of crawl.

The *brombólo,* the may bug, can easily die in his sleep, and since he is always napping, he is always somewhat at risk of dying.

But the *brombólo* is above all a climber; stick him on the War Monument up in Castello and he will grab onto the marble and begin to climb patiently. He climbs by taking advantage of the faint roughness of the stone and the troughs where the names of the dead are inscribed. He falls off without warning, and you can hear the little blow as his cranium hits the foot of the white cliffs. The *brombólo* doesn't die when he knocks his cranium; you put him in the infirmary with a diet of soup poured directly over him, he eats and sleeps, but often, given that this is his nature, he will die in his sleep with a full stomach.

We still remember our best *brombóli* affectionately, especially that outstanding one named Soga. The others would start climbing the War Monument from the bottom right edge, and they'd get to Zanella and Vanzo right away, less often to Sterchele or Saggin, sometimes even to the first Pamato. One time one of us pushed a beetle into the middle of the list of *P*'s, of which there are ten, and then he fell, knocked his cranium, and subsequently died in the infirmary.

But Soga would immediately move to the left side of the monument; he would climb past Lain, past Lappo, he kept going past Galizian, the brother of my Aunt Lena, past Festa, so high now we could barely reach up to protect him with our hands. When he passed the two Destros, both of them dead on May 16, 1916, we couldn't reach up to him even on tiptoe, and so we'd step down from the base and just watch.

He was alone now. Alone with De Marchi, Antonio, born in 1895, and with the other De Marchi born the year before that; alone where the sun's rays glanced off the stone and it said Cimberle. We were afraid for him; we watched him climb from row to row up there and the rows never seemed to end. How many dead were there from this accursed town?

We feared for Soga, sent into harm's way like that for no real reason, as tiny up there as a tiny man climbing that mountain battleground, il Dente del Pasubio, like that name that you can just see up at the top, Agosti, Alessando: Sandro's uncle and his namesake.

✦

There was a epidemic of these beetles of ours in the year 1598, and a plaque was duly stuck up in the parish church:

> While the *brombóli* were destroying the vines, the
> community of Malo, having made a vow to St. Ubaldo
> Bishop of Gubbio to celebrate his feast day every XVI
> May each year, was liberated . . .

So the eighteenth century abbot and chronicler Gaetano Maccà records. Let me add that when you attached a string and rotated the *brombóli* in the air, they dissolved in a vaporous cloud, like wild chestnuts given the same treatment. They also emitted a sharp cry—normally they're silent—perhaps in memory of the slaughter of Saint Ubaldo.

We didn't collect them from the grapevines, as perhaps our fellow townsmen of three or four centuries before did, but from blackberry vines, where they looked like blackberries. They made fine school companions and an excellent medium of exchange; they were harmless, slow, and sleepy. It astonished us to think that exterminating them could be a virtue, although that seemed to be the case.

Slusaróla (firefly); *ligaóro* (lizard); *ciupinàra* (mole); *sitón* (dragonfly). While the petite bourgeoisie dealt primarily with insects, the people also coped with reptiles and amphibians. Mammals belonged to everyone, some to one class more than another. There was the *ciupinàra*'s secret crawl that we once saw Nane-of-the-Vegetable-Garden detect.

Nane was separating the hemlock from the parsley. "Stop right there!" he said, and took out his knife. His mouth was making that kind of grin where you can't tell if the person has bitten himself out of intense concentration, or is just laughing. He bent forward and was listening to a faint rustling underground that we couldn't hear; all of a sudden he took two big steps, knelt down over an invisible moving target a few meters away, and stabbed the earth.

When he got up he really did seem to be laughing. He dug around the knife handle and just underneath was the *ciupinàra*, harpooned on the big knife blade. Its little face was pale pink, like a creature that is always in the dark. Its fur was bloody and caked with dirt, and it was blind. The little paws that were used to scraping hung inert, and impaled on the knife there under the blinding sun, it looked like a stuttering messenger from the land of fresh, damp tunnels underground. Nane, too, stammered, and the whole thing spoke to us of stuttering, of an afternoon's painful choking up.

Nane grew hemlock in his garden and mixed it with parsley for the sheer joy of being able to separate out the ill-omened stronger green leaves. He also grew the glossy, evil castor oil plant with whose beans we secretly poisoned the tips of our arrows.

✦

Among all those things that kill, the viper is by far the most fascinating. I found one dead under the little cascade near

Castello and took it home with appropriate care. I knew that heat could bring a drowned snake back to life, and so I laid the viper head down to dry out on the hearth in our kitchen. This creature is known to have superhuman powers—even several days after one dies, if you touch its head with a finger, it will bite and pump its poisons into you—and I was afraid it might come alive all of a sudden. So we nailed it to a board with U-shaped nails from the neck to the tail, and propped it up vertically before the fire.

The viper spat out drops of water and began to dry off; we watched it carefully and when it began to move and slither backward, escaping the nails, an epidemic of goose flesh spread over our bare arms and legs. Standing very still and clutching the sticks and rods we had armed ourselves with, we waited for the viper to drop on the hearthstone so we could hit it. But when it got halfway down, it died again and lay utterly still.

We forced the mouth with pliers and propped it open with little iron rods that vipers can't bend. I searched for the fang, which is hidden at the back of the mouth, and with the help of a penknife and great care, tried to extract the fang and poison sac intact so we could lash them onto a special arrow tip destined for a certain enemy, who luckily was never hit. I say luckily because even if the little gadget mounted on the tip to puncture the poison sac hadn't functioned, I expect that merely seeing my arrow fly through the air and hit him would have been enough to make him die of terror.

After the resurrection and the second death, the viper, now with a single tooth in its mouth, ascended to the Empyrean and became a Numinous Mystery. The Empyrean was a large bottle full of vinegar in which we stuffed the viper tail first and corked it in. It stayed there, a spiral with its head up near the cork, and we worshiped it daily. After a while it began to rot and come to pieces, but the pieces, connected by filaments, stayed more or less in place. The vinegar turned cloudier and cloudier. The Empyrean bottle was kept in the cellar so the servant girls wouldn't become nauseated. Soon the viper could no longer be seen in the cloudy, rusty liquid and the whole Bottle was Viper, and we worshiped it by removing the cork briefly at certain ordained times of the day. In the revolting whiff that emerged, you could perfectly distinguish a faint scent of violets beneath the stink of putrefaction.

✦

When all is said and done, humble people are closer to nature. Sfojàda would put silkworms in his mouth as if they were chocolates, and for a half a glass of wine he'd swallow them.

Sfojàda, Lòba, Squala, Bèna, Cicàna: they were a whole generation, an entire male race marked with sinister grandeur. They went around barefoot wearing hose pipes of cloth that hung far down their legs; they were familiar with things that exploded (Bèna was missing a hand); they were heathens, bold and indomitable.

In their pockets they had knives and pruning hooks; they played games for money in groups on the steps of the Casa del Fascio; they walked around lazily, almost reluctantly. They would gather in Prà and Cicàna would begin:

"First, you see the hand closed in a fist, and it's dark all around and the hand is lit up. Then this hand very, very slowly opens up and you see a beautiful, glittering jewel, this big. This jewel sits in the middle of the palm of the hand; the hand is *rùspia,* rough, and the jewel is *lìmpio,* clear, and sharp. Then the hand begins to rotate and the jewel rotates too, and you see the rays . . ."

Cicàna was a great raconteur of films, even those that ran to three or four episodes. His versions went on much longer than the originals, and he had a vivid grasp of camera angles and of tactile and visual effects. He knew all about the strongman

Maciste, the Thief of Bagdà, and the Mark of Zorro. The sub-
titles livened up when translated in dialect, and swearwords
abounded.

Cicàna knew an infinite number of curse words, and what
he didn't know he invented. One time he bet he could say 350
different swearwords one after the other, and he won his bet
without really trying. We listened enchanted: it was a sort of
hymn with a vivid feeling for nature running through it, and
with a lively spirit of observation.

It was afternoon, and we were gathered in the shade beside the last house before the Castello bridge. His extravagant litany brought before our eyes a procession of exotic
animals and our own small mammals, birds, fish, and reptiles,
the fauna of the manure heaps going about their business,
and the cheerful flora of the sidewalk, the big gobs of yellow
phlegm of the tobacco chewers and the scarlet ones of the
consumptives. You could see the cowardly *brombóli* turned on
their backs, rowing with their tiny legs, the rat trotting along
the top of a wall smelling the air, and the whip snake called
the *carbonàzzo,* wrapped tight around the farm girls' legs and
slapping them with its tail.

Wild and tame creatures, innocuous ones, ferocious ones,
big pachyderms and little fleas, right down to microbes and
bacilli that can't be seen with the naked eye. Beasts of the air;
buzzards on high; low, thick swarms of gnats; beasts of day and
of night, of clear water and murky abysses.

At the hundred swearword mark Cicàna left the animal
kingdom and moved on to plants, grasses, lichens, molds; at
two hundred he entered the inert world of inanimate matter;
at three hundred he began to touch the sphere of the arts and
the crafts, the structures of society, the play of human passions.

He ended with the microcosm of the human body, the internal organs both attractive and repulsive, the wondrous bodily
functions, and having reached the agreed-upon number of

swearwords (Lòba was keeping count), he added a few supplementary ones, singing a hymn to Love, which however he called by another name. He was in high lecture mode now, and finally came to a halt at 371.

He concluded with a brief, solemn curse, in which the Name of the Creator modified itself. *Dio-Dio.*

Chapter 11

THERE ARE TWO ROADS up to Castello: a narrow switchback that runs along the rim of the valley that looks down toward Prà, and another that is wider, steeper, straighter, and flanked by plane trees. This second road intersects one coming down from town, also bordered with plane trees, at a near right angle—and the ravine in front plummets down to the creek.

It was dangerous to race down Castello's straight slope back in the days before the priest put in the steps. You had to turn right toward town very sharply at the bottom, and those who didn't make it had a choice: hit a plane tree or plunge to the creek bed below. You played the game with a bicycle, or with a sled in winter. You had to brake as little as possible and as late as possible, and we developed an even more daring alternative in which we stripped our bikes of brakes and chain. Innumerable playmates of mine ended up down in the creek. One who— too late—chose the plane tree, died up above on the prow.

Swooping down from Castello at the head of the group I yelled, "I'm Leduc!" When I came to the bottom, I tried to turn left without losing speed.

Flat on the gravel, I felt even more like the real Leduc, a cyclist of those days (it was probably during the month of the Tour de France, when we read avidly about the cyclists' ruinous falls on the downhills). It was another thing altogether when I got home and they cleaned my wounds. Howling, okay, but drowned? I was completely drenched, and from my eyes gushed two thick streams of salt and water. I had little thought for Leduc, and that little was "Go screw yourself."

Sliding, running, jumping, climbing, throwing stones: Each of our principal activities was a world in itself, with local traditions, rules, customs, and even an apposite vocabulary.

In nature, velocity comes in three classes: trot, gallop, and flight. Man can only fleetingly touch this last sphere, for example, when he shouts out to his companion in harness: Fly! It's a step beyond a limit, like the sound barrier. It happens in nature and in books close to nature like the *Iliad*, where horses fly and Achilles is by definition the hero who can touch the supreme limits with his feet.

Other more exact measures of velocity falsify matters. Our Achaean-Finnish tables with their estimates of one-hundred-meter times for the principal Greeks and Trojans (Achilles: 10 seconds flat) didn't feel right. And efforts to express those times in kilometers per hour were even more convoluted. Velocity is connected with the imagination, and so is jumping and all the rest.

We saw ourselves as mere scions, almost pygmies; we came after a generation of great runners, jumpers, archers, superb climbers up outsize pine trees, greased poles, and the immense plane trees of Prà. They used to send Gelindo up to the top of the highest plane tree. "See the nest up at the top, Gelindo?" Gelindo, who was a little thick, climbed quickly and clumsily, and when he had become a minute little thing up at the top of the tree they began to throw stones to show him where the nest was. They were good shots, and Gelindo, struck on the head with a stone, tumbled down head over heels from branch to branch and hit the grass hard.

He was still sucking in air, and they carried him unconscious to the piazza. A cart arrived quickly, and headed quickly to the hospital; they raced at high speed over the cobblestones, and Gelindo's head banged heavily on the planks of the cart *pan-*

pan-pan-pan. When he got to the hospital he had a fractured skull—from the cart, however, not the plane tree.

We humbly sought to imitate the models our world provided. To mount a washboard and fly over the rungs of a long ladder suspended over the void below the hayloft, then connect, at an obtuse angle below, with another long ladder that ran down to the dirt floor of the courtyard. The aviator is in place and ready, sitting on his washboard; the machine is held in place by two pieces of cord at the top of the upper ladder. The aviator takes a pair of scissors in his left hand and one in his right, ready for the double clip of the cord that will set the flight in motion. The ladder has been patiently rubbed with soap and has an evil shine. "Go!"

Gastone-Fiore always survived. He even survived the longest parachute jump made in our generation. We had all tried to make a parachute, with sheets, covers, old canvas tops for automobiles. We all experimented with umbrellas, but the practical problems and failed first tries helped avoid more serious disasters. Of course the uninitiated, copying us, took some risks: Gaetano and Annamaria were seized at the top of the San Bernardino bell tower with their umbrella open and ready.

The only one who actually jumped off the roof with an umbrella was Gastone-Fiore. As a matter of fact, he had tried to persuade the good-natured, obliging Sandro to make the first jump, telling him he had to conduct a technical inspection from the ground, but for once Sandro dug in his heels. It all took place in a flash: one minute Gastone-Fiore jumped, the next he was sitting on the ground under a broken umbrella. He was lifted up from that position and taken directly to bed. Today, he says he felt like he was in a comic strip: he could feel the red stars rising from his backside to his head and exploding against the ceiling.

Swimming took place in the *bóji,* the water holes along the creek. In the one that was called Rostón, Faustino executed the crawl, the breaststroke, the dog paddle, the "lightning-fish," "the stone," and the "dead man" so well that when he came out dripping I said to him spitefully and despondently:

"Not bad, not bad. But what about the sword? Can you do sword?"

"Sword is my *swim*," said Faustino calmly, and the expression, more than the news itself, shut me up.

◆

We lived for racing, measuring up, setting records, winning trials.

There were two editions of the Olympics in the run-up to the war: one in Los Angeles and Berlin; one in my grandmother's courtyard. We tried to substitute cow racing for the equestrian events, but organizational difficulties made that impossible; all the other main events, however, took place.

For the track and field events the equipment used in Malo was no different from that of Los Angeles. For the shot put we had to find a stone weighing 7.2 kilos, and we took apart long stretches of the wall at Maule, weighing the stones on the scale. Stones vary greatly in terms of their specific weight; there were huge ones that didn't make the grade, and tiny black ones that weighed eight kilos and more. We finally found the right one; two or three of us would lift it to the athlete's shoulder, wait until he regained his balance, and then let go. The athlete would toss the stone, and we would measure the length of the throw.

There were athletes of every age and height, and they all used the same equipment, but they benefitted from a complex handicapping system based on years of age and centimeters of height. For the javelin throw (three javelin lengths per year) we didn't have a field long enough so we launched them against the high wall of the drying shed at the end of the courtyard.

By coating the point of the javelin with mud, the result of the throw would be marked on the side of the shed.

We had heard of a game called golf in which you hit the ball with a stick, and we decided to combine it with soccer because it sounded rather stupid. For the ball we used a tin can beaten with a hammer. This we called *golcio:* golf + *calcio,* soccer. Tennis played with the hands instead of rackets was called *triaf:* the rules were complicated and could be modified in the course of the game. There were rules about how the rules could be modified, and the principal keeper of the rules was me. But it was a thankless role, and in fact my opponents always wanted to play on the side of the drying shed, where the hatchet was. You need some training to duck a hatchet, because the weight difference between the head and the handle makes it do *schinche* in the air.

✦

War. War with slingshots, bows and arrows, javelins, with our superb rubber-band cannon mounted on a Citroën seat and hoisted onto a wheeled cart. War today against the guys from the piazzetta (who surrendered without a fight when the cannon made its appearance); a glorious future war against the ones from Piazzola, and one day, those barbarians from Cantarane.

Our reserves of slingshot-grade *càmara dària,* elastic bands made of inner-tube rubber, were the largest in town. We were actually able to furnish supplies to the enemy, but only the red *lastic,* the worst quality. Black *lastic* was never sold. Our javelins had long triangular tin blades wedged to the point, our chestnut bows shot slender arrows with nails on them that could fly high into the sun. Our heavy crossbows launched deadly oxygen pipes whose tips we spent days filing to make them into surgical instruments. There was a copper tube on the crossbow to guide these missiles, and once, while I was using this weapon, the tip came out backward, whirled around crazily, and stuck in my wrist.

I was out in the field behind the church, and Colomba was behind me. The elegant filed point went neatly through my tissues and came out my hand. I was too frightened to do anything but stare at it, but Colomba took my arm between her two round legs, and pulling hard with both hands, extracted the piece of metal. I stupidly didn't think of the *Iliad*. There was a hideous green hole from which little drops of dark blood were just beginning to come forth. It was necessary to take me to the hospital, and then to modify the design of our crossbows.

✦

For several years we fought bitterly at Montesèlo behind town, partly in the acacia woods, partly on the grassy slope. Piareto's side, hidden away invisible on the heights, would ready their attack. They sent my brother Bruno out on reconnaissance, and we captured him. I ordered Mino and Guido to interrogate him about enemy strategy, but the prisoner refused to talk. I had him tied to an elm tree and personally delivered the question-ultimatum. It was like talking to the elm.

I turned toward Mino and Guido who were standing there embarrassed, doing nothing.

"Torture him," I ordered.

Between word and deed there was a short circuit; in truth I hated the idea of hurting my brother, who was smaller than I and lashed to a tree trunk, but the dark syllables of "torture" came to mind with urgent necessity, the valves blew, and I was trapped in the gears, in the dark.

Mino tried to seem martial. "Yessir," he said, "How, sir?"

One began with willow shoots, obviously. I pointed to the shoots.

Mino and Guido conferred for a moment, and then Guido said, "You torture him," and they declined to follow orders.

While I was cutting the willow shoots the bell up on Castello rang noontime, hostilities were suspended, and we went home to eat.

Guido, faced with impossible choices, had discovered the art of the double-cross decades before time, and he exercised it on two fronts: not only did he betray one side pretending to betray the other, but he also betrayed the others, by pretending to pretend to betray them. He didn't do it out of malice, however, but out of goodness and innate courtesy. Guido sincerely wanted to be on everyone's side, even at the cost of having to betray everyone.

He had a large, polyhedron-shaped head, and because of this we called him The Maia, meaning Big Head. His head slowed him down running, so we also called him Race Horse. Recently, he told me that this second nickname, although it was meant to be derisory, seemed to him, deep down, a nice name, and he secretly basked in it while slowly galloping across the meadows.

Guido faced two tough choices: between me and Bruno; and between us and the guys from the piazzetta.

Between me and Bruno one had to be cautious, because even though I was a few years older, Bruno had a dangerous temperament. Guido worked with me to draft chilly, irrevocable documents of censure and expulsion, and one time, after I'd reread him the text, he added quite spontaneously: "And so Bruno was left in his shorts," an expression I'd never heard and which seemed to me quite fitting. But then I also know that he often seconded Bruno's plans to get back at me— although he did speak out against the idea of murdering me in my sleep. Bruno and I slept in the same room, and he would wait for me to fall asleep so he could go downstairs and get the axe, but then he would fall asleep himself before I did.

As for the choice between us and the guys from the pi-azzetta, the problem was this: The Maia was one of our men, but in fact he lived at the piazzetta. To be fair, he seems to have tried for a while not to collaborate with the enemy, but one day those savages—the worst extremist among them be-ing Gastone-Fiore—captured him and locked him up in the pigsty awaiting trial.

The Maia kicked desultorily at the door; Gastone-Fiore, standing guard with a pitchfork, pretended to fear that he might escape, and decided he had the right and duty to stab him through the window. With a hunter's cool aim he hurled the pitchfork at The Maia, and the prisoner had to jump des-perately from one corner to another to save himself. Finally Gastone-Fiore lost his patience, opened the door and got ready to make the decisive stab, but just then his companions appeared. The Maia was pulled out mostly unharmed, and—stinking and weeping—he betrayed us.

Chapter 12

PER DOVE PARI TU: that was the question. Which side are you defending? Soccer was part of our lives even before we had perfected the art of standing up. They took me to the Solarium, I was received, stripped of my clothing, and pushed out onto the open field where our games were held. It was my first match; there was a furious tribe that clung together yelling "over here" and "over *here*," and in the middle you could just see the ball.

Your *prime di punta,* shot with your toes turned up, set off fitful upward motion, but mostly the ball rolled around on the ground like a top, spun as it was pushed around by awkward kicks, jumped in circles, and did *schinche* all by itself. I took off at a trot toward the center of the horde, but when I got halfway, they swarmed away, I braked, changed directions and took off again. I was having fun and began to think this is how you played, at the margins. But now the tribe parted, the violent shins connected, and the ball came hopping forward hesitantly—right to me.

As if in a dream I gave it a kick, and fell down. A furious player bent to grab me by the arm and shake me, and he shouted:

"Hey, which side are you defending?"

So, the thing here was to defend. But which side?

Balls get a *prima* (which just means a hard kick, either straight-out or on the rebound, either in place or falling down) and *prime* are often delivered with the toes, but you have to learn to *dargli di falso,* to spin the ball, and if you have Technique you almost always put a spin on it, and sometimes *di ranca,* with the outside of the foot. In Hungary they always do the outside spin. Strange people, but good footballers.

There's also the head shot: the ball goes up in the air, and the player runs off the field, head in hands, howling. The stitches make a particular point of aiming for the head: big, hard, bulbous things, they would stamp a scar on your forehead and tear out hunks of hair.

The ball was much loved and much hated, in part because of these stitches, in part because of the valve. Once the valve was secured by force of nails and teeth and a gob of spit went on it to see if it still made bubbles, you had to force it into the crack beneath the stitches. Sometimes the operation just didn't want to work, and the red valve slowly absorbed all our hatred, seriously risking castration, and the ball, having its guts torn out with knives. And even when the valve did submit in time, there was always an irregular lump on the ball's surface that multiplied the skinning and bruising power of the stitches. Players specialized in head shots—they were nearly always men of the people—were therefore very much admired.

✦

For a long time Ivo came to me at night: he'd be there in the foreground, over to the right a little, with that air of going full-steam-ahead slowly that heavy people have when they run, and his right leg was flexed at the knee, ready to make a stiff kick. He wore boots with nails on the toe, and he instinctively pursued that murderous strategy called *omo-balòn,* "man-ball": going after player or ball with equal fury. He was stocky, slow, unstoppable: I would wake up just in time to avoid the fearful kick coming at me.

Ivo grew up to be huge, tough, and cantankerous. He worked as a miller, and went around town snapping his whip with that self-satisfied air that so often seems to suit men with gruff, asymmetrical, knobby faces. A girl fell in love with him and copied out a message she found in a book in which a man declares himself to his "white dove." She made the necessary adjustments and read it to my cousins before sending it.

"Come back to me, come back, white dove, to your nest!"

Ivo on his cart among the sacks of flour was rather white, and the message had a nice ring.

As I was shooting to goal from two meters away after a long *fuga*, Celo-Vilàn cleared the ball, kicking me in the ankle. Conversation with the grass, two inches from my wide-open eyes: Grass, grass, what is pain, what is woe? Why does one seem to fly, though stretched out flat, and feel the pain, yet feel it's still to come, and all the while one's flying? Grass, grass.

She said she liked them, my *fughe*. "What wonderful *fughe*," she said, and the Danube itself flowed through the *gh*. She was driving me home in her little sports car, a smile on her face. Elegant, Viennese, the Commendatore's young wife was the most splendid lady we had ever seen, with her short black hair and lacquered lips.

She had made a visit to the Solarium and had watched one of our matches, sitting in a chair among the directors. The pitch had rows of mulberries and vines running lengthwise through it, and I had played a high-spirited game as right wing, often racing zigzag between the trees. After the game, Signora Mariella shook hands with the barefoot, exhausted players, smiling gaily, and offered to drive me home. We became friends, and subsequently she came to pick me up many times.

She wore short, close-fitting dresses, of silk, the delicious dresses of that time, and sometimes a cloche hat. She was protective of me, and I of her: a foreigner and somewhat fragile and isolated on account of her beauty.

It was a very civilized relationship of mutual aid that lasted one long and beautiful summer.

✦

Playing football we learned some of the basics of English, for example: *Au* (out), *Ossei* (off side), *Cros* (cross), *Còrne* (corner), *Tràine* (trainer), *Gol* (goal). We also learned to respect the rules and the men who incarnated those rules, for example, Massimino.

Small, sturdy, and very strong, Massimino probably wasn't a genuine bully, but in early childhood he had developed an ugly habit of beating people up. He began to practice on his peers (luckily he was younger than I was) in nursery school, and he went on doing it until he emigrated to Australia with his family after elementary school.

When he began his fourth year in school Guido found himself in class with Massimino, from whom he'd already taken many a beating through nursery school. Guido came from Maestra Prospera's (private) classes and Massimino from Maestra Pia's (public) classes, the latter being my mother. The class was divided into two teams that played each other in a fifty-goal tournament that went on for many days on the field that ran downhill in front of my house. Massimino obviously chose the high ground.

But Guido's team had among its young players two or three of the best soccer talents Malo ever produced: whimsical Ennio, a genius at scoring, Nello-Fiore, master of *dribli* and other plays, and so the goals against Massimino's team began to pour in right away. He fought back with penalties: the penalty, according to the rules, had to be repeated ad infinitum until the goal was made, and Massimino had no doubts on that point, and so from time to time the score evened out. When Prospera's team got to forty-nine goals, Massimino, who was one behind, immediately called two penalties (he kicked them himself), and Pia's team won 50-49.

✦

My team was founded on the existence of my ball. In Heideggerian terms, the *Dasein* of my ball was that of a wreck: a scuffed spheroid with many casual lumps here and there and a nasty wen under the stitches. However, it was a ball, a rare object, and around it grew up a team, with Piareto playing center forward, Savaio goalkeeper, a midfielder reinforced by a couple of guys who didn't pull their punches, and, a few friends in secondary roles. The rest of the positions were up for tryouts.

We would accept and reject applicants with great hauteur, I holding in hand the symbol of power, the ball, and Piareto with the scowl of a senior executive. An aspiring left wing, however, surprised us with an unexpected move: he put his hand in his pocket and asked how much the position cost. Right then and there we hatched the idea we might be able to get twenty cents, maybe thirty; Piareto thought we should aim high, forty or nothing. But the candidate, the son of a barkeeper, cut us off and pulled out a franc. That colossal bid made us lose our heads, and the coaching staff began to jump up and down with joy and hug the prosperous left wing.

Some of our friends were not great footballers, for example, Berto, but he had Technique, which consisted of the art of spreading your arms out harmoniously in the course of play. We knew that Technique was what real soccer experts prized, and it was therefore unthinkable not to give him a place on the team. However, because he missed the ball a lot even though he had this fine Technique, one day Piareto stopped the game and said: "But just because he's got Technique, who does he think he is, God Almighty?" And in a rush of athletic opportunism we threw Berto off the team.

The good soccer player's other fundamental quality was the *calcio-fisso,* the "hard-kick," which was not an action but an innate quality; you didn't do it, you had it. We all knew the names of those in town who did or did not have the *calcio-fisso,* and there weren't many of them. We used to joke that Pietro Badoglio—mascot and lines keeper of the town team U.S. Malo who wore his armband and cleats every day of the week—was counted among them.

They had been playing a friendly, and they let him try a penalty shot, and then they told him he had demonstrated he had the *calcio-fisso.* Every time they talked about it he would open his mouth and laugh soundlessly; the fact had entered into his consciousness, putting him almost at the level of the real players. One night he even dreamed that he had dribbled past Nello-Fiore, Malo's illustrious center forward. Nello was standing up, and he had dived right past him. Soon he had forgotten that it was a dream and spoke about it as if it had really happened, like the penalty kick.

◆

"Which of those players would you like to be?" I asked my Uncle Dino on the way home from an A League game he had taken me to see in Padua. Dino seemed annoyed, but why? Whatever the case, he mentioned a certain Foni. Now this Foni was not the most spectacular of the players I'd seen, so why him? Of the qualities this Foni has, I said to Dino, which one would you like to have?

"Oh, I don't know, his *touch,*" said Dino.

Fascinating. Not speed, not acceleration, not even the *calcio-fisso.* His touch! Dino's instinct for the heart of the thing, *la Vita.* I knew instantly I'd never have touch.

I would have been a right wing, had fortune allowed me to play on U.S. Malo. At left wing in my generation—before that brief, amazing meteor that was my brother Gaetano—there was Nani Mole. He was an ace with his head; he could stop the ball with it, invariably fooling his opponents who thought he only meant to head butt them. They say he used to practice crossing the ball with his head, but that's probably just a legend. However, he did deliver a penalty headshot that was aimed to the corner, but weak and easily stopped.

There weren't many other times when he scored with a header, except for that day at Marano when the Marano team had bought the game for eleven plates of pasta, and Nani Mole was the only one who hadn't been informed about the deal. Each time, our keeper let the ball through on purpose, then back it went to the middle of the field and Nani Mole ran down and evened the score. They tried to make him understand the situation, but he was all fired up, and there was also the risk that the referee would catch on.

So our team had to turn to making own goals: the defenders began to pass the keeper shots ever more difficult to block: from ten meters away, from five meters, from two meters. Unrelenting, Nani Mole kept on matching their score. At the end they were shooting point-blank into our own goal, and luckily one of these own goals coincided with the end of the game, and so we all, including Nani Mole, got our plate of pasta.

> The black-and-stars roll
> against them, never a goal.

They played in black jerseys with a white star on the chest, to the left. The song promised a fierce game *sul campo da lor* (at home; the pitch was behind Scuole Nuove, beyond the Solarium) and in general "victory over all the league / as the ball darts into the net."

And in fact, the "league" was our reign of glory. Today other little parvenu towns in this old association humiliate us and even play in higher categories, but we used to top the league back in the days when some of these winning teams had never seen a ball that wasn't a colored balloon at the fair.

Galliano, Checco-Scheo, Cilo: the defense was solid, the midfield was masterful, but the amazing thing about the team was their attack.

> A leap by Tonìn
> meets the *cros* by Kùbal-Kìn
> and in the goal it will lie . . .

What would lie in the goal? The shadow of a stunned kid, the helpless opponent goalie. Tonìn had my Uncle Dino and Nelo-Uvi on the right, Gino and Cine on the left. I don't remember the Kùbal of the song being in the wing from where the *cros* is kicked. Tonìn was a little fellow with devastating timing; I've seen few other Italian footballers with timing like his. We were battling it out in front of the goal as the ball sailed down from the bottom of the field; the little man in the black jersey moved quickly back and forth, as if all were running on rails. Then Tonìn jumped, the ball hit the net. Cheers.

The only adversary worthy of our black-and-stars was the team in the sky-blue jerseys of Arsiero. Even today when I pass the town of Arsiero in Valdastico, it stirs my blood. They were a disciplined, tough team of mountain people. One year we'd win the league, and one year they would. Personally, as often happens to me in these cases, I suspected that in the end they were the better team, and maybe that was why I resorted to prayer, all those *hailmarys* at the edge of the field.

A draw was pointless: at the last match of the season, if Arsiero was ahead, and we were second by one point, we had to win. We were 1-1 with five minutes to go to the end of the game, and I couldn't stand it anymore and tried to escape. I prayed walking backward; at the gate I stopped and prayed standing still. You could see the ball arching above the spectators back there. There was the usual turmoil of the game's end, but suddenly a turmoil within the turmoil could be heard, suggesting some real action.

Now. Now and in the hour of our deaths! Okay, *then* too—but meanwhile now, now. And in fact the turmoil exploded in that unmistakable way that signified a goal. The Virgin Mary had won us the league title one more time.

Away games were tough; away victories were almost impossible. The public participated in the match, and to a degree we of Malo felt was often excessive. The institution of invading the field was an important part of the match, but some towns new to the game tended to exaggerate.

I used to go to away games in the capacity of relative-of-the-bus-driver, and once I went to Velo d'Astico to another final match of the season. Every time the referee blew the whistle the other side fell deadly silent, and as soon as the referee raised his hand—if the penalty was against Velo—the crowd swarmed onto the field. The teams played for a while in the spaces cleared by the police, and then the referee wisely decided to stop calling in our favor (in any case the players themselves administered the most urgent punishments without interrupting the game). No goals though; and as usual, we needed an outright victory to surpass Arsiero in the rankings.

Middle of the second half. One of our players was knocked down in the penalty box, and the referee, in a moment of distraction, blew his whistle. He immediately regained his senses however and, instead of calling a penalty shot (that would have been fatal to both him and us), ordered a indirect free kick inside the box from an impossible angle. Such indirect free kicks rarely lead to a goal; the shot is invalid unless the ball is touched by a second player, either teammate or opponent.

The carabinieri cleared the penalty box and Kùbal (who was top scorer that year) lunged at the ball like a crazy man, and watched as it hit the shoulders of Velo's defensive right back (a brave and excellent defender, for that matter) and deflected into the net. The crowd, dazed by the enormity of what had happened, left us alone, but later in town the people of Velo came down on the streets, not so much determined to break the windows of the bus (that was normal), as to extirpate our team once and for all. We were trapped inside, in front of a tavern in the piazza, and were several times close to falling into the hands of our assailants.

But when the chief carabiniere unsheathed his saber and raising it to the slate-gray sky shouted sternly: "In the name of the King of Italy I order you to disperse!" the name of the King of Italy dissolved the people of Velo, and in the dark of night we were able to leave town, safe and sound with the championship in hand.

At the Veneto finals, after Uncle Dino scored a goal from forty meters on a free kick, I was unable to follow the game much. In my enthusiasm I had unleashed a hard kick at Piareto who chased me three times around the pitch, so that I could only catch a glimpse while running. When we went to the grand finals both Don Tarcisio and Don Antonio came: one large, one very lean, keeping their distance a bit from the rest of us, with a black umbrella to keep the sun off. It was unheard of to see priests at the game, but it fit the solemnity of the moment.

The outcome was a vile draw, and in the return match we lost because of two grotesque mishaps that befell the keeper. When they got back, Dino told me how it had gone. I was able to ask: "And who scored our goal, Uncle Dino?" I already sensed it, and in fact it had been him, and he told me that at the final whistle he had blubbered a little And most likely I blubbered a little myself.

✦

No more *tinfo:* there was too much to do, the day was full of things. *Tinfo* was something that in the big cities infected all the spectators at football matches, something like typhoid fever. People lost weight; they came out of the hospital emaciated and without any hair.

They were the four new things: *el tinfo, el tanfo, la rogna,* and *el sgranfo. La rogna,* ringworm: our aunts protected us by inspecting the skin between our fingers from time to time. *Sgranfo,* cramps, you got in the calves of your legs. *Tanfo,* foul smells, were all around us. They drifted up out of the manure pits and were spread by the *cagne,* the farts loosed by children in school and in church.

Children laid *cagne,* and they floated in the air, lazy and foul-smelling. Every child had a small secret lair in which *cagne* were stacked up. You released them one by one, and people laughed and wrinkled their noses until *la cagna,* rolling over and over, broke up and dispersed.

Piareto, Savaio, Bruno, Guido, and I had wooden swords with foils and leatherette masks with oblique slashes to peer out of, and we held long duels in the courtyard. They were exercises in discipline, part of a complex preparation for a glorious future. Best of all were the secret pacts, the accords and solemn oaths, the investitures and rites.

We had gotten into the SPA the workers had moved to the bottom of the courtyard so it could be washed. Sitting across the front seats of the car, we were perfecting one of our pacts, and I felt like Napoleon and Saint Ignatius Loyola all in one. I was explaining, exhorting, demanding seriousness and attention. All of a sudden Bruno let go a small *cagna.* I pretended not to notice, but the others were already showing fatal signs of distraction, barely repressing their giggles. I had to keep the situation in hand, and so right then and there I expelled Bruno from the club. But even as I was pronouncing the expulsion decree, Savaio, without meaning any harm, I think, let go another, bigger *cagna.* Everybody was laughing now, and they all began discharging *cagne.*

I expelled them all for evident unworthiness and got out of the SPA in fury. Alone, I said, alone. Better to go on alone than have to work with such defective material.

Even my rebellious Jesuits sensed that the moment was dramatic, but they were caught up in their convulsive laughter, rolling around inside the SPA infested with *cagne*. I walked off with all the dignity an offended hero could muster, but I knew I was in the wrong.

Chapter 13

MIDDAY, SUNSHINE, WHEN the summer still feels endless, at the bar in the piazzetta with a glass of white wine. My father and I not saying much, waiting for friends, observing people we know.

Utter, supreme joy, out of time, in the very heart of town, as if beyond the reach of death. I shiver under the sun.

✦

Things are in their place; the spaces are unchanged. How well I know the shadows of the houses as they shift here in front, and the angle at which the midday sun hits the piazza. At this hour Via Listón heading north is pierced by the sun and gives off a sort of blaze of light. Contrà Chiesa sits under a roof of shade; to the south beyond the piazza, looking out toward the Castello bridge, there's a little gulf of golden air where things seen against the light dissolve and flake off around the edges. The Castello heights, the church, the peak of Monte Piàn tremble in the light, the air sparkling with sequins. A few steps under the hot sun, down to the bridge, and you are in a soft, quivering confusion of greens and blues.

Here the hills that come up from Vicenza spread out to the west, pulling behind them a corner of the plain. That bay is ours. Our town is fixed to the spur that separates it from the lake of the plain. In front of us is Schio with its back to a wall of blue mountains, to Sengio Alto and the Apostoli, Pasubio, Novengo, the pyramid of Summano, and the long, high ridge of the Altopiano.

✦

The *rastellamento,* the German search patrol, stopped at the ridge, and now they were heading down toward Granezza. Thirty paces from here and you were out of it: the hollows flattened out, all those little internal horizons disappeared, the void at the edge opened up.

The world it had been so hard to believe still existed was laid out down there with a precision that annulled the distances; toys glittering between the stripes of the creeks: Zanè, Giavenale, Marano, Thiene, Villaverla. Behind them there was a throng of towns like Montecchi, Sandrighi; at the bottom, a swelling surf of Castelfranchi's and Cittadella's. The world that had seemed farther away than India or China in these last months up in the hills was here before us, and seen from the high rim of the Altopiano, it looked like a toy universe.

That town on the right, under the bay of shrunken hills, is where I come from. I can only sit down on the ground and wait for it all to become real.

✦

Coming here with me by bicycle from Vicenza in wartime, Lelio—maybe he had never been here before, or had never looked—observed the stage set of the hills on the left, and said, "*Sacramèn,* it's beautiful." Barbara thought it was marvelous, but she meant the buildings more than the place, our urban design, you might say. When she came here a few years ago, she got out of the car in the piazzetta, looked around and said, "Oh, but this is *wonderful*." Such appreciation is nice, and even deserved I think, but for us the town was neither beautiful nor ugly: it was ours, and so was the scenery. We liked it, but it didn't occur to us to call it beautiful.

The approach from the west is the strangest. It's as if an elephant, or some similar beast, had walked toward Schio dragging a harrow of little hills behind itself, and having reached the bend of the creek, which must have been full of water in those times, decided to drink a splash, and had extended its trunk. At this point, it began to sink (there was a swamp, you could see, to the south of the creek) and having sunk about three-quarters in must have then touched bedrock and stopped descending. Now it's all rock, including the elephant: Monte Piàn. You can make out the head quite well if you arrive from Thiene: you see its dark profile against the high backdrop of the other hills to the west. But to see the whole you need to move down a bit, toward Vacchetta, for example. It's a many-sided mass with the broad, harmonious, irregular planes typical of an elephant's skull, and it's set at the correct angle for an elephant on the march: trunk extended forward, half buried, half free; on top a wen with a few hairs sticking out (Castello) and right at the point, the town.

As you approach you can see that beyond this great head, Monte Piàn, there is no space at all, just a slender semicircle between the beast's shoulders and the high hills behind. You see a curtain of hills, a compact, steep, woody slope that seems to offer no way out right up to the rocky peaks a few kilometers to the north. But it's a false impression: coming into town and taking the road toward Contrà Chiesa that exits on the other side, just as you get to the church and the bell tower and before you even realize it, you've entered a new space. The gruff wall of hills before you and to the right seems to have drawn back, softened, and there's this new space to the west and south. Of all the spaces in this world this is the one that is most ours, a little piece of drapery pinned at the top by the bow we call Priabona.

The road from Vicenza through Schio and up to the Streva pass ran through town from south to north; now there's a new one that bypasses the town. This meets the road that comes from the plains of Thiene and goes on toward Priabona and the Val di Là. The big road from Vicenza had already been asphalted; the one to Schio was paved in my day. The roads to Priabona and to Thiene were packed dirt, already rutted by the traffic.

Minor roads were important in the life of the town; they still are, but far less now that people travel by motor vehicle, and wish to move themselves from here to there only in bland and practical ways. Minor roads were mainly for walking, moving along beside the carts and the animals, or at the most on a bicycle. They snaked through the fields or along the foot of the hills; they were narrow, with a good base of earth and compact white gravel. They hadn't been spoiled by the rare automobile on the roads.

There were also the *caviàgne,* country paths that didn't lead to towns but rather made "visits" to isolated cottages and peasant homesteads, or simply came to a stop in the middle of the clover, at the edge of a boundless territory of fields and ditches and crops. And so you'd stop there, your bicycle resting against a pile of stones, and all of a sudden you would hear the voices of millions and millions of tiny creatures, and late spring seemed to be a place, not a moment in time, and from the middle of this great, crowded place, the town to which the *caviàgna* returned seemed far away and unimportant, and for a moment you didn't know what to think.

La Proa separated us from this territory, just as when you reach a border and on the other side stands Belgium, or Holland. From the path that began near our house you quickly reached the vast, low, rocky, thorny shingle, and there commenced a no-man's-land that ran toward the towns to the east: dense countryside that belonged neither to geography nor history. Continuing along the paths that didn't stop in the middle of the fields and that didn't seem to be going anywhere in particular, the sensation you were broaching the unknown grew. In midsummer you needed something like courage to keep on going through the sorghum fields, on the lookout like an explorer for the embankment hidden among the acacia trees that suddenly revealed the Jólgora's wide rocky flow, as it cut across the countryside white and motionless with its current of smooth, round pebbles and stones.

✦

Our own creek was called the Livargón, but the nearby tribes also called it La Giara, and in truth it was mainly *giara*, gravel. It came down from the hills above San Vito, and there was a bend below the town, as if to circle us on the south at the foot of Castello. There was little water in it, and in summer it was nearly always dry, although it swelled a lot "at the moment of its greatest excrescence" as the Abbott Maccà would have said. When the water did run, it formed the little basins that were our water holes: the largest was called Rostón; then there was the pleasant Bojetto, the cheerful cascade of the Sojetti, the "Little Rocks" at Castello, further down, the small brown ponds of Lower Malo, and last, the water hole of Cuca.

The washerwomen kneeling on their boards splashed their sheets in the clear water; kittens, drowning in the water hole, would fan the pink veil of their eyelids over their pupils. Skipping stones bounced happily on the surface of the water; children built dams among the rocks, and swimmers draped in their huge cloth underbreeches emerged from the depths face up to make sure their hair was in place. Gastone-Fiore walked back and forth along the bank impatiently awaiting the high water. We were all waiting for the high water, our yellow buddy that would set afloat our rafts, canoes, and boats in progress on the shingle. But Gastone-Fiore, to whom the airways had more than once been denied or rudely blocked, had his seaplane, a heavy machine of boards nailed together, which the current was supposed to give the necessary push to make it soar up to the heavens. When the high water came, a team of friends dropped the machine and pilot on the crest of the muddy stream, but the weight of the nails made it sink to the bottom, and the pilot had to return to shore, half sword stroke, half on foot.

There were indescribably pleasant spots along the creek: acacia woods, meadows like that down in Prà beyond the double row of plane trees, a border of grass below the commons almost at the level of the creek. It ended at the ravine below Castello, with a spur of rock that had a trail etched around it in the stone. Above the rock was a rough fence of thorns that surrounded the old garden belonging to the priest, a garden that clung to the rim of the hill and was in fact inaccessible from our side. It was one of those perfect spots that you find in chivalric romances: grass, water, rock, the mysterious garden in the air, the high crag behind us, and the plane trees in the distance. On the other side of the creek were the walls and gardens of town, the rough backs of the houses (straight ahead is the one where my grandfather was born) the alleyways where no one walked unless it was a boy and his goat. There were further places I would later recognize in tales of knights and swords, brought to mind by the paths behind Castello: places like the Fontanella, Paraìso, the spring with its water bubbling up, the moss and the speckled shadows of the trees.

The ridge behind Castello was a maze of paths and *stròsi*, trails—and *stròso* meant adventure. *Stròso* mounts the rock spur, climbs the hummock, leads to the pine on top, penetrates, covers with branches, casts off the branches, stings with thorns, consoles with primroses. From the *stròso* you could rob pears, apples, and grapes.

> *Chi ze che ròba la ùa spinèla?*

> Who's that stealing the currants?

Fox grapes, dropsy plums, sour plums, peaches in shades of green that taste of almond, apricots?

Stròso of the corniola, the sour corniola; *stròso* of the wild medlars. Ripe hazelnuts, and in the green clearing, tender new walnuts, and blackberries.

> *Quale vùto, quele rosse o quele negre?*
> *Quel che vien vien! Quel che vien vien!*

> Which do you want, the red or the black?
> What will be, will be! What will be, will be!

Along those pathways we robbed, we explored; the pathway agitated, it excited, and we would come out running into the sun and look down on the town from on high, laughing, our faces smeared with blackberries.

✦

The space of town was held together by clasps of ditches and bridges: beside those across the Livargón creek, there was the bizarre little Rana to the west, and higher up, the mysterious Vedezai, which had evaporated among the fields, leaving not much more than the name. And the slope that went down toward Santomìo along the road that began at Ponte delle Galline was also ours, and up on the heights of town the road that goes to Case and runs along the Montécio wall. This last was a small shaggy oblong outcrop in the middle of the enclosed fields belonging to the Count, which were separated from our garden by a wall. It was like a handsome ship with dark, dark masts sailing toward San Vito; we faced the stern that rose in steps and had fewer masts. It was a luxury craft, shaped so it looked like a little hill in the middle of the plain, and like a ship it looked small when you viewed it from up on the hills, but when you went inside it was so big you could get lost in it.

Case and Santomìo are the hamlets that belong to Malo; we also have another one far away in the middle of the plain called La Molina, where near the end of the week you would find a white cloth banner stretched over the road. Written on it, all in capital letters, were the words: "THIS SUNDAY, MOVIES." My friend Piareto lived in La Molina in something like exile for a few years, after life's vicissitudes separated us. His parents had a bakery; I recently discovered that La Molina still has its own bakery. Everything changes so quickly today you can't be certain of anything.

"You mustn't expect a *romantic* paese like Marostica, my dear": thus an English traveler accompanying a friend to Malo around the middle of the twentieth century. *Paese:* town, country, home.

The *paese* hasn't changed as much as many others, but it has changed. Until the past few years it had scarcely been touched by the postwar industrial and commercial development, but now a little breeze of prosperity has blown in. A cluster of new houses has sprung up between the town and the new road to Schio; people in the center have renovated their houses, and many now have bathrooms; the taverns and the shops have been modernized, and there are lampposts in place of the old light bulbs crowned by metal plates that hung from wires.

This renewal began some seven or eight years ago. Before then, the only thing the town seemed to express (after the war) was weariness and decay. Observing the residence of Count Brunoro from behind the grates of my window when I returned home, I felt I was watching its death throes. In the high gate of dark wood there was a hatch narrow as a slit; the windows of the ground floor with their grates looked onto a moldy darkness, big rooms now used to store junk. Two bands of stone divided the ground floor from the first floor: here there were windows, few and far between, dark shutters that were always closed except for the one in the middle, where a hazy light filtered from the north-facing window on the other side of the room, across a huge, patriarchal hall. Somewhere inside, the very tall, silent, circumspect carpenter Signor Nicola worked. He had come to live with the family during the war.

There across the street at the Count's house, a door opened noiselessly, then shut with a snap. The Count and the Countess, ever so distinguished, old-fashioned, isolated from the rest of us, opened their umbrellas on the sidewalk. A cart stacked with hay passed the fork toward Montécio.

The scene was funereal: the green meadows were dying, as was the overgrown hedge, the trees with their too many leaves. I felt I couldn't communicate with anyone. Tiny cars racing their engines went by, stupid crows losing their feathers, a jackdaw.

Streets, people, buildings, all seemed to be merely aging, getting ready to die, becoming meaningless. It must have been 1953, and even then, my perspective was off; in any case, the town's modest return to life has now cancelled these impressions. A few years ago, having been away for a couple of years, we came back and found the new appearing everywhere. In this place that is both modernizing and falling to pieces, I said to myself, things from the past will come to have more meaning, not less. Chrome drives out wood; fake marble, stone; neon, the old light bulbs; bathrooms enter the houses; modern cookers replace the old stoves; radiators, refrigerators, and carpets are coming. It doesn't matter, for people have begun life anew, or maybe just continued on living. It's like Montale's "silver bells / above the town," and all the rest that can't be stopped, the old wooden beams, the red tiles on the floors, the plaster, the corridors, the cobblestoned courtyard, the old privy outside.

The houses in the center of town had a paved portico that gave onto the courtyard; from the portico you opened the doors to the ground-floor rooms and the stairs. The rooms had wooden beams and tiled or board floors. The kitchen was the most important room, with its stone fireplace, cooker, and oblong table where the family sat down to eat twice a day. Children did their homework here; Mamma, her sewing. Men were never seen sitting down in the house except at mealtimes. Once when Gaetano was gravely ill, Papà picked him up and sat down on the kitchen chair closest the door; he had a hat on, pulled down over his eyes, and was crying.

The bedrooms were large and bare, icy in winter, with iron bedsteads and metal mesh frames (for the children) or elastic weave (adults). The horsehair mattress went underneath and the wool mattress on top. There was a wash table in the bedroom with a pail and jug on top; in the morning, we dumped the contents of the chamber pot in there too.

The houses had huge granaries, almost like another house up there, light and airy with high, irregular ceilings. This otherworldly sphere had an importance almost impossible to describe; it belonged to a neo-Platonic realm. It was like the Sagrestia Nuova of the basilica of San Lorenzo in Florence: there was the intermediate zone of earthly things, bedrooms, kitchens, courtyards; down below, the dark Hades that waited at the bottom of the cellar stairs, the petrol pump in the garden and other openings from which gurglings of underground, liquid things could be heard. Up above were the neat, spacious, open, bare rooms of the granaries, a disembodied world where the Platonic ideals of broken toys and used objects resided, the world of essences that Michelangelo tried to reproduce in *pietra serena* at San Lorenzo.

The overhangs of the roof were wide and gave the house something of a scowling air. Safe and dry under the gutters, you could lean against the courtyard wall and watch the rain fall. Often the windows had grates, and the sun made rhomboid shapes inside. Each family had a sitting room full of unused furniture, the shutters always drawn. Unless someone was being baptized or there was an important visitor, the family rarely used it. If an unexpected arrival sent you in there, you would lead the way brushing a dead fly off the table, righting the photographs that had slipped in their frames.

The best houses had a tap with running water in the kitchen, or in the back room where the women washed the dishes. The kitchen sink was a huge slab of rough stone; above it, on a large shelf, hung big copper pails in which water drawn from the nearest public well was kept. In summer even those who had running water at home would send out for fresh water from the well. This water from the pails was served up with a copper dipper, and no water in the world tastes as good. Under the pails was a copper basin where you would wash your hands during the day, and those who didn't have a wash table in their bedrooms would wash their faces there in the morning.

The house was full of copper: pails, pots, molds, dripping pans, kettles hung over the fireplace. The polenta pot hung on a chain in the fire. Everything that had to do with polenta was weighted with importance: the hollowed-out block of wood pressed against the polenta pot with the knee to keep it in place, the stick with which you stirred it, the crusted parts that you grated directly from the pot, the huge board you poured it on, the cotton thread used to slice the polenta, which only barbarous, ignorant assassins would cut with the blade of a knife. Pellagra, the disease of the polenta eaters, was a thing of the past, but still very much with us in the collective imagination. *Pelagroso!* our aunts would call us with a smile, a teasing threat that no longer frightened anyone. Then they'd look around, to be sure there was nobody there from Isola listening, and add, lowering their voice, "pelagroso from Isola." We never knew whether aunts from the town of Isola said "pelagroso from Malo." According to our old folks, however, if they did say so, they were wrong. Pellagra had settled in at Isola and held on for a long time; we were mere observers. I make no claims about the matter.

The bathroom was unknown; two or three lordly families were reported to have one, and Flora saw one in the Cavaliere's house. When you were dirty you washed under the faucet in the courtyard, and in exceptional circumstances you had a bath in the tub in the laundry room.

✦

From the laundry room you went down to the cellar, inhabited by a furtive population of rats and visited from time to time by snakes that came down from the meadows of Montécio and left behind a pale greenish skin (I thought of them as little fairies transformed into snakes, and like fairies I wasn't really sure they existed). There were other things among the sturdy cellar shelves: vague things, adrift between the mold and the shadows, maybe buried just under the dirt floor, things that seemed, when you came down with a candle to get the wine in the evening, like they might be about to emit vapors. The heavy door was closed with a thick chain (still twisted after the blow it took in 1919 when the powder house of La Pisa exploded). There were heavy grates on the windows; the cellar was a place where you locked things up.

Houses were full of back rooms: woodsheds, storerooms, closets, junk rooms. Ours had the fabulous attic room above the body shop, piled with the cadavers of gear shifts, ball bearings, levers, pedals, rods, washers, chains, all smeared with clots of old, greenish-black grease like dried blood. You went up on the tallest of the spiral staircases through a circular opening, and through another circular opening at the other end of the great, dimly lit room you could look out and see the pine in the garden and the circle of the hills. You had the feeling you were *spying* on the world from up there, from dark toward light, from silence toward noise: this too was part of the world above, an observatory.

The stripped, bare bones of the engines were tossed into the yard next to the forge, where they stood in a pile under a mulberry tree and rusted when the rain came. Inside the perimeter of the forge, among the dunes of slaked lime, stood the fearful gazogene hut that if it exploded, would have blown up the whole town and wiped it out. When Villa Muzani—"La Pisa"—blew up a few years before we were born, the Virgin of Castello had intervened to protect us; the chimneys of the silk spinners shook, clumps of plaster fell down, glass cracked, but all things considered, nothing serious. "La Pisa," however, was two kilometers away and since the explosion, the villa is no more. The gazogene hut, with its big, flesh-colored metal cylinder, was not two kilometers away but right there in the forge, and so any hopes of the Virgin's intervention could only concern events *preceding* the explosion, a fact we didn't let her forget. The forge also contained the chicken coop and pig pen, as well as the rabbit hutches over the privy.

The privy stood at the end of the yard. There was no seat, although a wooden sawhorse stood in front of the door for my uncle with arthritis. It belonged to him personally, he had made it, and it was as strange and weather-beaten as he was. Sharp, nothing more than a blade to rest on, exactly how he used it nobody knew, because only Uncle took it in with him.

A few very special guests would be taken down to my grandmother's privy, considered more civilized because it had a tiled seat and a wooden lid (a round board with a peg in the middle for a handle). At Grandmother's there wasn't the normal heap of night soil but an underground chamber that you could peer into through a square trapdoor that we lifted with great effort. The stink of this secret manure pit was foul and mephitic—not robust and strong like the one at home, which was open to the sky. In any case, we would take those special guests down Via Listón to my grandmother's door, ring the bell (a bell with a metallic cord), make the introductions, say "Please make yourself at home," and lead the guest out toward the courtyard.

In most courtyards the privy was used by various families and, if there was a shop or a workshop, also by the employees. Urination was done on the manure pit: men in front of the little parapet around it, boys on top, and when the matter was urgent, girls would go there too. Absolute urgency drove everyone, even the women, down to the bottom of the garden.

The rabbits—the forge was their domain, and they were put to death there in front of the stairway up to their hutches— had a little porch out over the manure pit, and often when you were standing on the parapet, especially when it rained and you had to huddle close to the wall, they would sneak up and graze your ear, giving you the shivers. Getting up on the parapet provoked leaps, dives, and wiggles on the part of the manure-pit rats—a special breed of rats that were tawny and rude. We knew them fairly well (although they usually ran pertly away to hide) because we often descended among them, not voluntarily, but because it was easy to lose your balance on the rounded top of the parapet.

How risky it was to fall in depended on the state of the manure, for it too has its seasons, its natural rhythms: the phases of the moon would endlessly swell it and shrink it. Sometimes it was as dry and compact as a field during the dry season; at others it was a lake full of ugly black bubbles. One of my first memories of my brother is seeing him reappear at the end of the courtyard after a rather long absence down at the forge. That thing that one learned only with experience to take in one's stride had happened to him for the first time, and he was a bit shaken. He was wearing clothes made of raw silk, one of those little suits with flounces that buttoned down below, but you couldn't really distinguish the silk from his arms, his hands, his legs, face, and hair. He came down very slowly holding his legs apart and making little sounds like sighs.

Libera nos amaluàmen. Deliver us from *luàme,* from ordure. For many years my friend Nino thought that was how you wrote it. It seemed to him a fundamental and amazingly appropriate prayer; rarely did a prayer focus on a problem so well.

Deliver us from *luàme,* from perilous falls into the dung pit, so frequent, so unpleasant for your little sons and daughters. Deliver us from what *luàme* signifies, the dark splatter of death, the lion's jaws, the bottomless pit!

Deliver us from ungrateful death: the cat in the bag that the man beats against the wall with both hands, the dog in Piazzola with the scalding metal sphere coming smoking out of its belly, the bleeding pig squealing at the top of the courtyard, the silent rabbit, the sewer rat shrieking between the wall and the gate as the ferocious police-search closes in.

Deliver us, Lord, from this *luàme,* from the filthy gates of Hell!

✦

With all these hazards and these threats, the house, the home, nevertheless belonged to the realm of life, to the traffic of man and beast, to those things the day is full of. (Aunt Lena's hens shared the territory and practically the work done by the mechanics in the shop; they were all but mutations, clockwork hens.) The house was an organism far more complex than a home of today, containing all manner of products: grain and potatoes in the granary, wine in the cellar, hooks hanging with hams and salami, bunches of raisins drying, piles of wood, heaped-up bundles of sticks. A large garden brought a walled piece of countryside within; wisteria and calycanthus flowered on the walls; on carts and in wheelbarrows, in sacks and hanging on rods, life from outside turned up in the courtyard. There was ample space; domestic life mingled with the world of work, even beyond the shop. Men split wood, gardeners hoed, builders mixed mortar in the yard.

The house was at its most beautiful on certain autumn days toward evening, when someone was working in every part of it. In the shop, the fan belts made their laps, the files screeched, the drill buzzed. Uncle Checco was hammering on the anvil, Uncle Ernesto up under the roof was changing a tire on the SPA, Papà was over by the pillar using a blowtorch and you could see him bent over the long, feathery blue flame. Outside, the workers were getting the buses ready.

Wine was being made in the washtub with the last baskets brought in by the day workers who picked the grapes. In the kitchen Aunt Lena stood before the flames of the fireplace turning a spit loaded with birds; in the office, Aunt Nina looked over the end-of-the-month accounts. Young people sat with their books in the kitchen, children played in the entryway. I stood by the window that looked out on the courtyard, laid aside what I was reading, and felt elated.

✦

The main streets were paved with roundish, black stones that gleamed under the rain; in the center, the sidewalks were the ordinary ones, elsewhere there were two strips of pink stone with a dark border.

Who was it who had the idea, not long ago, of trying to de-baptize the street we all knew as Via Listón and rename it Via

San Gaetano? (In the end they compromised with Via Listón San Gaetano.) I gather that even Don Tarcisio wasn't happy about it. A misplaced zeal has led to sticking the names of saints and prelates on streets that in a more Christian era were simply called Barbè, Lòza, Porto, Lovara, Muzana, Cantarane, Capovilla.

There was already a Via San Bernardino (ours, next to the old church with the small, sober urinal on one side, the Borboni family camped in the sacristy, and a stovepipe coming out the window) and down at the end of town there was Via San Giovanni, and there was also a road called Chiesa, church. Wasn't that enough? Now there's no more Lovara; they gave it to Cardinal De Lai because it passed in front of the house where he was born. It could have been worse, though: there's Contrà Busìa, scene of the great feats performed by Basadonne long before the cardinal even got started. I have nothing against naming streets to commemorate our most distinguished local citizens. I'd be happy to see a Viale del Tar (after partisan Ferruccio Manea, nom de guerre, "Tar") and if anyone felt the need to fiddle with an old street name, a Via Listón Giacomo Golo.

◆

Everything is endangered.

"You want to bet they'll ruin the church of San Bernardino? Look at those holes! This time they're going to close it right down."

It was one of the most visible urinals in the whole province, right on the corner where the side of the church meets the front. When you used it, you didn't show your back to passersby, but your undefended side flank. Cicci would stand there for long carefree moments; he would turn his head, observe the traffic, politely greet the ladies.

The other one in the piazzetta, along the wall between Valentino and La Scopa, was torn down some time ago. But people still use it, the ghost of it, under the windows of Valentino. The dreamy faces of the users appear above the windowsill, peering in at the family sitting down for dinner.

And that handsome palace they were building behind the bell tower? Ampelio's mother, on her way home from mass, wondered who it belonged to. They had some trouble convincing her it was just the new public urinal. Once upon a time, such grand and sumptuous structures were inconceivable. Austere old-fashioned habits, small dramas of incomprehension.

The kid who came down from the mountains with his mother and saw Malo for the first time had seen a lot, too much. Everything seemed plausible to him, even that horrendous thing that was slowly advancing up Via Borgo. A fully loaded Sàura, a huge diesel hauler—a gigantic monster that took up the entire street. People weren't running away, they were pressed up against the walls.

The kid didn't have time to begin to comprehend. Squeezed against the wall with his mother (there was somewhat more space on the sidewalk on the other side of the street, but it was too late to cross) he endured the jolts of terror until the roaring Sàura was a couple of yards away, then charged into the middle of the street and disappeared into the monstrous jaws.

Chapter 14

WHY DOES THIS TOWN sometimes seem more real to me than any other place in the world I know? And which town: today's, changing so fast one can barely keep up, or the other one so familiar from childhood, and the part of it that lives on in those of us growing older? Or perhaps yet another one altogether, the town of those who were already old, who seemed antiquated and fantastic to my generation? It's hard to say.

Right now, as I write, it's impossible to say either "the town as it was then" or "the town of today"; time and tense wobble under my pen: it was, it is, a little more, much less. In some respects the change is radical; what was, is no more. In others, little has changed.

Even as the new ways take shape, many of the old remain, those remnants of town life that up until a generation ago were common to our provincial towns, and which for us were (and to a certain extent *are*) life tout court. It's a life that can only be mourned with generic sentimentality, except that here, where at least the overall plan of the streets, the houses, and the public buildings remains almost untouched, it is still possible to do justice to it.

The town of the past had its qualities: it shaped a human community that was modest but organic. We all knew everyone, relations between the young and the old were more natural, relations between human beings and things were stable, ordered, lasting. Houses, public works, furniture, the objects of daily life: all lasted a long time. Everything was encrusted with experiences and memories thickly laid one over the other. Domestic utensils had a sharper personality, you could sense the hand of the craftsman who had made them and the very parsimony of life lent them importance. Even children's toys were more consequential: fewer plastic toys, less foolishness. Everything cost and was worth more; even the marbles we played with, the toy soldiers, were treasures.

The seasons meant more, because they were experienced in the same places, endured in the same houses. Private life itself seemed to have more meaning, or a richer meaning, because it was indistinguishable from one's public life. You came into life with a well-defined public persona. Who are you? A Rana, a Cimberle, a Marchioro? And which Marchioro—Fiore, Risso, Còche, Culatta, Culattella? Where a surname was not enough, there was a further appellation to define each person's identity. You were inside a tight net of genealogies, of hereditary occupations, of traditions, anecdotes.

There were *signori,* ordinary folk and the poor, but much of life was shared by everyone (in many ways more than would be imaginable in England, for example). Public services were shared, language, schools, public houses, churches, the confessional. Food was not shared, and often, seeing what the poor ate, I felt the shock of a difference I would later call *class.* Among our elders, the epitome of success was measured in food: "He eats well."

Life was shaped not only by various de jure institutions but by innumerable other de facto ones: *la compagnia,* one's draft year, wine, even profanity. Profanity was a rather important institution, by no means just an expressive aid for the inarticulate, although there was that aspect to blasphemy, especially the kind of cheerful, serene blasphemy that probably makes even the Almighty and the saints laugh. But real profanity is angry. It dethrones the supernatural and expresses a basic judgment—crude but independent—about how the world works. Officially our blasphemers would never dare to suggest that the blame lay "up there" when things went wrong, but in the very act of profanity, they did just that, embracing the side of heretical good sense against that of conventional piety. The liberated young fellow who cursed for fun (and the humble man who cursed out of spite) showed the very young what wicked, intriguing defiance looks like, they sent a delicious shiver along the divide between what one really believed and felt and what one was *supposed* to believe and feel.

In speaking of these matters, it is probably not appropriate to unsheathe the word "culture." Only in one sense did we have a town culture: in our traditional customs, our manners—a system of very well-defined relations and values. It goes without saying that what is strictly speaking considered culture—intellectual culture—either didn't exist or was imported from the urban centers where it was generated.

And yet we did have our own town customs, a set of values very often different from those officially in force: time-honored values that were primarily rural and of the people, combined with some borrowed ideas of urban, cultivated origin, assimilated and transformed in our own way. In so far as these habits made up a culture (an articulation of one's way of life), it was exclusively a spoken culture, lacking any written texts. It had, however, the power of real things, while the official culture, expressed in writing in a foreign language, seemed an empty convention (although incontrovertible, like illness) and remained an abstraction until its secular or ecclesiastical arm moved in.

Behind the town you could feel the stability of an immovable, hardheaded peasant majority. And in some way we were the urban flower of this peasant society. Town and countryside were still mostly a single entity, but the town decanted and refined country customs. It is not easy to document how town folk carried out this complex mediation, above all for reasons of language. The language in which we carried out our mediation (not that we were aware of doing so, of course) isn't written. And the language we in town use to write—and in which all Italy writes—can easily betray us.

✦

Between the code of conduct prescribed in the official written culture, and the town's real manners, the gap was great.

On the back of the cover of an old school notebook dating from the year before I was born, I find a "Ten Commandments for Daily Life" that begins thus:

> 1. Love your schoolmates for they will be your workmates throughout your life.
> 2. Love your studies . . .
> 3. Bless each day with some useful and good action, some act of kindness.

Up to this point, we are still within the specific virtues of the student; we then pass to those that will adorn an entire life: dignity, truthfulness, rectitude, generosity, loyalty, decency. And then there are the correlatives to avoid: obsequiousness, cowardice, credulity.

It's an admirable document, but what relevance could it have had for the students of Malo who wrote in these notebooks? This was a moral code that might have made some sense in an urban center, where perhaps there were mothers and fathers who really believed in civil rectitude, kindness, tenacity, and so forth, defined in that way. There must have been an urban, bourgeois Italy where these words, at least in part, corresponded to manners. But in Malo?

In our town circles, these words remained just words. "Love your schoolmates": this was not a serious maxim, no one seriously tried to make us believe, in our own language, that we must "love our schoolmates." When we scuffled with those schoolmates, sometimes adults reprimanded us, at other times they took our side. In the abstract, schoolmates were neither to be loved or abhorred; the injunction to love made no sense in dialect (and for that matter, it is a strange injunction even in Italian, and not even my teachers in Vicenza and Padua were able to teach me what it actually meant). Schoolmates were like everyone else: you got along with some of them, with others you didn't, and it varied day to day.

And that was more or less how it went for all the rest. I've taken the first example my eyes fell on among the Ten Commandments, so as to have a concrete example of one of the many explicit codes of conduct, either secular and civic, like this one, or directly inspired by the moral teachings of the Church (in this sphere the most important sector of official culture).

All are equally distant from the real codes of conduct that people followed, although they were not written down anywhere. I don't mean that these latter were the opposite of official culture, that people were openly immoral and ill behaved, just that our conduct was not inspired by the models put before us.

✦

Rectitude counted rather little. I refer, to be sure, to ideals, not to deeds. It goes without saying that the proportion of the upright to the not-upright is more or less equal everywhere. The expression "an upright man" does exist in Malo, but to me it always had a special inflection, such as an expression like "he has such a polite and sensitive voice" might have elsewhere. Rectitude was a virtue, yes, but it was marginal.

The principal virtues pertained to the circle of the family, and were connected with the necessities of life, or with work.

The word "duty" in the moral sense is unknown in dialect; we have instead the word "need," in the sense in that there's no escaping something, as in one "must needs die." One must needs work also, for oneself, for one's *dòna*, one's woman, for *el me òmo*, "my man," for the children and for the elderly who can no longer work. You must needs work not eight hours, or seven hours or ten hours a day, but practically *always*, perhaps with pauses, interruptions, or slowdowns but continuously and without looking at the clock, more or less from when the sun rises well into the night. You must needs work from when you cease being a child (and the girls worked at home even as children) until when you've been old for quite a while. You must needs work when you are so poor that working all the time you are barely able to survive, and when you are less poor and could work less. Here again, I refer not to deeds but to ideals, for not everyone worked this hard: there were the do-nothings, the slackers, the perfectionists. But the central principle recognized by all was that you must work for your family with all your strength, bear any burden, any sacrifice.

A proper Italian Ten Commandments should have begun like this:

1. Remember that you must work for your family, and that your family comes before everything else.

By far the greatest part of people's physical and spiritual energies went into work. For most, life was extremely hard: it was hard in the fields, in the foundries, in the craftsman's shop, in the spinning mills, and it was very hard indeed for the women at home and in the family. And even the jobs considered least demanding—the shopkeepers, the tavern keepers, the merchants, the traders—were very hard by today's standards.

The four silk mills were the biggest industry in town, and all the women of the lower classes sooner or later worked in them, with hours, wages, and working conditions that today sound almost unbelievable. When the mill was running, there was a loud, continuous din of antiquated machinery, and behind it, the sharp lament of the deafened spinners singing:

Santa Madre, deh Voi fate
che le piaghe del Signore
sìano impresse nel mio cuore.

Holy Mother, make it so
that the wounds of the Lord
Are pressed on my heart.

Polenta with onions, polenta with watermelon. The spinners came out at noon and went back when the siren sounded between 12:30 P.M. and 1:00 P.M. Not all went home for this brief lunch hour; those who lived far away sat down along the sidewalks on both sides of the street and took out their bundles of yellow paper with the polenta and its marvelous condiment!

Besides the spinners, there were also the *scoattìne* and the *ingroppìne,* names of sheer fancy. *Scoattìne! Ingroppìne!* Hard to believe, when you saw those women and girls with faces the color of silkworms.

Replenished after a morning's work, they went back inside to their basins of boiling water until evening, shouting their invocations to the Holy Mother of Heaven, begging for God's wounds.

Silkworms were raised at home, weird little "horsemen"—as they were called—they proliferated like tiny black seeds (during the "sowing") and gradually became miniature caterpillars, and then you would see them grow rapidly and spread out on the wide, dark, warm shelves of the trellises, invading our houses, gnawing ever more vigorously on the mulberry leaves.

Life for these creatures with their bellies full of silk was like a fever: it shot up every day, exacerbating their hunger. Level three, level four: the tiny rustle you could barely hear if you listened very carefully became a steady vibration, then a roar. Up on the mulberry trees, the men and the children stripped the leaves ever faster, they appeared with their sacks full, buried the frenzied beasts under an avalanche of glossy leaves that were ripped to shreds in minutes.

Now the horsemen were eating furiously. A few went to pot, developing a kind of silkworm consumption that extinguished their fever. The silk rotted inside and liquefied, bloating their translucent skin; if you pricked them with a pin the beast would deflate, sending out a spurt of slime. The rest, paralyzed by their fever and by all that eating, grew torpid and were taken out to the "woods" (where the sticks were piled up in the barn), and where, in a few days, in the dark, the windows papered over, the secret miracle happened, and the lustrous little golden baubles came out to float on the branches.

Tending the silkworms was one of those extra jobs that were mainly handed over to women so they wouldn't be idle (they merely had to give birth to up to a dozen children, raise a half dozen, cook for everyone, wash, iron, sweep, make the beds, empty the chamber pots, wash the dishes, sew, mend, patch the clothes, look after the chickens, take care of the sick, pray for their husbands, go to church, and bicker a little with the neighbors). How they also went out to work in the mills I never understood.

In the evenings they had their *filò*. In the countryside, they went out to the stables; in town, to their kitchens. There the lazy things would just fool around, doing their knitting or even playing bingo, or in the summer, sitting in their doorways doing absolutely nothing, looking at the crowds coming home from the taverns.

Men, for their evening entertainment, would go to the tavern to play cards. Television hadn't yet arrived and neither had neon lights or *beverages*. There were dozens of taverns in town, all of them serving the foxy-flavored *vino clinto,* with its hint of American grapes, and our own dark red wine. If these taverns, sociologically speaking, were a blight, they were however more attractive places than today's bars with their televisions (also, sociologically speaking, a blight, I think). The taverns had heavy oblong tables, big straw-backed chairs, a wooden counter, an open fireplace. In the same room, or in an adjacent one also open for business, was the tavern keeper's family kitchen, and going to the tavern was not so different from dropping in at a private house.

The aspects of work I've dealt with up to now have to do mostly with what Hannah Arendt, in her fine study of the matter, called "labor," as opposed to simply "work." Meaning: exhausting work, toil, the *tribulare,* as we use that word in dialect, characteristic of a peasant society, work compelled by utter necessity. This typically includes work in the fields, domestic work, lowly and subservient jobs, everything that has to do with just sustaining life, following the rhythms of the seasons, of day and night, of birth, growth, and feeding. It is that work that must be done merely so that one can eat, consume, or rest upon something; work that must be done every day, every month, every year. Man's original punishment and bondage.

Such is Arendt's "labor," but any activity can become toil when you are forced to carry it out under hard conditions and at a hard pace, and that was what happened in Malo.

We lived under the sign of Necessity, and it was from that imperative that the image of the Virgin in Castello took its meaning. Placid, florid, round, that pregnant Lady symbolized all that a community of *laborers* would dream of. Playing in Castello, I sometimes found myself in church alone, when no one else was there, and I would go and stare at her and ask her: "What are you thinking?" She would continue to smile that smile with her big, untroubled eyes. Now I understand that all she was thinking was, "Beyond Necessity, there am I."

✦

I don't remember whether Arendt writes about this, but the virtue that corresponds to this type of work is composed of endurance, industriousness, the will and the strength to work hard. Among us, this virtue was well known: "He's a worker" was an expression of high praise for my father, and it meant someone who consumed himself with work, who never stopped. But it was not the term of highest praise my father would use speaking of a worker. The highest praise was "He's *good*, he's a good workman," and by workman he meant not the industrial worker, but anyone who made things, the artisan, the one Arendt calls *homo faber*. And here the highest virtue was technical skill, craftsmanship.

For we were not a rural society, we were a town, with its arts, its creative work based on skills, not just on endurance. And it was because of this that we felt we belonged to a world: Arendt argues with admirable clarity that the solid and real "world," as distinct from fleeting and illusory "nature," comes to life when the craftsman imposes the things he makes between us and nature. *Res:* thing, from which comes our word "real."

Perhaps this is one of the reasons why growing up there felt so natural, so authentic, and why today (even knowing very well that new forms of community life are both inevitable and desirable) it can seem that in certain fundamental ways there was more to life back then in Malo than in our modern cities, either in Italy, or beyond.

Town was a structure genuinely built to the measure of man, literally to the measure of our fellow townsfolk, and therefore it fitted the natural scale of our lives. What was there had mostly been made there, while today things descend from on high, factories plummet down from the heavens of a greater economy, bringing new shapes to things, on the one hand civilizing us, on the other, dehumanizing us. New roads appear as if from thin air, companies and machines from outside build them, and ways of dressing and living also come from thin air, through the pipes and channels of TV. Once things didn't fall from the sky, they made them here.

I was talking with my father about bathrooms, running water in houses, electric lights: about when these things first appeared in town. He remembers quite clearly when the first bathroom was installed, the Count's; he had been a boy and had worked on it himself. When he was a child, water still came from wells, both public and private, like the one in my grandmother's courtyard that was still working in my day. When public water pipes first came to town, he and a friend of his got the job of manufacturing some kind of join or gusset, and they made the whole lot themselves. They would get up at four in the morning, even at three, and finish work well into the night.

Thus it was we ourselves who made the things of our world, far more so than today. Ideas did come from outside, but they were thoroughly assimilated in the physical working out of them. Everything was humanized in this way. Today the chrome-plated faucets, the vacuum cleaners, and the bathtubs arrive and my friend Sandro puts them in the shop window and then he sells them and that's it (and let it be said that Sandro is an excellent craftsman, a worthy heir of craftsmen of yore, but today, that skill of his seems as much a hobby as anything else, a personal talent, like the ability to do magic tricks with cards).

Our Ten Commandments would thus continue as follows:

2. Prepare yourself for labor and toil; nearly all must toil.
3. Learn to be good at your work. No one is more
   respected than someone good at his work.

The fourth commandment would apply to women:

Be tidy. The slovenly woman merits no esteem.

Among the older generation, just about the only criticism ever made of women was pronounced against those who were not "clean"—and here clean meant not personally washed or tidy, but rather good at keeping the house in order, the children washed, the clothes well mended and patched. When a woman wasn't clean, she was *untidy*, and in extreme cases it would be said (and my father still says today), that a woman was a *luamàro*, a cesspit, which was to say she was *most untidy*.

As I don't wish to compile a list of commandments but merely illustrate some points, I'll stop here.

✦

The all-powerful factor dictating relations between families was what we called *l'intaresse*, one's interest, and naturally one's own family came first. Against this code of conduct, neither the laws of the state nor the moral precepts of religion had anything like the power of decorum ("it's not done"), of what could set off community sanctions—and that might be profoundly different from what the law prescribed, but also from what religion preached.

In all that concerned *l'intaresse*, the state was almost universally considered a troublesome foreign body that everyone had the right, and almost the duty, to defraud. Stealing was frowned upon by all, but only in the private sphere: the classic, furtive chicken thief, or someone who stole cash from a shop or from the sideboard at home. But *l'arrangiarsi*, "getting by," taking advantage of the resources of any sort of public entity, even any sort of impersonal entity, was quite widespread, and it was also fairly common to "get by" at the expense of other families with whom the gardens, courtyards, stockrooms, basements, and barns were shared.

The first type of getting-by was spoken of openly as something natural and normal, and many boasted about it. The second was not only not mentioned in public, it was vigorously denied. It was almost a rule that you would lie if necessary, and you lied with great signs of the cross and distraught faces. Lying, as with stealing, was condemned in the abstract but often practiced in the concrete. "Liar," like "thief," was an insult, but lying and stealing in practice (in the cases described above) weren't perceived by the protagonists as deceit or larceny. Someone who was unusually correct in business dealings would be called "honest," a quality considered both admirable and a bit unwise, a luxury and a refinement on the part of an eccentric, usually a gentleman, that is, someone who could afford not to worry about the consequences. The opposite of "honest" was not "dishonest" but "someone who looks after his own interests." The town equivalent of "dishonest" would be *un poco de bòn*, a no-good, meaning someone who cheats in those spheres where it's not permitted, or cheats without any real necessity. The chicken thief is neither honest or dishonest, he's a thief.

These selective examples of conventional morality should suffice to describe all other cases. As a rule, goodness was not associated with such conduct or with other analogous aspects of behavior; it was more a psychological category than a moral one. *Bòn* suggests a kind temperament; *cattivo,* "bad," means litigious, inclined to argue, one who gives a hard time to underlings, who's ready to kick and punch. Goodness was not associated with religious devotion; on the contrary, "Church" people were often suspected of a distinctive kind of nastiness. But it was here on this terrain of "goodness" that the moral content of our religion could be understood by all, in the generic admonition to be good, something like a translation into dialect of the gospel's invitation to kindness, tolerance, generosity: in short, to love one's neighbor.

The canonical sins—envy, pride, wrath, greed, etc.—were thought of as psychological traits, not moral concepts. As children we were taught to accuse ourselves of them during confession, and we did so scrupulously, but growing up they seemed irrelevant, like searching our consciences about being "disobedient." One could recognize the corresponding qualities in people, but they seemed morally indifferent; they were more like natural traits of the individual, such as body size or a cross-eyed gaze.

If *l'intaresse* was the all-powerful factor dictating relations between families, it wasn't however always present. And although work was hard and filled each person's day, that didn't necessarily mean the individual was isolated from the rest of town; to the contrary. Each one looking after his own interests and his own work, people mixed with other people in a series of disinterested relationships.

This was the space of our freedom. Work itself, the day's necessities, looking after one's own affairs, the brief intervals of rest, a mere walk down to the piazza to buy something or deliver something or call someone, was enough to put each in touch with all. Not only did we have a public persona, but we took part in public life. Much of what one did was done before everyone's eyes: it was known, evaluated, commented upon—and belonged not just to us but to the town. Here, the hard law of Necessity did not obtain; one could improvise, fool around, observe how others lived and improvised and fooled around. People took part in the common life with pleasure, disinterestedly, simply because they all shared the public space of town.

A tradesman's shop was practically an extension of his house and family; it was almost always "open," and in any case there was no real distinction between open and closed. To buy something, you only had to walk into the courtyard, barely excusing yourself with the family seated for dinner in the kitchen.

Workshops, too, were almost always open: the blacksmith with his sooty face; the hardware man with his copper; the shoemakers cutting their ripe-smelling leather; the farriers (there was one right in the piazza, and two others in town);

the carpenters, whose neat, precise work done on neat, clean surfaces appealed to me; the butchers, who hacked at sides of beasts and split the bones with their cleavers; the millers dusted with flour; the bakers who worked in the middle of the night, so that those who rose before dawn could stop by and ask for a piece of fresh bread, as my father once did, and they gave it to him, those shapes in their white aprons before the flames of the oven, but when they turned around you could see that the aprons were open behind, and they were naked as the day they were born underneath, showing off their smooth backs and buttocks glistening with sweat. And there were the spigot makers, the tub makers, the coopers, the stone carvers, the carters, the clog makers; there were the traveling knife grinders, and the chair menders, the umbrella fixers, the mattress makers, the pig butchers, and all the rest. Barbers also worked as tailors, and my father still can't get over the fact that someone can make a living as a barber, and yet they do today, and even support a family. Many of these trades have all but disappeared now, and others have evolved: last year there was still a wood-burning bakery oven in town; today, I'm not sure. The very existence of all these trades, and the way they were woven into town society, made life more various and animated.

The streets and squares were our agora; our language, unlike that of Attica, was not written, but it was rich and flexible, and with it, as if in a mirror of words, we could create a gladdening picture of life made up not just of trial and toil, but also of encounters, adventures, of inspired amusements, reflections, events free to happen.

✦

Our language was made of overlapping layers; it was a work of intarsia. Beside the broad division between the rural language and that of town, there were many other gradations by neighborhood and by generation. Eccentric demarcation lines divided the various quarters, even the courtyards, the entranceways, the very tables at which we sat down to eat.

At home we said *sculièro,* spoon, but at Aunt Lena's it was *guciàro.* Papà said *ùgnolo,* "simple," but we said *sìnpio.* Long phonetic waves lapped down the generations; Uncle Checco never said *gi* ("gee"), not even in proper names, but always *ji* ("yee"). For that matter my father always said *jèra,* not *géra.* Even the morphology of the words slotted one into the other: if we had fought in World War II, *gérimo soldà,* we "went in the army"; but when it came to the First World War, the verb was *gerìvimo.*

In no more than the small flourish of a final *a* on the first-person singular imperfect (not *o* as we say in Italian) you could hear all the archaic sweetness of dialectal propriety. Down at the cafè, discussing various observations each of us had made in nearby towns—one of us at San Vito, another at Marano, a third at Isola—the Commendatore, a man of the world, spoke up at a certain point and said, *Me trovavaaa a Sàn Rafaèl . . .* and that *a* at the end sounded irresistibly lovely to us, although it's quite normal in proper dialect.

Language moves like a current, and normally its noiseless flow is totally silent, because we are in it. But when some emigrant returns we can measure the distance from the point where he stepped out and climbed the bank. They come back after ten years, after twenty years in Australia or in the Americas, where they continued to speak the same dialect that they spoke here with us and which we all spoke; they return and they seem to be people from another town or from another age. Yet it is not their language that has changed; it is ours. It's as if the words too are returning to their homeland, and are met with peculiar feelings, often after some hesitation, sometimes even some embarrassment.

When my Aunt Candida, who is married and resident in Como, comes back to see us, she says *chive* for "here" and *live* for "there," expressions all the aunts and uncles abandoned decades ago. The unappealing *ròda*, wheel, which to us is city talk from Vicenza, has virtually steamrolled our local word *rùa*, although at least we still have our *ruèle* (little wheel) and our *ruàre* (wheel tracks), our watchmakers nicknamed Ruet-te, "Wheels," and the grocer whose name is Ruaro. Ruette, being a good-humored epithet, you say it with the double *t*. The use of double consonants, like Russian verbs, is difficult to explain to outsiders. In general, the double is used to highlight, to imitate, to pretend to say one thing while you are saying another; it's a kind of linguistic *schinca*. And then if we venture into the question of when the double *ss* and the double *zz* are used, the rules are practically useless.

This language of ours, although not codified, even though limited to a small territory (someone from the Val di Là already speaks differently from us), although by no means unanimously agreed upon and in constant seismic agitation, is nevertheless not an instrument to be derided. Users of the Italian *koiné*, passing through, are sometimes tempted. But we can always reply: "There's no way we can put this in writing, but as long as we have wind in our lungs we too can make you look like fools, you *pajazzi*, you clowns!"

To appreciate the difference between *pajassi* and *pajazzi*, you would have to come and live here for a couple of years.

Chapter 15

BEFORE THERE WAS MALO there was a place called Maladum (which means Malo) and because of that we should be known as *Maladensi,* which is our Sunday name, but there is no special weekday name for us, just "the ones from Malo."

Living here, you would be told this was an old, old town, (leaving aside the *very* ancient past of Pieve di Santa Maria and of Castello), but from books you also learned that in centuries past we were far more important than we think.

"The Vicar of Malo rules over six *ville,*" says Francesco Scoto in his *Italian Itinerary.* The Abbott Maccà, who does not seem very enthusiastic about that statement, does acknowledge that "Malo is made up of four townships, which form six parishes, to which we give the name of *ville.*" And from his list we learn that besides some of what are today considered our hamlets, we also ruled over Isola, Castelnovo, Monte di Malo, and even Torreselle and Ignago. No offense intended but I'd be glad to give up places on the plain like Isola and Castelnovo. But Torreselle and that little nest on the mountain top, Ignago— those, I'd love to have.

The sources say that we too were a *villa,* and we won't object, but the truth is ours is a real stretch of territory, a town. At the beginning of the nineteenth century there were five hundred families here, and 2,400 souls, while my generation grew up in a town already two to three times that big, but no longer growing, and many other smaller towns and villages have nearly reached our size.

I don't know what we did to the Vicentine Exiles who occupied and sacked us in 1263, nor what happened to those who, roughly in those same years, "*fuere capti, et imbriati per illos de malado*" (were captured and tied up by the people of Maladum). In 1314 the Paduans, after the usual rude sacking, burned us down; at the beginning of the 1400s we were Venetians; in 1514 General Alviano's troops descended; in 1915, it was those of General Cadorna; in 1918, they were the soldiers of His British Majesty, who ate huge geese stuffed with jam. These Englishmen had almost no teeth and got as drunk as our worst winos, and even worse. But they did teach a bit of their language to the population, and people still remembered it in the years of my childhood. That was how I learned to say *si* in English. You said, *oyez! oyez!* In 1797, "the French overturned the Malo government," and in 1945, it was overturned again, but briefly.

✦

It's good to know that, let's say, on the fourteenth of April 1239 (it was a Sunday), our townspeople were summoned in front of the church by banging on the doors: "*ad sonum tabule . . . Ut mos et consuetudo est hominum maladi.*" At the sound of a wooden plank, as is the custom and habit of the people of Maladum. And thus it happened once again on February 2, 1279, which was *zòbia,* a Thursday; on *luni,* or Monday, May 30, 1306; and many other times. It would be a mistake to think there were no church bells, even though the inhabitants continued on for a while convening their gatherings in this other way. Documents show that the bells were rung as far back as the beginning of the fourteenth century.

Who knows how cold it must have been that January 14 when they gathered "*sub portico caminate Ecclesie sancti benedicti*"

(Saint Benedict being our parish church). *Sabo,* it was: a Saturday. What did they have to say to each other?

I'll bet that meanwhile in the houses, while the women cooked up an Ostrogothic hodgepodge in the fireplace (because we were founded by a "leading chief of the Goths around the Year of our Lord 500"), the little girls played with their Romanesque dolls, and the little boys with flint stones. One foolishly asked: "What day is it today?" And the other replied, as people still do:

> *Sabo: in boca te cago*
> *in boca te pisso*
> *dimàn te guarisso.*

> Saturday: in your mouth I shit
> in your mouth I piss
> Sunday: I'll fix you up again.

Of the seven, the most welcome of days! Hearts soared in anticipation of that thaumaturgic Sunday.

Chapter 16

THE PARISH CHURCH WAS REBUILT in the nineteenth century, but the old bell tower is still standing. In front of the rectory stood the old stables, and a bit beyond that was the nursery school. We're now in Cantarane, and the road continues on toward "The Bridge" par excellence, near Priabona, and the tavern that marks the end of town. Behind, to the right, is the cemetery. Cast your eye around in the cemetery and you can take the measure of this town. You walk among the tombs recognizing the names and the faces in the small enameled portraits, comparing the dates.

It's like strolling through a crowd of people you know: the town's recent history and part of its past is summed up in the benchmarks of these stones. Some faces I don't recall very well, but they all know me, at least they know which family I come from. As that old man in the tavern up there at Priabona told Gaetano when he guessed who my brother was: "The Meneghellos are like the Chinese, they all look the same."

About our ancestors, the reports are fragmentary. One was a priest in a nearby town, and he fell in love with the parish priest's mistress. The parish priest paced up and down the garden reading his breviary; from the window of the rectory, our ancestor pointed his shotgun. It was the hour of sunset, and the air was clear and calm; the shot hit the bull's-eye with impeccable precision.

There was a Meneghello who owned some fields up here at Monte Piàn, and there was his neighbor who every day on his way to work, drove through those fields with his cart and oxen, and Meneghello—our degree of relationship isn't entirely clear but we sympathize—did not approve. One morning he was out early cutting the grass, and the neighbor drove up in his cart and Meneghello stopped him.

"This is the last time you come through this way, understand?"

"I'll come through whenever I please."

Meneghello raised his scythe and rested the blade on his neck. "Well then I'll cut off your head," he said.

"Cut it off," said the neighbor, and Meneghello gave a snap to the scythe handle—and was transferred to the penitentiary.

✦

According to one old report it seems that our family can be said to be divided into two branches: a mercenary branch based in Monte Piàn, which is us, and a Jewish branch.

My grandfather was racing along the roads of Verona in a horse and trap, chased by the guardsmen. He saw an open gate, turned in, and said to the gatekeeper with his stripes: "Close that gate please, they're following me." And the gatekeeper closed it.

"Who are you?" he asked my grandfather, who was drying off the sweat.

"Meneghello," said my grandfather.

"Hmm," said the gatekeeper, "The master is also called Meneghello," and he went out and summoned him. He was a small, courteous fellow. "Meneghello? Where is it you're from?" he asked my grandfather, and Grandfather said, "from Malo."

The small man immediately had his bearings. "You people are the mercenary Meneghellos," he said, "the ones from Monte Piàn. You went up there to settle after the end of a war, when there wasn't any more work for you. We people from Verona are the Jewish Meneghellos." And this is what we know of the two branches of the family.

In Monte Piàn today there's a Vitale Meneghello who deserted during World War I, and the carabinieri were unable to find him. However, at a certain point his wife became pregnant, and since she was considered a woman above reproach, the lousy carabinieri surrounded the house, and they found Vitale in the hayloft.

At that moment, they weren't shooting deserters, and soon Vitale returned home, but the carabinieri still got their revenge. Every year from then on, Vitale would put in for a hunting license—hunting was his great passion—and every year they would deny it to him. Forty, fifty years have passed, Vitale's now in his eighties; wars, empires, monarchies, fools of all kinds have come and gone, but Italy still won't allow Vitale a hunting license. Which doesn't mean Vitale doesn't go hunting, however.

Grandfather always came out looking good when he was being chased by the guardsmen. There were only two smugglers in the area who could move up to two hundred kilos at a time; one of them lived in Barbè, the other one was Grandfather. With a sack on each shoulder Grandfather would ford the Astico, which isn't all that deep, but is mighty swift and cold. If he had just one sack, he could easily disarm the guardsmen with his free hand, otherwise he had to knock them down with his foot and run off with his goods.

When I knew him he was already highly respectable; he had made some money with the silkworms and bought himself land at Isola. He traveled around with his trap, wore a wide-brimmed hat, had large red handkerchiefs, and ate rye bread on account of the diabetes.

Grandfather's brute strength was terrifying to behold even when he was just fooling around. Once when he was young he had gone to take part in a church play in a town in the Val di Là; Grandfather was playing Saint Peter. While the actors were putting on their beards and costumes under a shed next to the theater, a few mocking remarks escaped from the curious crowd that had come to watch. This is how things are done in our part of the world, but those of us who come from Malo suffer from the fact that the name of our town often strikes people as the height of hayseed.

The mockers had no idea what would have become of them had Grandfather decided to strike back, but luckily he didn't get angry. On the ground, there lay a monstrous big oblong block of stone that was destined to be raised with winches and pulleys for some future construction. Obviously, you would have needed a team of big, strong builders to lift it.

Grandfather put his arms around this monolith, picked it up off the ground, and carried it around for a while. Then he put it down, upright. People said their Hail Marys. Later, the church play was much applauded.

We probably owe it to Grandfather if we Meneghellos, besides having similar faces like the Chinese, are almost all pretty speedy. Grandfather could run faster than anyone else in town; everyone said he could run like the wind, but when he went to try out elsewhere, in some archaic athletic competition, he met a fellow, "a guy from Brescia," who could run faster. The same thing happened again and again with my uncles and with us grandchildren: there was always some outsider, some Bresciano from hell, in other words someone clearly superhuman and *hors concours.*

Grandfather saw his Bresciano move alongside, then pull a meter ahead, then two meters. He knew he had to put his all into it, and he did, but the other fellow was still ahead of him. There in the middle of his lane, Grandfather was filled with a boundless admiration that you could still hear when he told the story fifty years later. He saw the nameless Bresciano fly past him, and he noticed that his eyeglasses on their elastic (for this exotic creature ran with special glasses) were flapping in the wind behind his back.

In his last years, Grandfather walked with some difficulty, carrying a stick, then he ceased to go out at all, merely dragging himself from room to room, and finally, he sat immobile in a chair. He no longer spoke and only bothered to eat; he ate everything that was put before him, stopping only when there was no more. Then they would push his chair over near the window in the front room, and he would gaze out at the street, tears coming down. He was still a threat to the ladies, though; woe to any he managed to get his hands on. So much so that my Uncle Dino, always open to modern and reasonable solutions, wanted to hire one just for the purpose.

His death throes lasted a while. His sons, daughters, and many grandchildren were all in the house. Toward evening, Aunt Nina saw an owl on the windowsill and began to shriek in a creepy way, but it was mostly pro forma, and also perhaps because she knew that when Grandfather died she would be the eldest in the family. Otherwise, there was nothing mournful about the occasion; to the contrary, there was a striking patriarchal naturalness to it all.

Grandfather's breath came slowly but surely, and the nurse said he might live for many hours yet. She said: "That's a good machine, they aren't many like that in town." In the middle of the night, I was alone in his room, listening to the rhythm of that good machine inside my grandfather's broad, smooth chest. Everything felt stylized: the large, half-empty bedroom, the nighttime silence, the lamp that still burned at the bedside, the death of the patriarch absent any illness, the long battle that was similar to a ceremony. Suddenly the rhythmic panting stopped, and there was a loud, hoarse rasping, and it was clear these were the last breaths. I called the others, and they all came in time. Aunt Adele bent over Grandfather as if she were possessed, trying to take advantage of the supreme occasion to get him to pronounce the right prayers: *Jesus . . . Joseph . . . Mary . . . be with me . . . my death.*

The unusual pertinence of the words redoubled her zeal. "Popà! Popà! she shouted, and began again: *Jesus . . . Joseph . . . Mary . . . with you . . . my soul . . . in peace.*

Absurd as the scene was, it was surely innocuous, but my aunt's behavior must have rubbed my father and his brothers the wrong way, because one of them dried his eyes, said, "Quit that, stupid," and Adele quit and Grandfather died.

The year before, when my grandmother Esterina was dying, they had made up a bed in a corner downstairs. Grandmother was a tiny, delicate woman, but near the end, her days were agitated, as if she were engaged in a fight. She struggled to sit up, caught sight of Death standing in the other corner, shouted to us to send him away. My grandmother was very devout, and I was surprised by her resistance, by the energy in her fragile arms as she defended herself.

✦

My grandfather's body type and some of his strength went to my cousin Giacomo. How strong is my cousin? No one knows for sure; all we have are hints. When his friends decided to leave without him and got into the car in front of the bar in the piazza, Giacomo grabbed the car by the rear fender with one hand—and they didn't drive off. These big men are often good-natured, and it's a good thing, because if they were aggressive like the rest of us, we'd be in trouble. Giacomo is a man of peace: when two of his friends scuffle too much, he will pick them up like two bundles of sticks, one under one arm, one under the other, and go toss them in their respective courtyards. One evening he went down to the cellar to get some wine for his friends, and he came back with a huge bucket full of wine. His friends laughed (a bucket of wine!), and one said, "I bet you can't drink it down in one go." Giacomo had been drinking all evening and was in the mood for fun; he put the bucket to his lips, and he emptied it. He's not the type to get drunk, although once he explained to me what to do if you have the tendency to become inebriated. Before going out in the evening, you take a pound of butter, you melt it in a pan, and you drink it.

✦

In my family there was a personage who was almost metaphysical, called My Grand-Lord (he wasn't my grandfather, but he was always referred to with the possessive, like a Milord) of whom I know little apart from the fact he existed and was called that way because he looked like the Lord. His all-but-total absence of qualities always appealed to me.

The records relating to those who were already old when the old people of today were children take us far, far back into the nineteenth century, and a stroll around town offers a look at the fragments of that world. Across from the thickets of Proa stands the house where my great grandmother Candida grew up: those bricks with their herringbone pattern in the portico are the same ones she played on as a child, and it was through that gate that she went, a girl dressed in her fine clothes, to mass on Sunday, and on that step in front of the eighteenth-century doors she would have chatted with her male admirer. In front of the scree coming down from Castello, on this side, stands the house where Grandfather was born; the creek that is now just a tiny trickle between the stones rushed down and destroyed it when Grandfather was four years old.

Our main link with that world (besides the houses and the huge beams of the old bridge over the Proa from which Grandfather certainly jumped down along with the other children of his century) was Aunt Gègia, Grandfather's sister, who in my day lived alone with a crazy daughter in a bare, clean little cottage here in Contrà Loza. She probably wasn't any poorer than many others, but for me she personified poverty: I knew she had been left alone with four children and that for a while she had gone to work in Switzerland. She toiled at the literal margins of the agricultural economy: collecting dandelion greens in the ditches, gleaning from the fields, raising rabbits for which she collected grass. She undertook great expeditions on foot (I have no idea why, but they weren't charitable expeditions) down roads and across fields, to towns so far away it had never occurred to us you could get there on foot, carrying a couple of slices of polenta, a few onions or some cheese rinds, a flask of wine.

It is strange how certain particulars can sometimes give us a lightning sense of what a person is; in the case of Aunt Gègia it was the itinerary of these travels of hers on foot, and above all what she ate, the little parcel with the polenta and the onions.

The story of Aunt Gègia—not at all an unusual story here in town—exemplifies some of the typical harshness and misery of life in the past. Her father died when she was a girl; her husband died an alcoholic after several years of marriage, leaving her to raise her four children alone. One of her children died of tuberculosis, after having left his own family; another also abandoned his wife and small child. Her youngest daughter was mad.

There were tales like this in many families: if not an alcoholic, there was someone with tuberculosis, or a mad person, or a halfwit, or a father who had forgotten to come home, or some other such misfortune or equivalent "cross to bear." Such things are rapidly forgotten because families tend to censor all that is considered unseemly. That the father of one of my aunts had not been seen since my aunt was a girl is something I learned only recently. The brother of another of my aunts, whom I myself saw just after he got out of prison, was hardly ever spoken of. He'd been inside for almost twenty years for having pointed his shotgun at a friend and fired. He was a young man, and worked as a baker and a hauler. The other, a bit older, was a pharmacist.

They were courting two sisters, and one of those rivalries must have arisen that have partly to do with the fine points of social status, and partly to do with the meanders of the psyche. And so one evening the young lad at Il Ponte tavern took down a hunting rifle, went back into town, learned how to load the gun, then went to La Scopa, had them call the pharmacist, and when he came outside, shot him dead in the dark. And then, as they tell it, he went home and said, "Papà, I need some money, I have to go away for a while. I shot so and so." When I saw him he had just gotten out of prison; he was wearing a cloth beret, looked pale and weak and had a hoarse voice. He died soon after.

I went to have a look at them in the cemetery a few days ago: they were buried in their respective family tombs, right next to each other.

Aunt Gègia had big bones and hard features. She was already very old when I knew her, but tall and robust, wearing the long gray skirts typical of her generation. She was cheerful, exuberant, and a pessimist. "Soon I'll be eating my radicchio from the root end," she would say, enjoying the idea. She had a strong voice and a boisterous laugh; she always seemed to be shouting. There was in her a strength I've seen in few others; at seventy, even at eighty, she continued to live as if she were thirty years younger. She couldn't allow herself to age; she was a woman alone who had to gather grass for the rabbits and look after her mad daughter.

We recently heard that my grandfather's brother was sent to jail. We asked our father, and he said it was the punishment for eccentric, lively people like Uncle. But who sent him to jail?

The priest.

And what did Grandfather's brother do? He had cut a plug out of the priest's watermelon, and had done his business inside it. The priest cut open the watermelon, and said, wrinkling his nose, "It was Meneghello who did this." And he had him sent off to jail.

He turned up again twelve years later, at night, and great grandmother Candida was very surprised.

Grandfather was the errand boy for the baker, Grandmother was the daughter of the owner. When they got married Grandfather had either just turned seventeen years old, or was about to. In any case the two of them had less than thirty-five years between them.

Christian marriage is a sort of mission *in partibus infidelium,* to the land of the unbelievers. Males are naturally pagan, and it is the job of the Christian bride, not so much to convert her husband as to save his soul. The savage male drinks, gambles, swears, molests women, gets into fights. The missionary wife does not try to counter these habits, she just takes care of the essential, that minimum of masses, sacraments, and worship necessary to remain on good terms with heaven—so that his soul can be picked up directly on his deathbed.

In this final task, which is often posthumous, as well as in every other aspect of her mission, the Christian bride can count on the help of her good daughters. Faith is largely transmitted thus, along the gynecological line; trying to face down the men would be absurd, like trying to explain algebra to a cannibal, but as long as there are women, there is hope.

My grandmother's case is typical. Grandfather's life began 1866 years after the Incarnation, in a place of long-standing Christian and Catholic tradition. Yet it can be truly said that in terms of his actions and his habits, the teachings of Christ and the Holy Roman Church were about as influential as those of, say, Hermes Trismegistus. The same, more or less, could be said of Grandmother's male sons: although they were raised as devoutly as the daughters, as soon as they reached adulthood they would begin to curse and swear, and in general to live like all the other males, while the daughters instead were all good Christians.

Worship obviously followed the contours of one's personality. The brightly colored holy cards with gold frames, the prayer books, the coins to buy the souls of little black children, the rosary in its silver case, the embroidered black veil: Aunt Nina's religion was made of such things. Thrust into a world peopled by men of haste and few niceties, she retired into her ideal of refinement, following the example of devout young ladies from the best families.

It was the world of the prayer books, of black silk stockings, of hot chocolate after Communion. My aunt was a spinster, but she had a certain feminine grace and coquettishness (ruthlessly trampled on by her brothers), and as a young woman had been the prettiest of the sisters. There had been a regrettable sentimental attachment during the First World War: as you would expect with a "captain," that is to say a distinguished person, albeit a deceiver. She had her own core of personal independence, which belonged to her ideal of the well-bred young lady: she had her own small job in "The Firm" and her own small wages, and she would take modest vacations and go on the occasional pilgrimage.

She would get the *caldanelle,* the hot flushes, when we made too much noise or when her brothers reproached her, and above all when the Firm's accounts didn't balance, as they didn't every time she added them up. What were these *caldanelle?* A comic but real kind of fluttering around; a flickering reflection of the world, but in infrared and microscopic; a heat inside that didn't register on a thermometer; an incipient intolerance that could easily grow absolute. Aunt Nina's religion was also a bit like this: distinguished, but with a hint of the *caldanelle.* In other temperaments, religion took other forms.

There were the genteel devout who would pray for the less devout and let God take care of their eternal destiny; and there were the severe devout who wanted to get directly involved. Severity was practically universal when faced with *resìa,* heresy, however. Grandmother's daughters and daughters-in-law were all but unanimous on this point. There was a small nucleus of Protestants over at Case (a few had gone to Germany to work and come back with this interesting novelty), and they carried out a mild sort of proselytizing by distributing copies of the Bible, in Italian. One was left in our kitchen. Aunt Lena took charge of the operation:

"Everyone out! Take the children away! Children out!"

The kitchen emptied out; even the cat, a beautiful animal called Plòmbe, exited. The Bible sat on the table, sending out black rays.

Aunt Lena went to get the tongs from the fireplace and moved with cautious steps toward the door, her eyes fixed on the Bible. She made the sign of the cross, then acted swiftly: the Bible was picked up with the tongs, transported, stiff-armed, to the other room, and tossed into the flames. The Bible was not merely a bad book; it was the word of Satan, evil stuff.

✦

My Uncle Checco, Lena's husband, knew the King of Italy personally, because he had landed on top of him while pole-vaulting, that time he dislocated his shoulder. They were holding a military track and field exhibition before the King, and my uncle was chosen for the pole vault.

The King, impressed by that spectacular athlete who was my uncle, had decided to watch the final jump up close. Uncle, wearing heavy boots with cleats, leg bands, and a helmet, made it over the bar easily but fell to one side, right on top of the King, and one of his boots clipped off a little piece of the monarch's right ear, the one you didn't see in his profiles on the coins of the time.

Uncle also knew Mussolini quite well; they had worked together in Switzerland, but lost track of each other after the war. When Mussolini came to speak in Vicenza, my uncle was in the crowd at Piazza dei Signori. Mussolini saw him and interrupted his speech to shout "Checco!" My uncle waved to him politely, muttering "Beni, you dirty dog, you!" and then Mussolini continued to address the crowd. That evening they were able to spend an hour together at Schioppi. "If you only knew, Checco," said Mussolini, staring at the gas pump in front of them, "how fed up I am!"

Uncle Checco has been old for a good while now. Tall, thin, and wiry, full of horrendous ailments: we all thought he was about to die many years ago when he had to stay in bed for some weeks; I pictured him creaking and disintegrating in that cold room with its tiles. And instead one day he got up and came downstairs, well again. Roberto, his oldest son, had been called up to the army, and Checco had to go back to making his "rentals" with the agents, day and night. The authorities also went after him about some rumors of contraband, which in our part of the world belonged to the realm of folklore and was considered almost more to be encouraged than repressed.

This was during those last years before economic well-being hit us on the head with a kind of delightful blow that made us lose our bearings. Until a few years ago you still had to toil and struggle to make a living, and to me it seemed a miserable life, but Uncle was used to it and paid no heed.

✦

"Uncle Checco's back with the pickup," said Papà one evening at the tavern. "He's been out all day, and what do you think he's made, maybe 1,500 lire?"

"What do you mean 1,500? You mean over and above?"

"Come on, dimwit," said my father. "But Checco was happy, he was singing!"

Singing! The news hit me like a slap, turning the tables on all the things that our professor of theoretical and moral philosophy at the University of Padua liked to call, sweaty in his excitement, "values."

I wished I could talk more with my uncle, but how? It was never clear whether we had a language in common; I don't mean the words, but the concepts, and certain elementary signals suggested we didn't. When he'd arrive with the pickup, he'd swing left off the road into the gate without making any kind of signal he was turning (all that recently invented nonsense) and obviously without looking: that was how he drove and how he had always driven, since long before the engineers at the Department of Motor Vehicles were born. And that was how he lived, too: following his own rules somewhat, a bit closed and distracted, and sometimes you didn't know whether he knew we were there, or who we were.

"Uncle Checco, have you got a cigarette paper?" It was just after the war and cigarettes were scarce.

He gave me the paper, and I put the tobacco I had on it. There wasn't much. While I was spreading it around with a finger, studying the problem, my uncle stopped to watch me.

"I'd better give you some tobacco, too," he said, and gave me a big pinch.

I began to fiddle with the paper. Producing messy spindles, lopsided eggs, funnels, misshapen cones, lumpy spheres.

"Give me that," said my uncle, and rolled me a cigarette.

"Lick it." I licked it, took the cigarette, and put it in my mouth. I searched for matches in all my pockets, and then Uncle took out his matches and lit my cigarette. He was looking at me as if lost in thought, and I didn't know if he saw me.

"Want to spit it out?" he said. So, he saw me.

✦

Uncle had a dash of inventive genius that made him deserving of a better life. He loved to come up with clever little adjustments, homespun solutions. If there was a lean-to that was wobbling, and the foreman said to put in a post to hold it up, Uncle would immediately think of a way to do without the post. He could stabilize a wooden structure with great ingenuity, making springs and suspension bars, grips and clips, each of which clung to the other with just the right counterforce until the whole stood up without resting on anything in particular. Sometimes the lean-to would fall down all the same; other times a fly cable would transfer the load to other parts of the adjacent building, and you would have to build a counterload or tear down a wall.

Uncle Checco was not merely an ingenious person, he was an inventor, a real craftsman. His work was based on imagination and fancy, and his solutions always left us wondering. You felt they were adventurous; Daedalus, I'm sure, had the same character. His ingenuity was greatest when it came to mechanical things and building. Transformation was his kingdom: turning an automobile into a tractor, a lathe into a compressor, a motorbike into a saw—here Uncle was unbeatable. When he was younger and an active member of the Firm, the main problem was to keep him away from the new cars. His eye would instantly zoom in on the possible ways to improve any new purchase.

"The new Lancia's not bad, but it could use a little work on the front suspension. You see these struts? I was thinking that if we cut them off here and soldered in the ones from the Nove . . ."

He made such adjustments all by himself, banging and swearing down in the forge. The result mattered, but the process mattered more; I suspect that in such moments of irresponsibility as we all have, he dreamed of a machine that was entirely made of adjustments, a clever and useless combination of winch, taxi, and asphalt roller, with carbide headlights.

In recent years he has almost stopped making adjustments; he takes a stool and sits for hours next to Roberto's van, deep in thought. Now, these ramshackle modern vehicles weren't badly made, but there were so many little adjustments you couldn't help noticing were needed. Following the thread of his calculations, Uncle would get down on the pavement and slide under the van, and there they would find him when they came calling at mealtime. They tell me that in these last months he's even taken to sleeping down there in the garage, next to the van.

Chapter 17

THEY WERE FOUR BROTHERS (along with three sisters), and the last one, Dino, was much younger than the others. The older three had already begun working before the First War, all with some enterprise and daring.

Uncle Checco had even lived in Switzerland from the age of fourteen to eighteen, and had traveled around Europe some, even as far as St. Petersburg. For a couple of years in Switzerland he had trained to be a modern mechanic in a sort of professional school, but when he began to move around his real forte turned out to be his skill as a blacksmith. Beating the iron on the anvil, something he had learned in Malo before leaving home, was an art already scarce in Switzerland, Alsace, and other places he visited.

At the inn in St. Petersburg they stole everything he had, even his clothes, and the innkeeper, who was a good Russian, gave him a new set of clothes including a high-collared shirt and derby hat, and in this peculiar dress he continued to wander from one forge and workshop to another. His adventures would need (and deserve) a book all on their own, beginning with his student years. He was a very good student, and at the end of year four in elementary school he passed the year "exonerated," meaning exonerated from paying the fees, and there were only four students in Malo that year who earned the exemption.

He was a handsome young man, tall and proud. My father, who was eight years younger, could recall how good-looking and modern Checco had seemed when he came back home from Switzerland. He was dressed like a young gentleman; everyone clustered around him in amazement. Later he went down to the courtyard to tie up the horse, and when the animal shied, he let out a oath. Grandmother Esterina heard him, and she began to weep silently.

"Ruined," she said.

All the brothers had a certain spirit of adventure. The other day with my father, we looked at his driver's license, and it was numbered in the 140s, one of the earliest issued in Italy. Uncle Ernesto must have had one of the very first. He had begun driving in 1908 or 1909, and my father a few years later, but certainly before they were twenty. Ernesto worked as a driver, or *sofèr*, for private automobile owners, while Checco had established a mechanic's shop where he adjusted, repaired, and modified bicycles and other such vehicles, my father assisting, mostly at the lathe. I went to look at that lathe recently, and it is still there in its place in the corner at the end of the shop. They bought it already used between 1906 and 1908, but it's still a good machine, with old-fashioned crank handles and a four-speed engine. I asked Papà how good a workman he'd been, and he said that in the 1920s there were already specialized workers better than he was, but it's clear from many other things I know that he was pretty good.

He had learned to work the lathe as a young man in Marano, but he had begun working even before that. He completed just three years of elementary school, but he expressed himself amazingly well when he wrote letters to us children, putting the dialect expressions in quotation marks and conveying his sense of humor with a delicacy I envy. It seems they often relearned to write as adults. When he was about twenty he went to Verona to make his "masterpiece": that's how they called it, with that unexpectedly accurate name. He says he was impressed above all by the beauty and modernity of the lathes there; he had never seen such splendid ones—but he quickly got his bearings.

The masterpiece he was assigned was what's called an "endless screw." He prepared the piece of metal, measured it, and made the marks you need to make to turn an endless screw, and at this point, the supervisor who was watching him already understood that he was good, and said "You can stop there."

✦

The Firm was founded just after the Great War. They had a small supply of capital in the person of my grandfather, and the large capital of their youth, their desire to work, and their artisanal ingenuity. They didn't have a gift for business the way Grandfather did, and never became rich; they were well-off but always in a precarious, *pro tempore* way. Their well-being was based on their own work, on the initiatives and gambles taken by small artisan-entrepreneurs, including, to begin with, that *arrangiarsi*, that "getting by," that was typical of the wartime years.

My father worked as a *sofèr* for a command post, and he would tell Checco (who was exempted from the draft because of that shoulder of his) about various auctions, deals, and wrecked equipment to be salvaged. Checco would set out with Grandfather in the car they had then. The sales agent my father knew gave sensational discounts, with a smile (my father was the kind of man people liked; he was small, dark, and lively and looked good in his uniform). When they departed with their new purchase my father would load on a couple of tins of gasoline they could sell on the side and some extra tires. A few days after their return Uncle wrote to my father from Malo: "It goes like the Wind, and makes a kind of Whistle. When we got home we were Drunk."

They would go and recover military vehicles abandoned upside down at the bottom of a hill or at the foot of a ravine. A Puch *sassì* (chassis), a G.M. engine: Checco had his work cut out putting things together again. In theory such private salvage operations were slightly illegal, but what is not illegal in Italy? One time in Bassano, where they had salvaged a magnificent *sassì* and were towing it, they got very hungry and foolishly stopped at the hotel to eat. They had already gotten out of their rig when they realized that right there in front of them was the carabinieri barracks, with a carabiniere on guard at the gate. Uncle Checco crossed the road and said to the carabiniere:

"Would you mind keeping an eye on that *sassì* while we go in and have a bite?"

"Not at all," said the carabiniere.

◆

The repair shop—the Ufficina, they called it—stood at the top of the courtyard, next to the Garage, the Portico, and the Forge.

Ufficina, it reminds me of an anthem:

> *E la pace del mondo, o gelatina!*
> *Il Tricolore canta sul cantiere*
> *Su l'Ufficina!*

> And the peace of this world—O Jelly!
> The Tricolor sings above the yard
> Above the Ufficina!

Closing my eyes, I could see the *tricolore* flying on the point of the roof, over by the garden, and the sky was a dazzling blue. The first line evidently meant either/or. The *cantiere*, the yard, was a place where you sang—*cantare*.

The Firm occupied the space around the courtyard with the black paving stones, which ran downhill slightly from the shop toward the street. The backbone of the thing, juridically and administration-wise, was *la linia*, the weekly coach "line" that meant that even in prohibitionist Italy you could possess your own buses. There were two "lines": one from Malo to Thiene (on Monday, driver Checco) and one from Malo to Valdagno (on Friday, driver Ernesto). For both drivers the "line" was essentially a modern way to go and shop or look at the market in these two nearby towns. The passenger service was an extra, an accessory that the driver took along with him. My uncles thought of the schedules, stops, ticket prices, and the route itself as essentially personal matters, to be determined each trip according to the circumstances and their moods.

You sensed they were a product of a time when automobiles were rare, and the driver-owner seemed not only privileged, but a kind of sorcerer to his peasant-client. Uncle Ernesto particularly liked this role, which he played with great brio and infallible showmanship. As for collecting fares, the brothers disliked any complicated calculations. Their idea was to come home and empty their pockets, and say to Aunt Nina "Here—you count it."

Ernesto had handlebar mustaches, curly reddish hair, and you could see from his face that he was one of us, but he had grown up round and a bit plump. He had no children; at home he was orderly, domestic minded, and quiet; away from home, easygoing, jolly, and a live wire. And, he drank.

Our parents were out, and Uncle Ernesto had no trouble at all persuading us to go along with him.

"Where are we going, Uncle?"

"We're going to take a spin."

He put us in the OM with the 13 VI plates, and off we went. There were six or seven cousins, boys and girls, and the smallest were only infants. Uncle sang as he drove, he made us laugh;

he had a great time and so did we. We stopped at the tavern La Pace, then at Il Ponte, then at Il Boro, then at the first establishment in Priabona, then at the second. We'd pull up to the tavern honking the horn, leap out over the doors yelling, and invade the bar. Uncle would order himself a quarter-liter, and for us, some fizzy drink into which he mixed a finger of red wine from another quarter-liter pitcher he ordered on the side. Then he'd dance, if he could with the tavern owner's wife or the serving girl, or if not, with a broom. From time to time we'd go out in the bocce court to pee, and Uncle would help the little ones. Then off we'd go, hooting the horn, on our way to the next tavern.

So the afternoon would pass, and the sun would go down over Feo, and evening would fall, then night. By now we were tavern crawling in the Val di Là, and Uncle was articulating his words with difficulty, but the more drunk he got, the more solicitous of us children he grew. He would order a big plate of minestrone for all of us, the minestrone the peasants ate, with spaghetti in it, and he would feed the sleepy ones himself. Quite a few of us were falling asleep now, toppling over with spoon in hand, and Uncle would make little beds for us on the benches with his overcoat and his jacket, with borrowed blankets, and he'd lay the fallen to sleep and tuck them in well, and then go back out for another turn with the broom.

When Mamma and Papà arrived in the middle of the night, I couldn't help but notice their scowling faces, like someone who's had a great fright. I noticed they didn't even speak to my uncle as they took us one by one and put us in the Venti in which they'd come: they almost seemed unhappy that Uncle had taken us on an excursion!

In later years Uncle Ernesto had reached that stage of advanced alcoholic intoxication in which a couple of glasses of wine would go right to his head. He was fun when he was sober and even more fun when he was drunk.

He continued to drive the bus until after the war, and his driving, especially on the return trip and on mountain roads, was always the most memorable part of the ride. "One-handed curve!" he'd announce to his passengers. "*Turnichè!* Hairpin turn, no brakes!" "Sharp right with eyes closed!" and he did just what he said.

He drove well. One Sunday we went to Priabona to watch a race for sport and touring cars in the hills, and as the contestants appeared at the bottom of the road where it snaked back and forth a couple of kilometers away, we studied the power of the cars and the ability of the drivers and tried to guess the names of the most famous ones. We immediately picked out a black sedan barreling up the hill: was it Taruffi? Villoresi? Actually it was Uncle Ernesto, in a rented 1100. He stopped at the peak, to applause, although he was irked because (he said) he had to pass quite a few out-of-towners who were making a slow ascent. "They should stay home on Sunday if they don't know how to drive," he said.

My father was less happy behind the wheel. He preferred working at the lathe, and my image of him is in his patched, turquoise-colored overalls behind the table, the floor striped with curly, thin silver ribbons. When he drove, my father would have preferred to be a simple *sofèr,* or driver, as we later learned to call it; sometimes he even dreamed of putting on a hat with a visor so as not to be confused with what he actually was: the owner of the car and leader of the outing.

I had heard the word "driver," but I had never used it before upper school. In my first year (this was in Vicenza), the priest who taught us religion said to me: "Meneghello, are you from Malo?" I said yes, and he said, "I know your people; isn't your father a driver?" I said yes, and blushed. "Driver" suddenly sounded like some kind of servant; back in Malo the question of what my father *was* had never come up, and if it had, I would have said, "He's got the mechanic's shop, he's one of those who run the buses; he works in the shop and drives the buses." It may have been the first time that I saw the town and all of us from the outside, and the effect was somewhat disconcerting, though it wasn't the town's fault.

Many years later the last of the brothers, the modernizing Uncle Dino, applied himself to this question of the firm's name, and came up with "Coach-Concessionaire." Technically it was accurate, and it sounded important, but it was a little peculiar.

The Firm's earnings came mostly from the rentals, not so much of small automobiles (the ones Uncle Ernesto liked, but then every client had his preferred brother and requested him) but from the Sunday and holiday rentals, those adventurous outings aboard open-topped buses to the sanctuaries, the places dedicated to the Holy Virgin, the caves and the falls (where water "falls"), the various Wuthering-Heights of our hills. We sometimes went along, mixed up with the clientele. At the Madonna of Corona there was a place where the bus, as it climbed the hill, gradually came out onto a sort of balcony, and before you there rose a huge blue mountain—the Garda, which is actually water, a lake, but which seemed to be standing upright, not lying flat.

These outings were the biggest jobs that came their way, and there was something passionate and cheerful about them: you rose before dawn, heated up the engines in the courtyard, took off to that pure hum that engines made then, when they ran on gasoline and not on diesel, and came back the following night with a stack of cash.

The history of our vehicles can no longer be written; the memories and recollections of the names and the colors are woven together in a crooked confusion. You can just barely make out the origins, an archaic universe of Standard-Bajard and the Fiat-Zero that gave birth to the yellow Tipo-Due. It wasn't always easy to distinguish between an automobile and a coach in those days—not to mention the intermediate fauna that had been American ambulances before Uncle Checco got his hands on them—and some cars were almost coach-size while the coaches weren't much bigger than cars.

Then came the Mesozoic Era of the 15 Ter, the Oligocene Epoch of the Uno, the Cinque and the Venti (the OM survived right into the early Tertiary Period alongside forms of life that were infinitely more recent), and then, in the middle of the Pleiocene Epoch, the SPA suddenly appeared.

The SPA was a huge monster, a mastodon, a deinotherium, a platybelodon. One day we heard a sort of low, continuous roar outside the gate, and we ran out to look, and there by the Count's wall, mountainous and quaking, was the SPA. It was magnificent. It took an hour to get it in the gate, in reverse: nobody thought it would clear the gate but it did. It was for the SPA that they decided to tear down the stone arch of the gate and leave the square hole that has been called the gate ever since—a shame, but necessary because the SPA sometimes scraped the arch and broke a window.

Then came the insipid age of the Balilla, and the banal buses of the late Quaternary. The age of the ill-omened "Companies" against which we little firms struggled to compete. There was the one called SITA (which really meant *saetta,* the small thunderbolt you found on the ground after a lightning strike, a pebble of salt) and there was SIAMI (something like a *scimmia* or monkey), and there were the buses that did the valleys: Val Pantena, Val Pestilence, Val Porno. How could we compete?

The drivers wore hats, the bosses were functionaries in whose offices my uncles would never have dreamed to set foot, and Dino, when he went there hat in hand, felt somewhat embarrassed. Things were getting tougher as the years went by, you heard of debts, the management on the part of my older uncles was growing ever more fanciful, and there was talk about looking for something secure—in short, you could feel that the end was near.

The Firm's last great adventure was the expedition Uncle Checco and my father made to Africa with a hauler. We always had a yard full of haulers: the buses often ended up in that department after Checco had gotten his hands on them. But this was no mere hauler, it was a tow-hauler (without the tow winch, however): a 34 Fiat that was practically a Sàura and even ran on diesel.

Monsignor came to bless it late one afternoon and off they went. They stayed in Africa for a number of years and made good money; they would come back from time to time, lean and tanned, and were able to return home before the war began. Uncle Checco was bothered by the hyenas, and he says he used to sleep with one arm outside the tent so that it was easy to strangle them.

Africa made an unforgettable impression on my father: the huge distances, the majestic landscapes, the place names, so cheerful and clearly enunciated, foreign, but not so different from our dialect: Dessie, the Cobbo plain, Lake Tana. For my father, this is Abroad: it's something we noticed during his recent visit to us in England.

"How far is it from here to Addis Ababa?" he asked casually.

"I don't know," I said, "Maybe four thousand?"

"Are you crazy?" said Papà. And soon we got used to the way he referred to London.

"How many inhabitants are there in Asmara?" he asked once, out of the blue. I understood immediately that he meant the provincial city where we live. When we took him to Windsor, I pointed out that the royal flag wasn't flying over the castle, and explained that meant the queen wasn't in residence. She was in Addis Ababa, thirty kilometers from Windsor.

Chapter 18

THE FIRST TIME PAPÀ saw someone brush his teeth was in Turin, when he went in the service.

"*Mària Vergine,* what's that fellow there doing?"

He was brushing his teeth.

The draft must have been one trauma after another in those days; already in my time it was different, although there was still the overall trauma of being drafted. It was like being hit over the head; it destroyed your sense of time: days seemed to go on for months, and at the end of a week, the week vanished into thin air. Everything was intense and unreal; you could hear your fatigues rustling all by themselves.

When they sent me home on leave I came down from Merano through the Val Lagarina, and then by train from Verona to Vicenza. In theory I was a fairly sophisticated young man, but when the hills of home and the names of nearby towns came into view, it was like being hit on the head all over again. In my father's case, the trauma had the effect of making him remember everything—names, streets, taverns, prices, conversations, the hours of the day, the days of the week. It had the opposite effect on me. Our family knows more about Turin in 1913 than about Merano thirty years later. I served seven months; my father also served seven. Years. At the end of it he must have been fairly sophisticated himself.

In his early years in the service they hardly ever let them off, but later he sometimes got out on leave. Uncle Checco—one day when he was in a storytelling mood—told us about the time he was working in the shop (he was exempted from service for that pole-vaulting injury) and he saw a military vehicle take the turn through the gate into the courtyard, my father at the wheel. When Uncle went out to greet him, he saw a man's head severed at the neck between the left fender and the radiator.

"Who's that?" said Uncle sternly, pointing a finger. My father got out to see, and knocked his fist on his forehead.

"*Orcocàn,* that must be the carabiniere I hit at Castelfranco."

Uncle, with all the authority primogeniture confers, told him he must take the head back to Castelfranco, and my father went.

We liked Uncle's joke so much we went to tell it to Papà. Papà laughed too, and said: "Unfortunately, it wasn't at Castelfranco, but much further along, over near Conegliano, and I only had one day of leave."

Papà was in aviation, but he worked as a *sofèr.* He was stationed at the headquarters in Udine, right in front of Mamma's house, and he often drove officers out to inspect the lines. One time, all that came back with him was a beret with the stripes on it. When Papà got up again after the explosion, that was all he could find of the fellow.

He sometimes transported big name personages, whom he would toss into a mix of names that included his fellow soldiers attached to the command—Ortiga, Quondamcarlo, and Fiorina.

"So did you ever speak to this D'Annunzio fellow back then?"

"Oh, sure. Sure I did."

"And what did he have to say?"

"He said, 'Wait here for me.' "

Sometimes Papà would wait for hours.

"And did he at least give you a tip, this D'Annunzio?"

"Are you kidding? He was a first-class cheapskate."

When we were small, however, what made the biggest impression was that Papà had been in the service with Baracca, the ace World War I pilot.

"Papà, what was Baracca like?"

"Extremely tall."

It's not always easy to communicate with my father, because the things he takes for granted are not the same things we take for granted, and furthermore, he shamelessly censors anything that doesn't fit with the way he thinks we understand things.

"Papà, you never told us that there was a brothel in the house in Contrà Grisa that belonged to Grandfather."

When he refused to say anything one way or the other, we showed him the entry in Don Tarcisio's diary, and we repeated to him what Signora Meggiolan had told us that very day. We used to make pilgrimages from street to street to find the vestiges of our elders, the simple houses in which they lived their simple lives. Contrà Grisa was down at the end of town, in an area we didn't know very well.

"Signora, which was the house here that belonged to my grandfather during the First War, the gray one, or the yellow one?

"The house of ill repute? The yellow one."

Now it began to come back to my father: he had been a soldier, and had learned about it when he came home on leave.

"But it looks so small, that place. How many women were there?

"Oh, I never set foot in there. Ask Bepi who always spent his entire leave over there."

The whole thing seemed so peculiar to me. "I wonder how they decorated the house?" I said to myself out loud.

"Oh, it was classy," he said, "it was all plastered with mirrors."

Then he began to laugh too, and there was no more need to ask Bepi.

◆

"But did you really take part in the March on Rome?" I asked, out of the blue, one day at table.

"Only as far as Isola," said my father. Isola is four kilometers away, to the south. So he was going in the right direction. "At Isola I told them my child was sick—that was you—and so I went back home. Also what's-his-name, he also took advantage of the occasion to turn back. He said he had a stomachache. But Uncle Ernesto took my place."

"So Uncle did the March on Rome."

"Yes," said Papà, "he went ahead with the others in my place."

"In other words he really did go to Rome."

"Ah, Rome—no. They stayed for two days in Vicenza, and then they came home."

Vicenza is sixteen kilometers away, and it too is in the right direction.

Dino, who had a nice sense of the ridiculous, made a big sign, hoisted it up on his shoulders, and walked around the center of town. It was 1940—year XVIII in the Fascist calendar that began with the March on Rome in 1922—and the sign said:

"This evening my nephew will speak on the radio."

There were comments.

"He was promoted *littore?*

"Must be a good job."

"As I always said."

I spoke in the evening. I don't wish to say anything here about this episode in my life, except that in a strange way the whole town was brought into it, because I said very proudly that I had been born the year of the March on Rome, and that several 15 Ter packed with squadristi, driven by Papà and my uncles, had taken part in a noisy celebration.

I suppose my grandfather went to listen to me at the tavern, among the crowd of customers. Most likely he was proud of the way I spoke, without paying much attention to the content, and I'm sure that the mention of the 15 Ter, those family vehicles so unexpectedly evoked on the radio, must have moved him.

There was the red 15 Ter and the green 15 Ter: two open-roofed buses with benches for seats. To me they were like two large, cheerful girls: the Red was Este and the Green, Flora. The Puch, instead, had a gray top, a sort of small roof held up by iron columns, and she was a foreign lady, angular, no longer young, quite reserved in nature.

In the entryway, between the people coming and going on the street and the sound of the engines, I can just hear a few phrases of the conversation between my father and a visitor at the gate. Small talk.

"Yes, I saw Perìn, I saw him when they interrogated him, the day before they hanged him. After the interrogation, they brought him to my cell, and his face was all black from where they had beaten him, and it was pointless even to ask but I said, 'What now?' and he said, 'Ah, they're going to wring my neck.' He already knew."

Perìn was the only one of those who were in jail with my father at Schio who was hanged: down at the curve toward Castelnovo, wearing a sign that said "Bandit." Various others were finished off in other ways.

What a strange thing a civil war is: there was my father, a squadrista of the first hour, in this Fascist jail, and there was the jailer who had agreed to take his messages out, also an old-time squadrista. The messages said:

"Don't even think about sending the lad up because they'll butcher him."

The lad wasn't me this time, it was Bruno; I was off in other parts.

Chapter 19

AS A RULE, WE IN TOWN could tell the difference between the serious, scrupulous storyteller, like Mino, and the ones who made things up. But with the elders you had to be more careful: many a time we heard incredible tales that sounded like pure invention but were later confirmed as fact by independent and reliable sources.

I can only say that in the past, things happened that today are very unusual. It seemed incredible to us that when *they* went out on their motorcycles, if Bocchino were riding an old Garelli and misjudged the curve at the bridge toward Breganze, and the Garelli slammed into the parapet on this side, that Bocchino might continue the journey via the airways to the other side of the creek. But in fact, that's just what happened. When they got to the piazza in Breganze, his friends realized that Bocchino was missing, and they went back to look for him. He had flown over the creek and was resting in a bush waiting for the concussion to subside; the Garelli was stuck on the bridge, out of commission, and they took it away on a wagon.

Riding motorcycles was much more fun in the past. To begin with, there was that business of the transmission with the belt, and this belt would loosen during the ride, and from time to time you had to get down and—I never understood which—either tighten the belt or stretch the bike. They would start up on foot, pushing, and at first the engine would catch only sporadically and as if strangled by inertia, but when the bike got going, it went fast.

It seems that machines like the Aìesse and the Borgo, and the complicated Frera, went faster than the chrome-plated playthings of today. It would be pointless to question the fact that Checco Agosti made it to Mantua in an hour one Sunday, including those stops for the belt, because the entire older generation knows he did.

And furthermore, back then motorcycles did something that ours on today's roads don't: they would *shimmy*. When you hit a rough surface, the bike would begin to make little warning signals when you got beyond a certain speed, quick hints of disobedience from the handlebar, and the novice cyclist could mistake the effortless way the bike then took the next hundred meters for a complete recovery. It was a fatal error.

All of a sudden the handlebar would say "no" for the last time, and catastrophe would strike. The motorcycle would begin to seesaw, then it would get convulsions, stick out its chin, and threaten to topple, then the back wheel would start to kick, and the machine would do battle with itself in the air.

When the bike shimmies, you mustn't try to control it; you just look for a patch of grass.

Over at Isola, even in our times, there were a couple of hundred meters of road surface with "troughs," tiny undulations every ten to fifteen centimeters that would have made a tank shimmy. Some would slow down to walking pace, others would push their bikes, especially on the downhill toward Vicenza because in that direction the critical phase happened in a very unsuitable place, with stone walls on the left and the creek down below on the right. On the uphill toward Malo, the terrain was more favorable, and you could take more risks. Countless cyclists got thrown onto the field between the old cemetery and the new.

Annibale, who was the greatest motorcyclist in town, didn't even think of slowing down on his way back from Vicenza; he would roar through Isola at eighty kilometers per hour as if he were riding the horns of a bull at the rodeo, ready to fly off at the old cemetery. Then he'd pick up the bike on the grass out front, saying he saved a couple of minutes that way.

The brokers drove Guzzi bikes with gas tanks hanging down and swollen flywheels like moving goiters; the bikes made a slow, quiet *put-put* noise, and in between you could hear the scraping of metallic parts. Handkerchiefs around their necks, they drove their Guzzi's proudly at walking pace. Erminio, sitting in the doorway of his shop, made signs to one of these fellows to try to let him know he'd lost the cushion behind the seat. The broker turned around.

"*Ostia!* And the woman?"

He had to turn back to look for her up on the road to Case.

When Papà lost Grandmother Esterina, he knew it right away. He heard a kind of rustling noise and turned around, mostly out of curiosity. Grandmother was huddled on her side down at the end of the straight stretch; she hadn't gotten hurt at all, but she was lying there very still and composed in the middle of the road, like a little parcel.

The family bike was an Indian, with gigantic handlebars like oxcart handles and a footboard long enough to take a walk on. Nothing about it suggested speed; the huge engine made a good-natured *cik-cik-cik* noise, and you felt like you were traveling in a big wagon.

Dino's personal bikes, however, were dedicated to the cult of speed. We would race along on the little Guzzi, me perched behind the seat, and between Isola and Castelnovo Dino would inform me:

"Ninety-five per hour . . . ninety-eight . . . one hundred!"

The little Guzzi could just barely pass one hundred, although very elegantly; the racing model Sarolea could do so in third, but boorishly; and last came the Norton Turìs-Tropì—"Tourist Trophy"—with its deformed tank like an overdeveloped organ. It—she—was a sort of lofty, morose prima donna who would rarely let you put her in fourth, and when she did go into fourth, seemed to be acting out a great drama. But with gusto; she had style.

Sometimes Dino took me with him to meet his lady friends, so that I could get some experience. He used the respectful *Voi* with the ones he held in highest esteem; he'd say, "Do be kind to my nephew, he's just a beginner." None of the bikes of those times had suspensions, and a ride on the fender, even with a cushion, was hard on the back, but the Sarolea and the Norton Turìs-Tropì were mortally rigid. After a couple of kilometers you'd get the first, famous stab in the side, and from then on every bump would take your breath away.

✦

The season of our own motorcycles came late, after the war, and was brief.

On a Sunday outing to Vicenza, you could hear the notes of three sporting bikes: the song of Ruaro's Alce was easygoing-gregarious: happy, healthy, silly. The 4-Bolt that Aldo was riding produced a vigorous chord rich with truculent vibrations; my Twin whistled with incomparable grace.

On the straight stretch, the Alce would raise her voice, the 4-Bolt began to knock from side to side—pure ring of steel on steel. At this point the Twin, front wheel lifting, would speed past the hysterical zone of the shriek straight up into those spheres that belonged only to her, where the great, unadorned ideals of noise and motorcycle hummed.

✦

When Dino was in the service, there was dread and dismay in Grandmother's house, a darkness to the rooms, a tacit pride mixed with grief, like when you have a son in prison. The women would read his letters aloud, and one time one of Dino's girlfriends came to measure out on the ground the length of the jump he'd made in a military athletics competition. They kept repeating the distance—it was five meters and quite a few centimeters—with simple-minded wonder, and when they measured it out on the kitchen floor, they had to move well out into the stairwell. Dino, however, had come second: a filthy rival of his from the Bersaglieri Corps had jumped even further.

He came back home on a leave with a new worldview and (it must have been his last leave before he was discharged) with a bayonet. This weapon—in those days I called it *lo stilo*—seemed to me the very essence of danger and bravery, a sacred object that I got him to let me hold for a moment in Grandmother's kitchen. It was almost as big as I was, and unsheathed it was a silent, terrible, real, adult thing; it even had grooves "to let the blood run off."

Dino's new worldview encompassed a touching desire to read books, and these would figure in time among the non-school books that I, too, read. Many were books about "life": Alexis Carrel's *Man, The Unknown*, a *Sexual Encyclopedia*, novels with titles like *Life Belongs to Us* and *An Adventure in Budapest*. Among the Hungarian and American novels, the best were those by Jack London (pronounced Lon-DON), whose heroes I identified utterly with the figure of my Uncle Dino.

He taught me, among other things, that a woman is a fortress, and that it was all about laying siege to her and taking her—and then you no longer knew what to do with her. This was not just the usual vain male wisdom, but something like a discovery that vaguely saddened him. It was from him that I heard the first exacting definition for those he called "inverts." I thought it was a clever term, both scientifically and linguistically; it must have come from a book. As for the thing itself, Dino had encountered it, touched it with his hand as it were, while he was in the service in Milan—in a crowded cinema, leaning against the side wall deep into the film, his hands behind his back. Strange people the Milanese, a mysterious land of snares and traps was Milan, where years later our own Plinio went in his impeccable clothes to consume his "coldsuppers." Dino got frightened and ran away.

In Dino, my family expressed a surge of modernity; he was dynamic, curious, eager to learn and know. You could feel he was a new man, that he belonged to another generation from that of my father and my older uncles. There was an air of romance around him that didn't seem to pertain to the town, something urban. He smoked Tre Stelle, hummed—a bit tone-deaf—"Mimì's a Flirt" with great feeling, explaining to us the emotional significance of it all. Flirt: it was a concept he knew all about. Among his women there was one he liked *just as she was,* no smell of Coty, no rapacious penciled eyes, and there was another by the name of Nanù who seemed tragically sad, but maybe her silent suffering was merely playacting.

When they were showing a good film at Schio or Vicenza, we'd get on the motorcycle and go see it. A film was good when it dramatized some tension involving Life. Dino had a special feeling for the *how* of living, for the *meaning* of life: what emerges in a crisis, women who rebel, characters who make themselves change or clarify their relationships with the family or with society. He would write to his girlfriends rarely, but at length, with the aid of a dictionary. "Only once every six months," he advised me, "but exhaustively." He wrote with dash and impetuousness, and his handwriting looked very much like a famous hand of the era. Polish and culture was what he admired above all in a woman—that, and force of character.

Many of his lady friends had high school diplomas or university degrees; they were, in short, more educated than he was.

He treated us nephews like sons or younger brothers, teaching us the ways of the world, and he would have liked us to be good at sports. He bought us boxing gloves and a *punci-bàl,* and followed my first bicycle race on his motorcycle.

After a few kilometers the rider in front of me blew his nose in his fingers and I swerved, in surprise. A large heap of riders and bicycles piled up. Dino had stopped to look, and as the fallen slowly righted themselves in a huge cloud of dust, he was cheered to see I wasn't among them. Finally there was just one rider on the ground—me. They took me to a pharmacy in Monte di Malo where they taped me up from head to foot, so much that Dino, as we were coming back into town, decided to take off half the bandages so as not to frighten the family. The other half still made quite an impression. It was Sunday, and there was a large audience in the piazza; I was on the backseat of the bike, and another motorcyclist behind us was carrying my beautiful, twisted bicycle. For a moment I feared Dino might take the long way around, but luckily he went straight downtown.

✦

Without mentioning the word "glamour," I told Rita, in the car with me on the way to Schio, how I used to feel when Uncle Dino took me to the cinema on the motorbike in the evening. Breathing in the scent of his Tre Stelle, listening to the bracing song of the engine, I felt the night contained the very essence of life. I asked Rita if she had any similar memories.

There was one: an aunt from Valdagno who came to visit one time, a self-possessed, commanding woman who wore a hat with a veil. In the family, she had a reputation for being very distinguished, and she lived up to her reputation. They made her coffee, and she drank it without lifting her veil, filtering it through the mesh. For the first time in her life, Rita felt she had met a real lady.

◆

From this Dino of the 1930s, another man would later emerge. During the war destiny assigned him the last residual asset of the old Firm, a Sette transformed into a pickup with a wood-burning engine, with which he made prodigious expeditions in the upper Po Valley, travels worthy of a Jack London hero. At night he and my cousin Mamo would travel without head-lights; by day, Mamo would sit up on top of the load to look out for airplanes, jumping down often to stretch his legs be-cause the wood-burning Sette went very, very slowly, and on a modest uphill if they didn't push it, went backward.

They were machine-gunned by the Americans, requisitioned by the Germans, swamped by displaced people. Sleeping, eat-ing, starting the engine, putting out fires, fixing broken parts: everything was a problem, yet they came back safe and sound every time. But Dino changed: certain obstinate traits of his emerged, a hint of a quarrel with Life (the most compelling of his paramours), a late passion for hunting, a tendency to stand on points of honor.

Some time ago now, he took to pronouncing the word "knock-out" as "*conàu*." They told him you don't say it like that, but he replied, "I say *conàu*."

And he still says *conàu*.

◆

I would have liked to reproduce something of the relations we had with Dino with his own children, but it didn't work out.

As a boy Dino used to mock his son Ilario, calling him "the carnival barker," because he had a great passion for attending town fairs. Whenever there was a fair in a town nearby, Ilario would disappear from home and be gone half a day, sometimes all day. He went on foot if he had to, alone, and I don't think he did anything special there: he would look at the stalls, the colored balloons, the real carnival barkers with their baskets of sweets as brightly colored as a bottle of *rosolio* liqueur; he would listen to strangers shouting and buglers squealing; he would wander around for an afternoon, hands in his pockets, in the reign of freedom.

This passion of his was silent and inarticulate. The child did not even try to justify himself, as if he knew he could not be understood. You sensed his personality was inaccessible, hidden in some remote place where no message could arrive.

One time he exasperated me by telling some lie and I slapped him too hard in the face. We were in their house, in the entryway, and that act, that excessive smack, created in both him and me a suspended moment, an interval of surprise.

For just a second, before he began to cry, I saw another Ilario, one who looked at me without rancor, and with no real fear: not a lying child, but a person who had been injured a very, very long time ago, very calm. I watched his eyes fill up with discouragement, and as his white cheek turned red I regretted what I had done, and then Ilario began to cry like any other child, and I walked away.

Chapter 20

TONIGHT WE FOUND OURSELVES still awake at 3 A.M., and Sandro with us, and we decided to go over to Monte di Malo and watch the sun rise. We went around town and woke up Gino, Franca, and Mino, but from their windows or their balconies all declined, and so we three went alone.

We had to wait quite a while in the piazza at Monte di Malo, and finally, there where the rent in the night sky was getting red-hot before our eyes, we saw the sun itself emerge, and watched it for a few minutes, a small fluid ball, and Katia shouted, "But it's alive!" And so it was: it seemed to swim, a globe of molten matter that floated and whirled above the rim of the clouds. Then it took off and began to climb, and we could no longer look at it. I imagined the heating up of distant engines, the great volume of force converted into the slow climb of heavy masses in the air.

Turning around, I saw the church tenderly lit up by the rising sun.

✦

We would come here to Monte di Malo to train on our bicycles, either directly, or via Priabona or San Vito. Each route had its seasonal, monthly, and weekly records that we sought to beat. The climb was hard work, and rather lonely.

The loneliness of the long distance runner is nothing compared to that of the aspiring cyclist doing uphill training for the Tour de France. To tell the truth, it is an awful loneliness: the physical effort sends poisons to every part of your body, the pain darts to your sternum, then over to the left, and needles pierce your heart. A braid of muscle twists up, then some of the guts in your belly, now a vein in your neck.

There is something disgusting about a throbbing, tortured neck vein, and the very will to endure it grows shaky, because the poisoning has reached the central nervous system. The cyclist, in a hypnotic haze, begins to act in a mechanical, unpredictable way, and his agitation drives the bicycle here and there at random. All this is felt as a kind of loneliness.

Such is the experience of the cyclist on the uphill, determined not to stop before reaching the peak, and not even at the peak, when the bicycle magically grows lighter and begins to fly downhill on its own, and the woozy rider spins on, a gentle buzz behind him, pinches of sweat dried by the wind to rouse him.

Sometimes even the little ones have to endure this torment on modest uphills. When my brother Gaetano was very young he was persuaded to join us on his little bike to ride up to Priabona. Long before he got there he was already numb, and could no longer hear the encouragements of his tormentors; we, meanwhile, were sorry we'd made him come; we knew it was too much. He got there in a state it would be embarrassing to describe.

Without saying a word to anyone, I took Bruno, who was maybe thirteen, on the most terrible of the uphill trials, the pass between Monte Pasubio and Monte Cornetto. It was already quite unusual for me to do this route as an adolescent, and I knew that with Bruno, we were going to exhaust ourselves. I gave him the Ganna twenty-four speed, a powerhouse, and I took Mamma's unsuitable Schwalbe. Climbing the pass with a woman's bike was a crazy enterprise, but, following just behind Bruno to urge him on, I didn't think about it. The problem was Bruno. After frightening me considerably during last few kilometers on the cruel and enchanting Ponte Verde climb up to the pass, Bruno arrived.

On the final rise of about one hundred meters that comes out onto Pian delle Fugazze, Bruno looked like he was about to die, but in a slow, painful zigzag, he managed to get himself to the top. There was a pile of gravel up there, to the right just as the road levels off, and the bicycle landed on it, and so did Bruno.

He was lying on his side on the gravel still proudly clutching the handlebars, his feet still in the toe clips, shaking. His eyes were closed, and although his mouth was open, he didn't seem to be able to breathe. I remember distinctly thinking, "He made the pass," before thinking "and now he's going to die."

But even this was not the worst. The worst, the worst of the worst, was the torment of having to follow another vehicle, not a Tre-Ro or a Sàura, but the buses that on the plain could always maintain a small edge on you, a torturous few meters per hour that no human effort could ever overcome.

The pursuit of self-punishment must begin when the bus is still far away; when it arrives it always has a surprising surplus of speed, and as the back rolls past you must rise on your pedals, throw yourself into the slipstream, and let your bike jerk around like a madman's. Like a madman, you won't be able to see straight, and tossed into the slipstream you'll follow the bus blindly for a while. This is when the real torture begins.

The bus's exhaust pipe gives off a powerful, invisible poison that sinks into your chest along with the acrid smell of the tires, the oil, and the dust, and this poison rapidly combines with other poisons that are spurting abundantly out of every muscle, producing an acute sense of disgust and desolation in the victim. Where has the world gone? Is there anyone beyond this slipstream? What does it mean, to be beyond? What is more me—me, or the pincer that's grabbing me between the thyroid and the trachea?

The sound of the engine is strangely small and muffled; you can only sense its power in the smell. Although it feels as if you're being towed (and you know that if the bus were to brake it would leave no more than the decal of a man on a bike on its blue tin), it also feels as if you are somehow paralyzed. Meanwhile the fogged-out ghost of the bus slowly begins to distance itself from the bicycle wheel.

In a spasm of disgust and pain, you feel terribly solitary. What you are doing makes no sense, nothing seems to make sense anymore, and it is only later, after lying in a field and throwing up, that you begin to hope again, to make plans for being alive.

✦

The place called Feo, on the tuft of the mountains up here above Monte di Malo, didn't seem to us to belong to this world. According to our crazy notion, there lived in Feo a primitive race of men with their goats, their women, their children, and their chickens. There was also a priest, a school, a tavern, and once a year, the town fair.

As young men we went up there in the winter to ski, and one year when there was a lot of snow we stayed there quite a few days. At night, you would leave the tavern in wooden clogs to go to the empty house where we slept. There was the moon, and deep snow that seemed to be rose-colored and that squeaked under your clogs.

The week we spent there seemed unreal. Feo was a frozen paradise, and our astonished senses devoured the effervescent day and the dazzling night sky. Wonder became a belly laugh and we four big boys, turned back into children, indistinguishable one from the other, laughed all week.

Going to bed meant wrapping yourself up in scarves, ski masks, woolen gloves. There were five of us in the room: we four—myself, Mino, and the two Brunos—in one big bed, and the pig in his pen in the corner. We would climb up on the fence and piss on the pig. The pig, targeted by the streams issuing from these padded ghosts and made nervous by our perpetual laughter, grunted but didn't get angry, and you could see him steaming by the light of the candle.

This being together, this contentment, was all important. With friends with whom you spent time you developed stable connections; the friends became a Compagnia. You not only felt you were at the center of the world, you had special privileges.

The Compagnia was our school of life, our mother-space. A free association, a club without a clubhouse or rules, the Compagnia had stronger ties than any other natural or traditional association. It coalesced among old schoolmates, friends in the neighborhood, contemporaries, and it corresponded to the generations: it was in fact one of the basic ways in which we marked the generations in town.

The other mark was the year of birth, the levy year for the army, a recognized aspect of a man's personality. Just as we knew a man's name, we knew his levy year. Who was Gigio Urta? The milkman, the younger; the one who used to play with Colomba on the meadow; born in 1911. Nano Busa, 1912, used to play with Dosolina, and after we'd watched them play we went to tell Mamma about it. And Mamma said: "And what's it to you, you tattletales?" And she was right, but we were still interested. Colomba was pale, plump, and pretty; Dosolina, lean and winsome. The first levy year I remember well was 1907, and I also distinctly recall that when, somewhat later, the year 1911 was called up, I could feel the way time was devouring the generations. It seemed a bad joke that these big boys of 1911 had already been conscripted, and when the boys of 1912 were called up, I stopped thinking about it, although every year the slogans I saw on the walls continued to surprise me.

But it was the subdivision by Compagnia that divided the generations mostly sharply. Each Compagnia had its age range, something like a half-dozen years. There was very little overlap at the margins; the friends coalesced around two or three age groups, chosen probably by chance. A small, compact constellation formed, and above and below it, there was a vacuum. You had few connections to the previous Compagnia or that which came after; they were extragalactic formations, of which you could just barely distinguish the overall structure and see that it was similar to our own.

During the years of adolescence and youth, the Compagnia was the most important institution, the one that seemed to give a meaning to life. Spending time with your friends was the greatest of pleasures, in front of which all the rest paled.

"Time spent away from my friends always seemed like wasted time," says my brother. Going to school, doing homework: these were neither good nor bad activities, merely disagreeable because they took up time. Even meals at home were time wasters. As soon as you could you raced "out" to meet your friends, and only then were you happy. No other subsequent activity could ever be as perfect. This was our world, self-sufficient, utterly satisfying. Had we been able to keep things that way forever, we'd never have wanted anything different.

Today, urban society is much more conscious of such forms of association among the young; not only do we acknowledge that they exist but we acknowledge their importance; they are studied, described, and codified. In our town society, however, this was not the case: we all knew that the Compagnie existed, but we considered them incidental, marginal. We were distributed among various other recognized institutions and associations: we were the young people of Catholic Action; we were the youth of the regime. We also belonged to families and to our schools. But all of these good things exerted only a superficial influence compared to that exerted by the group of our chosen companions.

In essence, the Compagnia was a free association of peers, and normally there was no pecking order, and no real chiefs. Each one's capacities were of course known and appreciated, but the fundamental prerequisite was the pleasure you felt in spending time together as equals, as peers. Either you felt this pleasure, or not; when you did, your friends' personal gifts or defects became secondary things.

All this pertained to the central core of the Compagnia, but as in other societies of free men, there were also complementary orbits marked by gradations and differences. The small, compact nucleus of full members—Mino, Ampelio, the two Brunos, Guido, and a few others—was stable. This was the mass: a thick vortex of inseparable protons. Outside, on longer orbits, revolved the associate members, who were more numerous and who participated only from time to time and with lesser intimacy.

As for those passing through or new in town, the *metoikoi*, there was a certain initial coolness or reticence, but any who had the requisite qualities rapidly gained full rights and privileges. The qualities were always the same: not physical presence or strength, and even less intelligence or money (the Compagnia had very spartan material standards), but simply the capacity to be taken seriously, to be acceptable in practice. Anyone who was not taken seriously automatically joined the subclass of the helots. These latter freely accepted their inferior status (which was quite relative and not very perceptible), and if the Compagnia had meaning for them, they also had meaning for the Compagnia. On these half-members, we partners projected the image of our own full membership; we saw it reflected on them. Their weaknesses offered an inexhaustible subject of analysis and comment, a means to measure our own strengths. Because they accepted the values of the Compagnia, even their imperfect attempts to measure up to those values helped to strengthen the system. Every such association is something of a mutual admiration society, and here the helots really carried the torch. Bruno Erminietto, one of the most admired full members, had an outstanding relationship with the helots.

The helot was not just a flunky or a parasite, however; he could have quite a sharp personality. The most distinguished of the helots was Pompeo, who now works as a veterinarian in another town. He came to Malo rather late when he was already adolescent, and he had a certain literary talent; he was one of those young men who can write easily, and with a certain chaotic verve. This literary talent blossomed furiously and bore showy fruit, then rapidly decayed.

Corpulent, uncombed, lisping, the Pompeo we remember was the most peculiar young man in the world. He wanted to be like all the rest, and this was his mistake, because he lacked certain elementary capacities, such as a sense of balance (physical balance), and he never really learned to ride a bicycle, although he would move around on a bicycle, or rather swerve around from one place to another.

The outside world must have been far more unreliable and treacherous for Pompeo than for us. When it came to judging a distance, measuring a blow, a push, or a jump, he was at the mercy of a capricious universe, and not surprisingly, it was frightening. To us he sometimes seemed no more than a sissy, but under the circumstances, I suspect that fear was one of the most normal things about him. His body was capricious, obeying him only imperfectly and only sometimes. Even drinking at the spring behind Castello could be a problem for him; his elbow would slip into the water, he'd be seized by terror and clutch the bars where you hung the water pails with such desperation that he'd launch himself over the side with the force of his own arms and toss himself into the pool.

In that half-meter of water, you didn't even have to stand up to avoid drowning, you could kneel or even sit down. But the poor devil was by now prey to ugly, uncontrollable forces; the smiles froze on our faces and the rest of the drama took place in silence, broken by the little splashes around Pompeo, now completely submerged, huddled under the bars he was holding with such force that it was hard to pull him out before he drowned.

When he'd go to Rostón to swim with the others, he'd strip down to his bathing suit, but he didn't dare to broach the swimming hole past his ankles. On the concrete embankment there was a little canal half a meter wide and three fingers deep, wet by a film of clear water, and here Pompeo would go and lie belly down in the water. He was more damp than wet but it suited him, and he would move his arms and legs energetically as if he were swimming various strokes, enjoying himself, a little wild. It was hard to get him to leave. "How wonderful a nice swim makes you feel," he'd say, drying off his stomach and getting dressed with the others, happy, an equal.

Pompeo was intemperate: when there were no cigarettes and we heard that a shipment had arrived at the tavern in Boro, someone would send him out to buy a packet of ten. He'd be back inside twenty minutes smoking the last two, both at the same time. He wasn't completely intemperate when it came to substance, but he was utterly intemperate in terms of form. Not with all the senses and passions; he was very little intemperate with food; only slightly and only sporadically when it came to drink. But in his field he was absolutely intemperate, and the supreme field for him—for most of us, that field was lust—was smoking.

To watch him smoke was an education in itself; it evoked mercy and terror, it purified the soul. We are all changeable, provisory things precariously held together, but when Pompeo attacked a cigarette, two if he could, he would come visibly undone. His eyes would shrink until they seemed to disappear into the folds of his eyelids, his hair would flutter over his forehead, his head would loll to one side, you could hear his lungs pumping and the smoke inside gushing, invading his whole being in jerks, and his feet would grope around seeking dry land. There was no more Pompeo, just a huge infant coming to pieces, sucking.

He foolishly tried to copy us in certain things, he tried to impress Bruno Erminietto. One evening he appeared at Castello all excited, and we could see that something dramatic, something radical, must have happened. He was all out of breath because he had been running, but he managed to get out his message in a strangled voice, "I kissed her, *io-porco*." Everyone laughed and Pompeo didn't understand why.

He was always playing billiards, a hopeless pastime for someone so radically deprived of all sense of distance and motor skills, and he lost a modest amount daily. He'd go away in resignation, always repeating the same little prayer:

"Thank you *porco-io,* for today too, you have given us our daily bread."

✦

What did we do together? Anything, everything, whatever our whim, the hour of the day, or the season suggested.

On summer evenings along the road that leads to Castello, looking right toward the meadows beyond the creek, families out for a stroll might see ephemeral globes of light blinking in the grass. Not fireflies, not will-o'-the-wisps, they looked like little summer bombs.

There where the creek's shingle meets the tender shoulder of the meadow, we friends lying in a row would raise our legs in the air while the helot servant prepared the matches and gave the signal in a low voice. A bluish flame flared over each supine body in turn.

The Compagnia had no practical ends, it was a way of being, but obviously the members tended to do many specific things together: sport, amusement, and above all, the pursuit of sex. In practice this last became, at some point, the most important activity and principal function of the Compagnia.

I don't know much about when and how the Compagnia became focused on this matter, when, you might say, we specialized, because I was in and out of town during the crucial years, but I do know something. Without a doubt, the Compagnia was in this sphere the most important agent in our formation. For better or worse, it was in the Compagnia that one gained one's sexual education, and where that part of a man's character that depends on sex was shaped. The Family, the School, and the Church counted much less here.

The collective pursuit of sex offered a system of values that, in theory, could have radically redefined our standing within the Compagnia. But in fact, the outcome rarely differed much from the prior ranking of full members, associates, and helots. Those who were taken sufficiently seriously before they began to pursue women were unlikely to be inept with women, because the activity tended to be a collective, cooperative one that diminished the risks of shyness and awkwardness. At the same time, the partial members and the helots were more prone to various misfortunes precisely because they didn't have all the advantages of collective action.

✦

The mother-space, the sanctuary, the bosom. You were at ease here, slouched between the legs of the chairs, crazily intertwined with the girls. Back and forth, we'd scale the steep slopes of the sofa, inch down precipitous legs. The lights were dimmed, voices low; the mother hen—Compagnia was keeping her brood warm. It was Saturday, we could stay up late, go to the last mass tomorrow.

The Compagnia was essentially a masculine institution, though almost always with its complement of *tóse-fisse,* its steady females—auxiliaries recruited among the girls we played with as children, cousins, schoolmates, neighbors, young ladies we knew who were just a bit younger. While the Compagnia was active day and night, the auxiliaries would come along mainly in the evening for walks or get-togethers, and also for parties or outings.

Collectively the girls were treated as associates and friends, but at the individual level, one specialized. Protected by her associate status, under the wing of the Compagnia, the *tósa*-auxiliary could permit herself liberties that otherwise would have cost her irreparable social consequences. She could thus experiment with one or the other of us boys until the wheel stopped and some got paired off.

✦

There were some beautiful, daredevil girls among the auxiliaries: one with curly dark hair who was literally a Compagnia *militant,* who thought of the group as a kind of militia and her participation as a sort of military service. And there was also a fair-haired young lady who pursued adventure, starring in quick, repeated skirmishes, which although they were fairly spirited, were also planned with fundamental seriousness and practicality. She was a cheerful girl, but "solid": it was in Malo that I learned the ethical and cultural inflections of that word. I was over at Grandmother's, and there was a young priest, or a seminarian close to being ordained, who was talking about some author whose name I don't recall—someone who had refuted Kant, I think, or some such thing. He said this man's doctrine was "solid," and I understood immediately. Such was the nature of this auxiliary.

The average auxiliary was of normal height, attractive, and modest: she was superior, in her ideal nature, to all praise. Certainly there were also some unattractive ones: Strafànti (little beings that would dart in and out, flimsy, and amusing) and Casuàli (which meant ugly, awkward objects or furniture).

Rodolfino, aged seven, would join us without being aware he was guarding his sister. It wasn't his fault, but he was a pain. He had a little head crowned by blond ringlets and a small, slender body that ended up in two skinny legs, and altogether gave the irresistible impression of a wedge-shaped creature, or as we say here, a *péndola*. The nickname seemed even more appropriate when transformed into French, and so Rodolfino became *la Pendule*.

His sister was ample and curvaceous but often annoying, and those who were courting her would revenge themselves on *la Pendule* as he walked among us all unaware during our slow evening promenades, taking a barrage of *crogne* on the head. A *crogna* is a vicious blow delivered with the knuckles; the ones Rodolfino took were masked as affectionate pats, and he got hit mainly when his sister wasn't looking. Protected by his mass of curls, Rodolfino was initially proud to be receiving these signs of attention, but as the *crogne* grew sharper he was puzzled and began to wail. His sister quickly shut him up with some dignified slaps.

All this took place on the well-lighted parts of the sidewalk, but when we would move along into a dark area, the courtiers would dig in their pockets for the big keys that unlocked the front gates, and as they strolled along would hit him on the head, making a very precise little reverberation.

Two of the girls were magnificent: two sisters who I've since met—in another light, but unmistakable—in a celebrated verse portrait:

> The light of evening, Lissadell,
> Great windows open to the south,
> Two girls in silk kimonos, both
> Beautiful, one a gazelle.

The question of which was the most beautiful was very serious indeed: both were tall, slim, years ahead of their time in a certain type of adolescent beauty of which the cinema would later provide illustrious examples. For me, neither English nor Irish, the two girls of Lissadell owe their beauty to the syllables that surround them, to the syntactical arrangement and to the brevity of that bit about the gazelle. But the two girls of Malo, unassisted by syllables, derived their beauty directly from the long lines of their bodies and the light-handed, fanciful, rapid lines that brought into being breasts and neck, shoulders and face, high cheekbones and lashes.

Michela was probably the most perfect in terms of pure form; she had the simplicity and perfection of a young animal. Claudia was more of a woman; her beauty was indirect and much more complex, with tender passages, a hint of languor in her lines and heartbreaking rhythms to her face. On our way back from the mountains in the back of the pickup, Claudia was next to me, sitting on the floor. She put a hand on my knee, and I looked at her at point-blank range (we hardly knew one another) and sensed, worriedly, that I would have preferred to console her rather than hold her tight. Strangely, she understood the way my thoughts were going, and moved closer to me, laid her head on my chest with an air of great melancholy, and so we sat until we got back to Malo.

✦

Cotto, said Este to Flora as she rinsed the plates. Flora was drying. Este was making an effort to say *cotto* with two *t*'s, as she'd seen it in a magazine, but it came out with one and a half. *Cotto,* "cooked," smitten: they were talking about some young man who had been gently wooing a girl. This was how the females spoke about men, and their presumption, along with that affected city word *cotto,* aroused *cana,* our fury. Nitwits! Don't you understand that most of the time there's nothing to *cotto* but the heat of coitus?

Cana is silent and solitary but its wrath can erupt in thunder, while during the shocks of that state called *nervoso,* one hisses insults in an undertone, waves one's hands about, works the sinews of one's jaws.

Chapter 21

THE COMPAGNIA WAS ACTIVE across a wide territory that included several nearby towns; there were rural forays, country plunder, raids to San Vito and Marano and to our hamlets Vacchetta, Molina, Case, and Santomìo. Patrols would even venture beyond the rural circle, out to the big, built-up towns Thiene, Valdagno, and Schio.

The girl from Schio who had promised to bring along a friend was late for the appointment at Melonara. Ampelio had cleaned his teeth, others, their necks: everyone had made some special preparation, because girls from Schio are practically city girls.

Finally she appeared, riding a man's bicycle with a little cart behind like those for carrying milk, upon which her friend was sitting, in silk stockings and high heels. The friend was reserved for Bruno; she had been pointed out to him at the swimming pool, but far away and sitting down. Sitting down she wasn't bad, but when she stepped down off the cart, instead of getting taller, she got shorter, and with the heels and all, she was only waist-high. It was a disastrous evening; before ten minutes had gone by one of the girls from Schio had already said "Go screw yourself," and the other, "Jesus, you boys are in a hurry."

Many such enterprises were individual challenges, and although confidential and semisecret, they were shared in spirit. The friend who headed off pretending indifference departed in our name too, and tomorrow his success would be our collective triumph. It was great to have another confirmation of how clever, how resourceful we were! Of course, there were also mishaps.

Guido, a great Casanova, was heard one day behind a hedge, courting. He had put on a soft, sweet voice and was saying:

"I'm so much in need of affection."

He never heard the end of it. "Affection!" his friends would say, "Really, with that sow!"

Before the age of Ulderico arrived, Guido was one of the leading specialists in rural adventures, and generally in amorous expeditions, especially at night. He would go off very mysteriously, taking with him pregnant silences and a blanket, like a provident knight putting darkness between himself and innocent eyes.

Once, after one of these departures, his friends went to the cinema in Schio to soothe the sting of jealousy. A few rows ahead of them sat Guido, all alone, with the blanket folded up on the seat beside him.

Pesta—clumsy, good-natured, stingy, affable—came late to the Compagnia. He came from Belluno, he was a grain dealer, and had greater means than the rest of us, beginning with his pickup, which had once been a Lancia Augusta. He'd take a girl out "for a nice ride," and then he'd get fed up after a first, rapid stop under a tree by the side of the road. He'd get bored, and although it was still early morning, he'd take the girl home and dump her.

"Why?" the poor thing would say. She had bought a new scarf, and a nylon slip.

"Because. Time to go home."

"But what am I going to tell them at home? I said I was going on an all-day outing with two girlfriends."

"Tell them the girls died."

Pesta was a good fellow, but his moods were intractable. He had a constant headache, and took powders for it.

✦

The climate of the town Compagnia was healthy, it made you stronger, like my army captain used to say of Alpine duty: among conscripts, he told us, chest circumference grew on average a couple of centimeters, and he urged us not to let the average down.

Of those in town who ended up being cut out of a Compagnia—the sad sacks, the introverts, the weaklings—most would find as they came to maturity that they had no system of values other than that of the Compagnia, and that if they didn't wish to give up and forever be woebegone creatures (fainthearted bachelors, comical husbands) they had better make a desperate effort to link up with the group.

And you would see these unattached types, these latecomers trying to catch up at eighteen, at twenty, even at twenty-five and in extreme cases even after that. The truth and the life were there—there where the members of the Compagnia were languidly, effortlessly enjoying themselves, just lazing about. Here there was nothing but dust and anxiety: the unattached with their sweaty faces were patiently training themselves to swear, to drink, to rough up contenders, to seduce, and they were struggling day and night.

Many of them would be left by the wayside, but a few would make it. But then sometimes they weren't able to stop, and even after the veterans had decided to accept them, they would keep on demonstrating, every evening, every dinner, every woman, the proof no one was asking for any more. Bombastic oaths, huge meals, extreme—excessive—amorous exploits, the now-attached would continue to struggle, marching around and around the tavern floors.

The young man who returns late at night from an excursion, with his blanket rolled up and highly visible on the back-seat of the bike, his vague replies, his air of virile unconcern barely disguising an ardent, swollen pride. Another excellent day's work, another nail in the lid of his identity. And now, for the nighttime victory celebration, his prize—tripe soup, a liter of red, and a plate of roast at midnight!

✦

Ampelio was one of the three or four most important members of the Compagnia, the most refined, the best dressed. He was also the stingiest. Arriving on his motorbike from Schio, he would cut the gas long before the curve by the Count's house, so as to use up every drop in the carburetor. It was all perfectly calculated: the engine would die at two-hundred-and-some meters from his house, and the bike would continue on in neutral right up to his gate. The engine—he was one of the first in the Compagnia to have wheels, right after the war—was permanently starved, fed by the smallest *giglèr* in the province, a fuel inlet so tiny it was invisible. But to Ampelio it doubtless still seemed a leaking gash, a torn ventricle; his dream of a happy world was one where the *giglèr* had no hole at all.

It was inevitable that Cesco Pozzàn would take Ampelio's engine apart in secret and drill a hole as big as a mine shaft where the fuel inlet was. The bike, unaccustomed to all that booty, sucked in gas furiously and made strange noises like a falling-down drunk. On a full tank, it would go just under a kilometer and a half.

But you know how these skinflints are: they will go to any length to scrimp and save, but they are very, very attached to their own convenience. Ampelio's existence was full of rationed cushiness, of sybaritic expedients. His motorbike was a thing without any particular distinction, but it was richly mirrored, and Ampelio kept it polished, dust-free, immaculate.

On Sunday he would take his girlfriend up to the mountains, and, so as not to tire the bike when the climb began, he would make her get off and walk, sometimes along a shortcut, other times making her push on the steepest hills. They had a lot of outings this way without wearing out the engine.

Ampelio's relations with this girlfriend were famous in town. In brief, he neither wanted to marry her, nor to let her go.

In Malo, a girl had to act quickly. She had three or four years (up to about age twenty or twenty-one) to be chosen by a young man, and if she made a mistake, that was it. There was a period between adolescence and young womanhood when every girl was young and fresh, and her prospects were open to negotiation. That was the moment to aim as high as possible (without going *too* high) so long as she thought she could hold out during the inevitable long engagement.

When a girl knows her business, her ability to hold out can be surprising. At first it looks easy: the young man is all over her, he's hungry and thirsty for what the girl has to give, and no bothersome differences of social status, age gaps, hostile family—none of it can stop him. But then the long siege begins: the young man is not yet set up in life, the family isn't prepared to lift a finger, and indeed just prays the danger will pass (and if there's no dowry or at least a trade to fall back on, the danger is always considered real and present). The two besieged young people resist: his is a passive defense, more and more gloomy as he finds himself falling into habits he's already inclined to think he detests. She is the soul of the defense, for she cannot afford to let go, and usually ends up victorious. Worn-out and losing her looks, she steps up to the altar wearing white. Technically, she gave up the right years ago, but nobody is looking at the fine print.

This is the girl's victory. Far more rare is the man who can declare an equivalent victory over an unattached young woman who is still distinctly marriageable (one who's pretty and shy, for example), but beginning to wonder whether spinsterhood may not be her vocation. When this situation occurs, it sometimes happens that an older man, well-off but not well respected, pounces on the prey and carries her off practically without any engagement at all. Often this is someone genuinely seedy—very stupid, for example, or physically ridiculous. This is the man's victory.

In other cases, the girl simply remains without a husband. The young man drops her, and for someone who's been dropped by a young man, it's quite the rare event when things turn out well. Some girls try solutions beyond Malo—little jobs in the city, solitary vacations—or perhaps get involved in some clearly inappropriate affair, close an eye, console themselves. Most often they return home embittered and by now completely disqualified, and do as the timid ones who remained in town: embrace their destiny as no longer marriageable sisters and become aunts and daughters charged with taking care of the old. When all is lost, the most independent ones give themselves for free to ravenous young men who show up at night shoes in hand, battling with the squeak of the door and the creak of the stairs.

It was evident that Ampelio didn't want to marry her. She knew it; everyone knew it. It had probably been true ten years before, it had certainly been true for at least five. After that it became a scandal, then absurd, and finally surreal.

Over his dead body was he going to marry her, but just let her pick up her courage, as she did several times, and say, "Okay, let's call it off." Suddenly the uncatchable Don Giovanni Ampelio became a desperate, bleating little lamb.

She tried to go away without saying a word. Ampelio arrived downtown on the bus, carefree, his hair all pomaded up, but when he heard from his friends in the piazza that she had left town he was like a man bitten by a tarantula, he went wild. "Where did she go?" he'd bawl with tears in his eyes, "you have to tell me, I have to know; I have to find her, she has to come back." As soon as he found her and she came back, it began all over again.

In later years her only hope was to make him marry her, so that she could spend the rest of her life making him pay for it. Their bond of hatred now cut so deep you could no longer distinguish it from true love.

Chapter 22

IT WAS THE LAST ACT of Fiorenzo's wedding with the halfwit that always stuck in my mind. Maybe thirty years ago, up in Castello next to the war memorial, there was Fiorenzo dressed up as the bridegroom, Righella as the mayor in a colored sash, and I can't recall who else playing what role. After the ceremony, the speeches, and the photographs, the guests began to trail off one by one, then the officials, witnesses, and the bridegroom himself gradually disappeared, until the poor ninny in her Sunday dress stood all alone by the monument, clutching her little broom of flowers tightly, still smiling as the first pangs of angst began to gnaw.

The next morning she appeared very timidly at Fiorenzo's door, the new bride with her little milk pan, to claim her marital allowance.

I don't think the main point of this prank was to make fun of civil marriage—certainly the retarded girl herself with her milk pan demonstrated that she valued its importance—but that side of the matter did partly justify the girl's mistreatment, and of course such a parody of Holy Matrimony would have been inconceivable in church.

But you couldn't parody Holy Matrimony in fun, only in tears and calamity. Cattinella, who was married in church before the Concordat of 1929, was abandoned as soon as the bloom was off, and like so many other young women, pregnant. This was an industry all in itself: rather than mistreat the feebleminded who weren't of any practical use anyway, they raped and cheated the farm girls.

And so Cattinella came to us to work as a servant, in order to feed her son who was called Giovanni and who had her surname. She was small and patient, and her speech was twined with mountain inflections. I addressed her as *Lei,* my brothers as *tu.* It must have been a strange world for her, full of modern novelties and urban perils, the *Pullò* of colored wool, the *Cacào* in our milk bowls, our peculiar games, the strange *Alfa-Beta-Gamba-Svelta* lessons. She became very fond of us, especially of Gaetano who tyrannized her and once even made her taste what he was producing hunkered down in the laundry room.

She worked the way women worked in those days, like a beast of burden, but she didn't complain. Her dream was to see her son grow up and find his place in life, and then one day to go and live with him, so as to recreate as an old woman the family life of which she had been cheated as a girl. Meanwhile her peasant mother looked after him, and we saw him on Sundays, a shy and stubborn boy who didn't quite understand our games although he sometimes tried to join in.

When we moved to Vicenza before the war she was all but cut off from her son, whom she now saw only in summertime when we returned to Malo for our holidays. Her life in the city was hard and thankless; she slept in a little closet that was slick with damp, she rose at 5 A.M., cleaned the house, cooked for us (Mamma was out all day long): soups so thick they were almost rocklike, that you could pick up with your fork and wave in the air. When the war came she went back to the house in Malo.

Giovanni was by then a young man, nineteen years old in 1944, and Cattinella wanted advice. Should the boy present himself for military service? Should he be allowed to go with these partisans as he wanted to? In the end Giovanni went with those partisans, he took the nom de guerre "Zampa," and on the night of August 12 he was with the detachment up at

Malga Zonta. There is a photograph of the fifteen or twenty young men lined up in front of the mountain hut, hands over their heads, the moment before the Germans began to shoot. Giovanni is at the head of the line, in the foreground. He looks stunned, as if he doesn't understand the game, and he has a bruise on his face, inflicted, most likely, by a rifle butt.

Cattinella, who now lives alone in two humble rooms when she's not in the hospital, was able to obtain this photo and keeps it in a drawer along with pictures of us. On her dresser there's a photo of my mother; on her wall a framed portrait of the dead partisans, their faces in small round insets beside their names, and among them is partisan Zampa, Giovanni Tessaro, 1925–44.

I won't forget the first time I saw Cattinella after she had learned about Giovanni. It was down at the end of my grandmother's courtyard, near the stairway up to the drying shed, where we used to hide our weapons when we came to spend a day at home, in case they came to round up partisans. She was dressed in black, her face swollen and disfigured by toothache, and when I embraced her she neither spoke nor cried.

Every year on August 12 she goes up to the Malga Zonta, often walking all the way to Schio before dawn and then up to the hills on a flat-back. She listens to the speeches, she lays down her flowers.

✦

After the Concordat, the church wedding became an ironclad institution. It still had to be approached with caution, however.

"So, how's it going with your young man?"

"Ah, I have to take care. Because, you know, once he's broken the harness it's too late to have regrets."

The town girls soften their language with metaphors, while the mountain girls speak with a harsher tongue:

"Because—what can I say—when's he's done it with me, I'm fucked."

◆

Even among married couples who get along there are moments of friction.

"Whore!" says the husband to his wife. From time to time the wife too expresses her point of view. "You—don't touch me. If you touch me I'll give you a kick in the balls."

"Whore! Sow! Pig! You cow! You ugly slut! says the husband, who then turns to his youngest daughter who's whining and clutching her mother's skirts, and improvising poisonously adds, in a lower voice:

"You shut up too, you little floozy."

It's a fine family, respected by all, devout. It's just a family that converses in loud voices.

◆

The threatened kick is an ancient institution passed down from previous generations. The crazy woman's husband (both were in their seventies) was on his way out to catch the bus in the piazza. The crazy woman stood in the door, watching him. He was doing his best to hurry because the bus had already arrived, but as he was old and worn-out, he was dragging along. Mino was watching from the door of his workshop. The crazy woman raised her voice: "You lazy slob," she yelled, "if you don't move, I'm coming to give you a kick in the balls that will get you to the piazza before the bus does." The fact is, though, we are largely on the plane of words here, and these terrible kicks almost never take place.

More modern couples have completely abandoned the crude insults of the past, and express their feelings more demurely.

"Now that you're an old hag, when we go to the seaside, I'm going to take off my wedding ring because I don't want anyone to know we're married. Let them think you're keeping me."

What's considered a sin in town when it comes to matters of the flesh and sex? Some time ago I realized with some shock that while I'd been away from Italy the sixth commandment had changed. Living in a Protestant country I already had trouble answering friends who wanted to know why our Decalogue is missing one commandment and the last has been split into two to make ten. To my way of looking at it, "Thou shalt not commit adultery" in English sounds far less intimate and subtle than our "impure acts." But now, I see, our sixth commandment prohibits "fornication," a word that sounds distinctly peculiar in Malo. There is more than one *fornix*—arch—in town but in practice there are no fixed public females.

Perhaps there were disputes and discussions about this change in the bosom of the Church, and probably the reasons for the new formula were spelled out to the public. I don't know much about that aspect, but I must say that I have not been able to get my fellow townsmen to explain the point of the new language. Instead, I've gotten the impression that in practice this "Thou shalt not fornicate" continues to be understood by young catechism students and by adults as if it meant precisely the same thing as "Thou shalt not commit impure acts." In any case, I'll take this opportunity to explain what the sixth commandment once meant here in Malo.

First of all, it was considered the most important of all the commandments. Murder was a greater sin, but fairly rare; impure acts instead were frequent, and extremely mortal. At times we had the impression that the entire difference between living in God's grace and going to hell lay in that one sin.

With the sixth commandment, a distinction had to be made between the abstract part, with its absolute injunction of chastity, and the concrete part that specifically prohibited certain practical deeds that could be put down in a list.

The abstract part was taken seriously almost exclusively by children, who, as we know, reach the age of full discernment in this matter when they turn seven. At seven, we have the "use of reason," that is the capacity to distinguish between good and evil. The laws of the state, at least in Italy, do not fully take this into account, but in England until recently, children over the age of seven were still hanged in public—although not for impure acts, but for petty larceny.

Chastity meant seeking to live without ever thinking about the bodies of little girls and women, neither in their presence nor their absence. The word *nuda,* feminine "naked," was powerfully magnetized: *nudo/a* belonged to the Italian language; in dialect there was *nudo-nfante,* which means bereft of clothing, and thus in danger of catching a chill, while the practical equivalent of *nudo* in dialect would be *cavà-zó,* which however bears no sexual charge whatsoever, or *in camisa*—in one's shirt or underclothes—which sounds poetic but not very arousing. Merely to let one's mind wander voluntarily to the word *nuda* was seen as a breach of the sixth commandment. Saying it aloud was often enough to set off an orgasm. When the first American love films arrived, it was immediately obvious that these actresses and the men who courted them were very sinful. With faces like that, I said to myself, you can be sure that when those ladies get married, they will go to bed with their husbands leaving certain parts of their bodies uncovered—or worse, they'll be entirely naked. Although we had some knowledge of sex from very early childhood (long before we had the use of reason, when it wasn't supposed to be a sin) we didn't associate sex with marriage however, and the idea of these depraved actresses who did so, both revolted and attracted us. A moderately devout husband married to one of these must have many, many occasions for sin!

The habit of weekly confession, often right up to adolescence, gave our chastity a certain rhythm. There were "chaste" hours and days in which we kept ourselves scrupulously away from forbidden images, profane thoughts and opportunities. Then came the Fall: a magazine cover, a playmate's skirt revealing legs, a word—and down, down we went into the pit of conscious, active, almost scornful impurity for the rest of the week.

I don't know much about masturbation in Malo; for me, it was a phenomenon typical of Vicenza. It was in Vicenza that I encountered it (I was about ten years old) and learned its name. The name seemed all wrong to me, full of urban vulgarity; it conjured up visions of something strident, absurdly laborious, of tuneless noises. Apart from the brothels of Vicenza, the phenomenon was associated with the voluptuous figure of a Secretary dressed exclusively in red, with a brute named King Kong (who held an almost naked woman in his hand), and with the long tresses of a certain Sacred Virgin named Luana, who was nearly undressed herself.

Urban fantasies, urban practices: in Malo there had been impure acts "with others" and impure acts "alone," but it was always clear that the one was a continuation of the other; there were none of the brutal dividing lines introduced so coldly in the bright, crude toilets of the city.

It had always seemed to me that masturbation was typically *manibus turbare*, not *manu*—plural, in other words, not singular. The real failure of chastity lay in the Thought of the Woman's Body, and it was only because of this thought that what we did with our hands made any difference, as if they were urging our little sex organs to share the perturbation of our souls. To the question "Alone or with others" you were almost inclined to get polemical. What do you mean "alone," Reverend Father? What would be the sense of "alone"?

In the city, however, I learned that the men of Vicenza, not to mention the monstrous King Kong, did it like that, and what the technique was.

Masturbation in the confines of that pagan and amoral society of friends, the Compagnia, was another thing entirely: a lighthearted collective activity free of any connection with chastity, just one more of our common athletic endeavors.

My companions who stayed in Malo would get together in the pastures or on the slopes behind the creek and take part in clocked speed trials. Gastone always won. Ampelio, whose father would lock him up in his room to keep him from taking part in these contests, watched from his window, which looked out toward the creek, and did his best to participate from afar, although he was not in the running.

As childhood came to a close, the abstract and absolute injunction of chastity faded, and impure acts became in practice that list of things that signified mortal sin, while all the rest was simply ground for pointless perfectionism. That did not mean, however, that the field narrowed to the mere contemplation of adultery or of fornicators.

Besides those physiological acts that need not be spelled out ("material acts," we called them) anything that almost infallibly led there by touching or looking or showing was also prohibited—but always with a firm sense of the anatomical and physiological boundaries between the venial and the mortal. The notion of generic desire, that thing contemplated in the ninth commandment, was generally not associated with mortal sin; only concrete acts and efforts were held to be toxic.

As we grew up, the prohibitions had less and less to do with the way we behaved and finally, were mostly about the way we confessed. Confessions grew rarer, less regular. The problem of chastity gave way to those of habits and intentions. Why confess this morning when you knew very well that this evening you were already set to do the same thing you were about to confess now? Wouldn't it be more honest just to stay away from confession?

When this scruple was brought to the confessor, the reply was that confession (that is, honest confession) was always a good thing; that the sacraments exert supernatural powers on those who receive them; that we cannot know for sure whether, having received the sacrament, our wicked intentions might not be foiled; that the grace of God is anyway more powerful than human intentions; and that in short, it was no good rashly accusing yourself of sacrilege. And in that way, you went where you had to go in the evening with the consolation that you had already informed your confessor.

As the sway of Religion ebbed, Manners, which in my day reigned supreme in this department, advanced. A young man was expected to behave in a certain way with women; the woman ran her risks, and it was up to her to protect herself; and anyway men also ran their risks. It went without saying that the relations between one and the other were ruled by what was held to be natural law. They went at each other with knives, and it seemed—although it was not always true—that the man had the knife by the handle (while instead it was sometimes the girl). The two struggled to stab each other beneath the plane trees and under the porticos, in the fields and on the riverbanks—he, moved by the natural whims of vagabond Venus, she, driven by the demand for certain nuptials. The town stood and watched.

The ideal eternal history (as Vico called it) of our sexual education was thus spelled out according to the following ages:

> The age of Innocence and of Bad Things
> The age of Purity and of Perturbation
> The age of the Compagnia and of Erratic Coupling
> The age of Betrothal and of contests for Certain
>   Coupling

From this sequence comes forth Holy Matrimony, and here religion weighs in again on manners by imposing certain rules on the sexual behavior of the married couple—rules that can be enforced by means of the women's confessions and by refusing absolution.

The question of lust and lasciviousness (forbidden to the married no less than to others) is easily circumvented by means of casuistry probably handed down from theology texts but greatly expanded in barroom discussions. We all know that the purpose of marriage is reproduction, for which mere sexual congress is sufficient, and therefore any further lewd behavior is an impure act. However, if the husband, in good faith, determines that some particular lewd act is necessary to prepare the way for sexual congress with his wife, such homespun lewd behavior does not constitute an impure act.

This doctrine, in somewhat different terms, was explained to me more than once by my friends. Coitus interruptus, however, was perceived not as an impure act, but rather as a violation of a virtual Sixth Precept of the Church, a tacit addition to the other five. The ban is absolute, not to be violated under any circumstance.

Those who didn't conform to the town model of normal sexual education were almost always those who not only came from "Church" families, but also suffered from some real or imagined sense of inferiority, a marked timidity, the conviction, whether true or merely believed, of being ugly, unpleasant, or ridiculous. The signs of this were evident even in those, like Giacometto, who were otherwise lively and likeable.

Raised in a devout family, accustomed to take religion—"the rectory" as he called it—seriously, convinced moreover that he could never be attractive to women, Giacometto grew up without adequate sexual outlets, experiencing ever-worsening "nervous crises" until his marriage. He was married late, as often happens with those who don't serve in a Compagnia—late and without making a real sexual choice, largely to "resolve the problem."

But the problem arose again after he was married, in the matter of family planning. Times were changing, and Giacometto was a victim of the fact that an analogous change in manners had not yet fully taken place, not to mention that his upbringing made such thoughts repugnant. Once upon a time people accepted the children that God sent and tried to scrape by despite their problems; today, they're practically forced to make calculations, to set limits in advance. But how? Giacometto now speaks openly of these matters, and while he treats them very seriously, he also laughs and makes us laugh.

And perhaps that's how he was able to avoid *the madhouse and the whole thing there*. He's "walleyed," he says: one eye always trained on the bed, the other on the rectory. "Oh," he says, "the Lord was tricky when he created us!" He would never do anything the priest calls sin, but he's too responsible not to understand that he must also not have too many children. The directives from the rectory are simple enough but as Giacometto says, "technically" impossible to obey. His friends, laughing, suggest one or another infraction. It's a laughing matter to talk about, but the doing is no joke: Giacometto believes with all his heart in the distinction between what is a "natural" way to avoid conception and what is not.

With all mechanical and chemical devices barred, convinced by his friends that water is an excellent measure but unsure whether it's legal, Giacometto has ended up making a pact with time, a pact that hasn't worked out so well. "I give the Lord time," he says, and that's evident. He has seven children and, no surprise, he treats them badly, he insults and beats them for no reason at all, given the pressure he's put himself under for so many years not to bring them into the world.

It would be a mistake to believe that Giacometto's nerves and the atmosphere that reigns in his family are solely due to his sexual upbringing, for such matters are always complex and difficult to fathom. But it's certainly true that Giacometto's family (founded on the father's minor sexual martyrdom) is a profoundly bad environment for his children to grow up in, it does just about all the harm it can—short of the butcher knife wielded by Signora Orsolina.

This lady, a very devout Catholic, a widow with just one, grown-up, son, having fed numerous large bills to the devil that had possessed an ox down at the piazzetta weigh station, then one night discovered that the fiend was impersonating her sleeping son and stabbed him repeatedly with a butcher knife. The wounds were not fatal, however; the mother was sent off to the insane asylum, the son came back to town all bandaged up, returned to his job (he was an electrician) and, carelessly touching a live wire, keeled over dead.

When they end up stabbed or electrocuted (as I've often heard fathers wish for the good of their sons themselves, and for the good of all) the matter is closed, but many do survive, and that is why the influence of the family environment matters.

Giacometto's younger brother is many years his junior. Stefano, as he's called, is the only member of the family with an education, a seminary education, of course. When he reached the end of adolescence he decided he had no religious vocation. He spoke right up about it and made an honorable return to secular life. I didn't know him very well but enough to say that underneath, I sensed an authentic story of a misbegotten upbringing. As a boy, he had believed that the world he had decided to renounce was one thing—and instead it was something else. He returned to secular life with the honest intention of easing himself back in; instead, he was knocked off his feet.

He got rapidly drunk on his first experiences with women, joining forces—hastily, recklessly, here today, gone tomorrow—with various stump ends of the Compagnia, just aiming to learn as quickly as possible. Then he began showing off, as if he had to overtake the others in what, only a year before, he would have called depravity. He soon ended up with our main prostitute, and he was a client both desperate and madly in love—no mere client, that is. There was something excessive, dangerous (and touching) in this impossible passion, something the young men who don't put store by religion have lost touch with. The woman, provocative and much older, was his lust object, his friend, his protégé, and his ruin. It was clear it wouldn't last, and in fact it lasted less than a year. Stefano came out of the experience purified by fire, matured and ready for marriage, he thought.

He was presentable, well educated; he could choose his bride. He decided on a shy and pretty girl from a nearby town, the kind of wife the typical young man wants: graceful, innocent, unsullied. Within a year she had bedded all his friends, and then she moved on to the neighbors, the tradesmen, the boy who worked for the greengrocer, the electrician. Stefano found her in the dining room with a fellow who had come to the door selling figs, and now they are separated. Stefano went to Argentina. There are no children.

Giacometto and Stefano had four sisters, and the worst was Rosalia, who married a man quite different from her own kind, a charming, dyed-in-the-wool libertine named Giulio Sterle. Sterle is a tradesman, he comes from a fairly prosperous family and is the classical product of what's considered a normal sexual education in town. In his day he was among the leaders of the Compagnia, one of the most admired. He always had luck with women, here in town and beyond, but he never ruined any. He didn't pretend he wanted to get married as the worst ones do; he conducted amorous "adventures," imitating the movies and trying to add something more sophisticated than sex's sheer vitality.

He would fall in love quite sincerely, but always holding something back, warning that to be in love did not mean to marry, that he had no intention of getting married and could only offer love. Women would hear out such speeches and go right on thinking in their own way—otherwise there would have been no need for the speeches. In fact, Sterle offered more than just love: a big, good-looking man, he was cheerful and easy to be with. He was passionate about many things—horses, the mountains, the sea—and the women he fell in love with were treated handsomely. Rosalia, however, got pregnant. Their characters are so monstrously incompatible that Sterle has not been himself since he got married; he's lost his verve, and the energy that doesn't go into his work ends up in family quarrels.

The children have turned out badly, maybe because from time to time children just turn out badly, or maybe because in a family like theirs they are unlikely to turn out well. Their father insults the daughters and beats the sons; out of their presence he defends them with a sigh: they've been mistreated (by their teachers, by the police, by their neighbors, by the priest) *and* they are no-goods. The two theories somehow work together.

Rosalia is a sad, irascible woman. She, too, is at war with her children, yet you sense that if necessary, she would do anything—no matter how demeaning—for them. Her personality seems to be entirely focused in this one direction, the only part of her that is still alive.

Snug in her living room she rails against people passing by outside, convinced they are enemies of her cubs. When the school exams begin, as the marks come in and dishes get tossed against the walls, Rosalia becomes downright dangerous; she looks like she might step out and slaughter people on the sidewalk.

In a single family, children grow up under the influence of things both old and new, and the two are mixed up largely by chance. You might see two sisters, both beautiful: one a nun and the other—as we used to say here rather too carelessly—a slut. I knew the nun a bit before she put on the wimple, and she used to sing dirty songs, grinning cheerfully and showing off her voice with some vanity.

"Why do you want to take vows?" I asked her, not fooling around, but because I really wanted to know.

"Why not?" she said.

I said I thought it was a serious step and that she was very young. Had she asked any advice on the matter? She said she had consulted Don Paolo, who was perhaps the most admirable of our priests, an almost saintly man. Then she added with a smile, "I'd do *anything* for Don Paolo." I had no idea what to say.

I only knew the other sister by sight; she flowered early (they flower earlier and earlier) and was gorgeous at fifteen. And when she began to add the cut and style of urban fashions to her native grace and freshness, the first impact was stunning. But it all came too soon, and in fact she faded quickly and now looks old although she's barely twenty. As far as I know she's not a prostitute paid by the hour. She's a woman of the city, and engages in free trade. But does she do so with the necessary caution? Hers, too, was a serious step. Did she ask any advice on the matter, I wonder?

Chapter 23

NORMAL ADULTERY IS a fugitive passion; what we remember are the small, individual complications.

The married girl who, when her husband was traveling, invited a marriageable girlfriend to visit, and they slept in the same bed. The bed was large; two outlaws appeared (leaping from the wall outside onto the balcony), and they got in bed too. One was sturdy and blond, the other lean and dark; one was impulsive, one ironic, and both were very cheerful. *We must love one another or die.* The four of them loved each other in merry permutations, while the dog down in the courtyard howled all night.

There's a comic side and a serious side to acts of lust. The small world of the town intensifies first one aspect, then the other, and only fragments remain. These are not stories you can tell; the most you can make out of them are sentences.

The wife with her elbows on the windowsill is waving good-bye to her husband as he heads off down below the kneeling lover bites her so hard that it's arduous deliciously arduous not to scream just once begs the bride the young man has come to say it's over then here against the door closing it a little and keeping a foot in the young mother lying back on the divan shoves her tiny daughter out of the space that belongs to what's about to happen the little one doesn't understand and in any case is an infant and doesn't speak the signora who hasn't been seen for days appears downtown looking pretty a bit pale she stops to say a few words to an acquaintance reading the newspaper she says I think it was yours and adds smiling as if to say good thanks I was sorry to have lost it.

"You only want to have fun, and that's fine," said Emilia. She didn't say more; she didn't say, "While I, instead, love you"; she didn't sigh. There was a realism in her, a sobriety in matters of love that inspired respect and admiration.

Thirty years old, she had two or three children. When she could, she left the house at dusk, frank and open, a hint of briskness in her pace and of reserve in her demeanor. A polite "good evening," then around the corner of a little lane she went, passing effortlessly from the conventions of the well-lit sidewalk to complete abandon in the shadows. Standing up under an umbrella (it was a rainy autumn), she let herself be loved, and she loved, without any hint of fear.

One of these lanes is no more than an alleyway between two walls that runs from a central street down to the edge of the creek. There's a bare, empty space here next to the garden walls; in front, on the other side of the creek stand great leafy trees and a dark slope. Here the still, composed little figure would come to life in a tallying up of wet raincoats, her head tipped slightly back; her truth suddenly shone in the reflections; so possessed, so blessed the pool of her eyes, Signora Emilia earned her significance in a circle of perfect knowledge.

✦

Signora Emilia's seduction took place on a beautiful September afternoon. Her husband had just driven off with the Engineer in his car (the Engineer came regularly three times a week to fetch him), and they would be gone for several hours. The seducer knew this. The sitting seducer. Sitting at Felice's cafè he had chatted with his friends while he paged through the illustrated weeklies, waiting for the gray Citroën to go by.

The friends went off to take a nap; the piazza emptied out. He chatted some more with Felice's daughter; there was a half-yawn, an ostentation of laziness and boredom. Then the hour suddenly struck, inaudibly for the girl and for the fool squatting on the sidewalk beyond; inaudibly, except for a whistling in his ear, to the Engineer's traveling companion. And Signora Emilia? Perhaps a tiny crack appeared in her conscience, a phantom that made a celestial click? She'll have a vague memory of something tomorrow.

The hour has come, and the seducer, no longer sitting, is on his way. He walks through the town deep in its hour of siesta, the shops are closed, the shutters are drawn, there is nothing but sunlight on the streets. Here is the gate, the shadows under the portico, there is the door.

He stands a moment listening. He has a newspaper under his arm, he takes it in his hand, then replaces it under his arm. He pushes the door open and says: "*Permesso?* May I?"

Polite conversation, the coolness inside the house, an exchange of pleasantries between two people who have only just met, meaningless remarks. The signora sits at one corner of the table, she's wearing a light summer dress, she looks like a girl. She doesn't say much, but listens carefully, a model of composure and cleanliness. The young man walks up and down speaking of this and that. He stops in front of the signora, a bit closer than normal, still talking, and kisses her in the middle of a sentence.

She has a stern look about her: gets up, goes to the door, and opens it wide. The young man, leaning against the wall beside the doorjamb, looks out the window toward the building across the street and sees that, from where he stands, its windows are just hidden from view. Silently she leans toward him and they conjoin their limbs without any further preliminaries, keeping an ear out in case the open door should bring warnings of a sudden return.

When her young man was allowed to make love to the signora on her bed, she invited him to be silent, waving a hand at the flimsy wall because on the other side was a jealous neighbor. She was understanding, not to mention passionate; she knew—rare quality in a woman—that lust is indifferent, that it is an end, not a means. In crowded cinemas she would let herself be loved in the noisy darkness in the middle of the crush, from behind.

✦

One of our most prized stories was about a man who, having spied on his unfaithful wife for a while, finally succeeded in catching her in bed with the fellow. And without hurting anyone in the least, rushed out into the street shouting like Archimedes, "Eureka! I have caught her!"

As if overwhelmed by his good fortune.

✦

Then there is the ardent, desperate love of our elderly (that is, fifty- and sixty-year-olds) most often for florid married ladies no longer young who have recently arrived in town following a husband's business affairs or their children on holiday.

The most brazen of these ladies will allow themselves to be courted without ever entertaining serious intentions; in public they laugh and pretend to be unmoved, but deep in their hearts they are electrically excited by such conquest. Most likely, once they retire to their own hotel rooms, they exult in their nightgowns before the mirror.

Meanwhile our poor fellow townsmen, fathers and grandfathers with huge, old-fashioned mustaches, sit downstairs getting drunk alone with their hats on, exposed to public mockery, for when love is too intense it will always be scorned and derided. Often, when the tavern closes, these unhappy souls stumble out onto the sidewalk in front, waiting for a ray of light shining down from a balcony or the ghost of a footstep, some faint, neutral message from the beloved.

One of these *amateurs,* who was also a relative of mine, after cooling his heels for quite some time, suddenly surrendered to the tempest inside and staggering back across the street, went after the locked door with kicks and punches.

Outside of Holy Matrimony there must not be love, but everyone knows there is always a little. The voluptuous refugee in her forties, very urbane, was visited with evident admiration by the young, pale, silent priest. She enjoyed playing the muse, and there was something intriguing about this admirer in his cassock, so little expert in the ways of the world, so troubled. The young priest was honest and would not consciously have entertained even the tiniest indecent thought about her, but the ways of love are so very twisted! Genuinely admiring the earthly aspects of a soul, even of a different sex—there is nothing at all wrong about that, and one can also do good, bring an unspoken reflection of faith into a life governed by worldly matters.

So why did he blush so violently when a third person unexpectedly entered the room? You could see that things had moved forward on their own, and the young man was deep in an enchanted circle that he hadn't even known he was entering, and where he was now a bewitched prisoner. His eyes were black, indolent, and dismayed.

Some forms of love are less subtle and impalpable.

"Auntie, do you want to hear a joke?"

"Yes, little one, let's hear it."

"Grandfather Beni humped Rosina in the bath."

By now the houses have bathtubs. Once they didn't, and you washed only when necessary. The concept of a full-scale and premeditated *bath,* an ablution rite, was unknown, and when it first came to town it was a vaguely scandalous novelty because the habit of washing and urban sexual finesse were strictly linked. There was the lady, a refugee from a big city, who took it upon herself to cultivate and polish various townsmen, even young ones like Nello who was a rustic, intelligent lad and a quick study, and who was seduced by his teacher's obscure sexual charge.

"But signora," said his mother, "what have you been teaching my Nello? He's using up all my soap."

✦

"You've made a conquest," I say to the new secretary.

"She's a sly girl," he says.

"And very pretty."

We discuss her unusual features. The secretary tells me about her sly side, which he has studied with great attention, weighing her every little remark, her gestures, the tone of her voice. He remembers all the particulars: "And so I said . . . And she didn't say a word for a long time, she just stared at the ground, and then she said . . ."

The flirtation between the secretary and the Parisian broke off—ended altogether—on Sunday. Véronique, who's ten years old, left after having dragged him behind a pillar where she tenderly bid him adieu.

A middle-aged bachelor and great *bocce* player, Duilio, or Renga, as he's called, has had prepubescent girlfriends for many years now. They dally until his young fiancée turns fifteen, then Duilio neatly sunders the relationship and starts over again with a twelve-year-old. He's been through three already.

✦

What a good boy Signora Placida has! Having grown up among women, he always combs his hair and is not bad at school;

she's really very pleased with him. It's a wholesome life: home, school, and church on Sunday. He's diligent about his homework, and you almost have to encourage him to go out and have a little fun from time to time. After all, he's not even thirteen years old.

He does, however, know how to have fun. He walks down to the piazza, buys some sweets at Felice's, then goes to see Viola (although this part he doesn't tell his mother), and the two of them go at it for a half hour before supper.

Viola, separated from her husband and still young, has taken charge of nearly a dozen of our young townsmen between the ages of eleven and fourteen, to whom she gives lessons in love. These are no mere accelerated courses in copulation; hers is a real school promoting affection and respect between the teacher and her students. Some pupils, as you might imagine, are better than others, some are hard workers, others distracted, others backward, but from what we know the school is successful. It's amazing what you can obtain with children when you follow their natural inclinations.

The miniature men in short pants play games on the pavement, waiting their turns. When one comes out, pale and radiant, another steps up to the door, asking politely, "May I come in?" He's just polished off a big ice cream, his eyes are shining and his little undershorts already swelling.

Oh, three, even four times blessed! The way we used to go and steal pears in the priest's garden, and sometimes came to a halt mid-tree, clutching the trunk with arms and legs, quite near the fruit but distracted by how bizarre the countryside looked from our unusual vantage point through the branches—so, but rather more passionately perhaps, the little guest perched on Viola rests there for a moment, his legs bent like a frog.

✦

Bruno Erminietto went to Celeste's to try on his new trousers one evening. The trousers fit just fine, and the little client was taking them off when the lights went out.

"Oh, great," said Bruno, "they've cut the power." Outside, however, the lights were shining. Bruno turned toward Celeste, who strangely enough hadn't said a word, but he wasn't there any more; instead there was a strange sound, a sort of moan as if someone were suffering and begging mercy.

Bruno Erminietto, somewhat frightened now, heard a voice whispering his name, and by the light of the streetlamps made out a round, white apparition in the middle of the air above the side of the bed, gave it a little kick and ran off with his trousers in hand.

The most visible were Celeste and Plinio. Plinio was quite distinguished; he dressed elegantly and had a nice, measured way of walking. He loved to talk about a world he dreamed of joining: the drawing room, the marble stair, an elegant party, arriving a bit late, wearing evening clothes, feeling that all eyes were upon him, playing the role of a gentleman just a bit gray in the temples, proud and slightly lame.

These were mere dreams; more concretely, his idea of the ultimate in distinction was the *cenafredda*, the "coldsupper," a rite he had learned about among the sophisticates (he went to Milan from time to time), to be celebrated in place of that banal thing usually called supper. This was not in fact a *cena fredda*, a "cold supper," but a *cenafredda* pronounced, very rapidly and in Italian—something so recherché as to be almost sinful in and of itself.

Both Celeste and Plinio had thickset bodies and large heads, and the idea of their union "alone or with others" seemed comic to us. One evening, the friends in their Compagnia went out to watch.

Celeste came down the sidewalk in front of our house, turned right in front of the Count's property, went past the last weak streetlamp, and, just beyond the houses on the big road toward Schio, near the Vedezai bridge, went down into the field. His friends followed him cautiously, pushing a motorbike along silently and moving closer. When they turned on the headlight what there was to frame was crudely framed in the cone of rude light.

As a rule, a practicing Plinio is not barred from our civic life. He participates as an equal in the society of the town: at tavern gatherings, at banquets among friends, at dances, and often he will take regular part in a Compagnia although he will never quite be a full member. He is considered something of a comic figure even when, in the grip of murky desperation, like Plinio, he shoots the thing he loves, the shop boy.

✦

An elderly man, prosperous, active, pleasant. Not a man of great ambition, but one who enjoys life's pleasures: good food, excursions here and there, the novelties of the modern world. He's not "Church," but he pays his dues to religion; he has no enemies; never speaks ill of anyone; his sons and daughters have found their places in life; he's respected by everyone. Climbing the stairs to a little room on the second floor, from which the apartment next door is visible, he turns on a table lamp, and as soon as some women appear at the window across the way, draws their attention and boldly shows off his privates.

✦

Just for fun, they asked Cina, a bundle of tobacco-colored petticoats with a hay-rack of yellow teeth on top, if she, too, knew the temptations of the flesh. Cina, who is feebleminded and also very devout, surprised them by saying she knew them well, because at one time there was a fellow here who abused one of her sisters, also feebleminded, on the floor of their bedroom, and Cina grew disturbed watching them, and was tempted.

She came to work in our vegetable garden, and Gaetano heard her loudly singing various litanies about herself, then, at the top of her voice, gleefully, furiously:

"Long live the Pilgrim Virgin!"

Chapter 24

CRISTOFORO'S DREAM HAS ALWAYS been to get about a dozen women, undress them, and put them naked inside the woods at Montécio, with their hair loose over their shoulders, and then to go and hunt these women—he, too, naked among the pines.

If the measure of a balanced life is to realize the intentions of youth in maturity, Cristoforo has subverted the rule. He has tried in every way he can to realize the intentions of youth during his youth. Barely adult, a sturdy giant, he hurls himself naked through kitchen gardens and nettle patches toward the smell, the idea, of Clelia, who lives just a few houses down the road. He scales nets and fences, knocks over the peas, ravages the vegetables, gets scratched, stung, and blistered.

A huge bull of a man with a Cyclopic sex organ like a great idol that seems to nestle in his belly when he runs, he is a reserved fellow, not in the least vain, but he has these bursts of naked madness.

Naked in the garden spying on Clelia, hunkered down among the tall stalks of the pumpkin foliage, the pumpkins of his sex resting on the ground among the others, crushing the fragrant sage and rosemary.

Chapter 25

Sti ani antichi—co i copava i peòci coi pichi.

Those olden days—when they slaughtered the lice with a pickax.

THERE WAS A PRIEST HERE "in olden days"—that is, in the far-away depths of the twentieth century when our elders were children and my father, just starting out his working life, got up at 3 A.M. to collect manure from the streets—a priest who first said mass, then gave a simple sermon, always the same.

He would stand silently at the rail, staring hard at his audience of rude lice killers, and then give his message in three brusque salvos:

Bisogna . . . èssare . . . bòni.

YOU MUST . . . BE . . . GOOD.

This was the sermon. Papà remembered it clearly. I can't help but think that Don Culatta, this priest of ours, delivered a complete and comprehensive sermon. What else is there to say?

Slaughtering lice with a pickax is difficult and dangerous. Yet even this art of our forebears, derided in popular memory as the very symbol of backwardness, conjures up a breed proud and strong also in the little duties of everyday life, such as delousing—which even when I was in school was a daily necessity for many and an occasional one for us all. These forebears of ours with the pickax may never have existed in reality, but they did in our imagination, and so there was something real about them.

One time Don Culatta went on a trip to Tuscany, climbed up to an Apennine shepherd's hut, and asked for *puìna*. The shepherd said to his helper:

"Give this ignorant Italian some ricotta."

We say *go down to Italy* up here on the Altopiano too, but we also say *puìna*. Don Culatta was remembered for another sermon he made on Saint Joseph's day, not during his usual early mass, but at the last mass, per Monsignor's order.

"Parishioners," he shouted in a jerky voice, purple with the effort. "Saint Anthony . . . is a great saint." A long, red-faced pause. "Saint Peter . . . is also a great saint." Pause. "But Saint Joseph . . ." here, instead of words, he just whistled twice and returned to the altar.

Our elders remember these events vividly; like the time when, they say, the priest summoned Seleghetto and Seleghetto pounded his breast and said *mea maxima culpa,* and the stash of little birds inside his shirt went *pew-pew-pew.*

Don Antonio, who was then still known as the Capellanello, the junior chaplain, also preached with great economy.

"The Virgin Mother," he said one time as he settled into the pulpit, and then fell silent, bowing his head. He was silent for half a minute, utterly mute. Then he said, "the Most Holy Virgin," and fell silent again, his head down. Whole minutes went by, the hypnotic hush grew into an enormous silence, and Mino's grandmother was terribly embarrassed. Then Don Antonio slowly raised his face and said, "Let Jesus Christ be praised," and stepped down. To me, it was a moving sermon.

✦

I hear that one can even go to mass now in the evening. "It's valid," they assure me. I feel let down.

"I suppose you can also take Communion without having fasted from midnight?" I say cuttingly, as of something absurd, extravagant. But you can. You merely have to hold off eating for two hours. *Ostia*, where will it end?

Messa prima, messa del primo, messa granda, messa ultima: these were the masses that shaped our days. There was also a *messa del fanciullo,* a children's mass, but I had the impression it was something newly invented, an artificial innovation. But the other masses were part of the very structure of society, as much a part of our surroundings as the hours of the day and night.

The *messa del primo* took place between night and day in the winter; in the summer, during that luminous fringe of the day when the sun first strikes closed shutters and brightens empty streets. This was the mass for people who had things to do: tight ranks of mothers, elder daughters, tavern keepers and shop-keepers of the older generation, devout and industrious families.

The *messa granda* was for "Church" families, for the town's affluent purists and the flocks of patriarchal peasants. Religiously speaking, it was the truest mass of all, delivered by the senior priest who chanted (in an incredibly shaky voice, however) and who made his official pronouncements during the sermon. After mass, the farmhands would convene in the piazza, chatting in small groups, making a day out of it.

The *messa ultima,* at eleven, was the elegant version for the downtown middle classes, young ladies and gentlemen, couples of modern manners, older people who were not "Church," the upper crust, the authorities. Abbreviating the mass legitimately was a refined art. Everyone knew you could come in at the Gospel and go out at the Benediction, but according to a current of opinion that was fairly influential in my day, the real critical moment came at the ringing of the bells during the Elevation—and you could either enter at the first bell or exit at the last. (Some tried for a bold compromise, but in bad faith.) Attending the *messa ultima,* especially at the back of the church, was fun; you could take part in fine discussions, everyone facing the altar, you could make the girls laugh just when the senior priest came by. It was like talking during lessons at school. And the girls, all dressed up and wearing veils over their hair, were especially attractive. But the nicest mass of all was the first one.

✦

Messa prima, in the drowsy bosom of the night, the fantastical prehistory of that time called Sunday. Stars in the sky, a cock beginning to crow; inside, a golden penumbra and the candles' yellow haloes. A small gathering of the faithful, poor people, accustomed to hard work; the priest himself perhaps a bit rough; a brief and simple sermon. This religion comes *prima,* before the rest; it rises with the field hands, the mountain folk, the serving girls, the people who begin work at dawn.

Messa prima! It astonished me to think that every Sunday while we slept, before the night began to fade, this ancient thing—possible, it seemed, only in a time out of time, far from any link to daily life—really took place. I see the little community of the faithful standing for the *messa prima,* gathered before the altar in the early morning darkness. Each has a gnarled stick to lean on; they wear skins, their heads are shaved, all but a fringe of hair around the neck, like a high collar. One giant eye is fixed on the priest.

The sacristan, old Checco Mano, comes around first with a red collection bag (souls in purgatory) and then with a black (for the priest). The Cyclops deposit a handful of acorns, and sometimes, in the black collection bag, a few goat pellets.

Inside the church, a plane where things of the night slowly dissolve and become something else.

Religion and theology provide a background to profane life, too: "Up on the mountains, we're closer to God. Also in New Zealand, on the other side of the world, when they go up on the mountains. God, therefore, is round." For Mino, this wasn't a witty remark but a deduction as interesting as it was surprising. While he was explaining it, you could see the pleasure of discovery on his face. Mino wasn't what you'd call an unbeliever; this round God was his God, and the idea he was shaped that way made him smile even more uncertainly.

The young have to consider problems that never occurred to their fathers. Elijah flew up into space before the Russians, but where is he? The priests, though, tell us that perhaps that story isn't literally true, while instead we are charged to believe that the Virgin Mother is in heaven, body and soul. And so one day, as we go further and further out into space, we are practically certain to see her in orbit.

"Come to Prà after supper, to see the Virgin Mother? Any time after eight." These aren't tricks of religion; it's not religion that's being scoffed at, but the exhilarating weirdness of modern life.

Children, too, have an inbuilt theological sensibility. The little girl is playing with the cat, stroking it.

"Etto—little one, my pet!"

Affection overcomes her and she stretches for hyperbole, the only terms that seem adequate:

"Etto—my Holy Ghost!

Everything has its moral measure. "To hell, to hell with you," whispered Franca, scandalized and elated when she caught our cat walking with her tail raised high, in a state that neither merits nor obtains pardon: the cat wore no underpants.

At times, the theological question arose spontaneously.

"Could we put a point on iron?" asked little Roberto. I was trying to hit the barn window with the javelin I'd made, a length of reed on which Roberto had watched me carefully "put a point." It was after sundown, but still light in the courtyard.

I said we could, but it was more trouble. I kept up my throwing, without however, hitting the window. Roberto said:

"And could we put a point on the window?"

That struck me as funny, and I said, yes, in a certain sense, if you wished, you could. Roberto was ready and waiting, and he said:

"And God, could we put a point on him?"

I had to confess that I didn't know, that we don't know anything about that.

But if the Rangutang is the strongest creature in existence, and can beat any other, the fatal question arises: is the Rangutang stronger than God?

There are those who say that the Rangutang can beat God, and those who say that God, being omnipotent, beats the Rangutang—but just by a hair.

✦

What did people—do people—believe? What did "believe" mean in Malo? The truths of the Faith were something we learned in "Doctrine," which we attended on Sunday after lunch, called by a special bell, as well as in courses of instruction for First Communion and Confirmation. We learned the truths of the Faith by heart: the definition of God, the Trinity, Redemption; the lists of mysteries, commandments, precepts, sacraments, virtues, vices, and sins; and finally, the elements of the Sacred History of mankind from the Creation to the Concordat.

Belief meant two things; in the narrow sense, it meant accepting all of the Faith's truths. You were permitted to enquire, with moderation, what they meant, always keeping in mind that they were *truths*. Children enquired frequently; adults, less. Both "believed" without dispute. The very way the verb "believe" is used points to two types of belief: one can believe-in, and one can simply believe. To believe-in meant to accept an authentic definition. We read and memorized the authentic definitions of the Doctrine and believed in them, that is, we didn't question whether they were true, even when we had no idea what they might mean. In this sense, we believed in all the truths of the Faith.

But in the other sense—to believe something one has understood, to be deeply convinced that's how things stand—we adhered to a simplified theology, perhaps even a somewhat twisted theology (it's not my business to judge).

Strangely, the concept of God was not, as it is in standard theology, the basis of everything. We believed *in* God and in what we were taught about him; we believed *in* his goodness but without really presuming to understand it. What we believed and understood was that there was a supernatural law, a System of Necessity analogous to that which pertains up there, that one could in no way escape.

Our system was based on the concept of Hell, the horrors of which are no less comprehensible for the fact they can only be expressed in hyperbole. From hellfire a single flame (a sample brought by a damned person come to visit a friend) will bore through the hand on which it falls: this is a fire "compared to which the most searing earthly fire would be sweetly cooling." So they taught us with the appropriate citations in Doctrine. We saw that fire was nothing, it was just a taste—but that it was enough to stop at fire.

And furthermore, Hell was eternal: you endured its torments for ten years, then for another ten, then for one hundred, then for another one hundred, and so on.

In Doctrine, they told us:

Sa tulì su na manà de sàbia, quanti granèi che ghe sìpia?

"Pick up a handful of sand; how many grains might there be in it?

"Are there a half-million in it? And then, how many are there in all the beach? A million million? And then, how many in all the beaches of this world? And on the deserts? And under the sea, which is made of mountains of sand? And I say to you that if I were to tell one of the Damned, 'you will be scorched and stabbed with spears of flame for as many years as there are grains of sand in all the world,' the Damned would begin to holler with joy. Because when all those years will finally be finished, here's the thing: it starts all over again. And remember, tomorrow morning, you too may wake up Damned."

These points were reiterated in our grandmothers' houses, by the serving girls, by our aunts. No normal person doubted the literal truth of the matter: those very rare people who didn't accept it were not normal people, they were unbelievers.

However, the parallel idea of divine punishments in this world was far less certain. The absolute master of the other world was also master of this one, but he rarely intervened here, and many bad people got on just fine, while there were fine, devout women who suffered every sort of misfortune and pain, and some were literally covered with sores where they lay and waited for years for death and its relief.

You would see them on summer afternoons languishing in the courtyards where they'd been taken to find a cool spot in the shade of the houses. Their all-but-decomposing faces wore saintly expressions; they were covered with festering flies, and they endured this nuisance with mysterious forbearance.

What mattered, therefore, was the other world. Strictly speaking, it seemed one ought to spend one's whole life insuring oneself against the terrible prospect of eternal torment, and this was what many saints have done, and also friars and nuns. Ordinary people living in the world were at risk of sinning, and even the best of them sinned, if it's true that Saint Peter's own brother managed to sin 490 times and only at the 491st did Saint Peter have permission to knuckle-rap him on the head! One ought, at the least, to remain constantly on guard against the threat of Hell, and so women and children tried to do, and presumably priests—but not men in general.

They too knew how things stood, but they acted as if they didn't. Man is a strange beast: just as he does not live by bread alone, he does not live by fear of hell alone. Taken up by his work, his interests, his passions, he behaves as if the *real* world were the one in front of him—his family, his town, the fields, his shop, his friends, the women, the table laden with food— and not that other one where there are no fields, families, taverns, or towns.

✦

As for the normative framework of religion, it was founded upon the axiom that God, inscrutable and threatening as he was, nevertheless behaved both honestly and correctly toward us. He had created precise rules to assign men to heaven or to hell, and he was the first to respect them. The substance of religion was to keep those rules in mind.

In theory, they were spelled out in the Ten Commandments and the Five Precepts, but in practice the collective town conscience extracted its own simplified code, made up entirely of concrete duties and infractions.

It is absolutely necessary: to go to mass on Sunday; to take Communion at least at Easter. And (for children), to say your prayers.

It is absolutely forbidden: to curse and blaspheme; to touch the host with your teeth; to eat meat on Friday; to be disobedient (children); to kill other people; to commit impure acts of any kind; to steal; to tell a falsehood under oath. This list did not include several points that could be taken for granted, for example, that you must be married in church and not at town hall; as well as some others that emerged after the Second

War, for example, that you must not vote for the Communists and that you must not practice coitus interruptus in marriage. With these additions, the list of rules contains all that the town conscience considered absolutely indispensible to save one's soul: this was the strictly necessary.

A violation of one of these norms constituted a Mortal Sin. The punishment for a Mortal Sin was Damnation. There was, however, a technique to avoid this simple equation: the rules dictated that sins were automatically pardoned when they were confessed, or when the sinner achieved Perfect Contrition.

Eternal salvation thus depended on three essential factors:

> Confession when you commit a mortal sin,
>
> Achieving Imperfect Contrition when you confess,
>
> If you are on the verge of death and haven't confessed, achieving Perfect Contrition before losing consciousness.

But while the town's religious life was based on this rock, its surface was sprinkled with a rich humus in which sprouted a thick vegetation of venial sins, along with acts of devotion that were not necessary but advisable for three reasons: the need for a safety margin, concern about Purgatory, and the wish to obtain a higher place in Heaven. Of the three reasons, the first was probably strongest and most frequent, because human judgment (in determining whether or not a sin was mortal) could be faulty, memory could betray us, and a sin we neglected, without malicious intent, to mention in confession, could finish us off for eternity. It was thus a good idea to appease the Good Lord and above all his direct and most influential subordinates, both by exhibiting a scrupulous conduct in marginal matters (venial sins), and via supplementary worship.

No one I knew in town was really afraid of Purgatory, in part because there were theological uncertainties about the doctrine here: what would condemn you? Only venial sins that hadn't been confessed, or also mortal sins confessed without Perfect Contrition? Or all sins, even those confessed according to the rules but for which one must do penitence down there, reciting the prayers assigned by the confessor—although wasn't it reasonable to think that in the other world the Good Lord would concentrate, at least a little, on the worst crooks?

At any rate, people didn't fear Purgatory for themselves, but they were quite concerned to think their relatives might land there. There was some notion of decorum in this, more than concern about any suffering: it was like having relatives who were losers, for whom one felt a sincere duty to do something.

As for the highest seat in Heaven, the doctrine here was also very unclear. The notion of "achieving merit" was well known but hazy; in its active form it was the specialty of devout aunts, a sort of vanity on their part, and rare among normal people. In general, people who weren't especially devout didn't much indulge in the wish to go to Heaven; it was associated with images of church and worship and incomprehensible sentiments like "getting pleasure out of God."

On the other hand the notion of a safety margin was quite clear to everyone, although not everyone acted to put one in place. The safety margin campaign (on the two fronts of venial sins and supplementary worship) was fought by the light brigades (women) and cavalry (children). Men, except for a few grizzled Roman foot soldiers from exceptionally devout families, usually stayed behind the lines playing cards.

This was the reign of devotions, of extra communions, of rosaries, litanies, and *jaculatoria*, of novenas and triduums, of *fioretti* and first Fridays of the month, of processions and the exposition of the Most-Blessed-Sacrament, of abstinence and fasting, of the worship of the saints.

Many of these things had ancient and magical aspects to them, long roots stretching back to the days when San Gaetano was our parish priest more than four hundred years ago (and as Don Tarcisio told us, was greeted by the bells of what is still our bell tower and which was already then quite old) and even before that, when we were a tiny settlement devoted to the same ancient Madonna we have in Castello. There were the candles, the dim lights, the black veils worn by the women, the holy water, the benches with their straw seats, the incense, the sing-song voices, the altars for the saints, the nude, wounded body of Jesus Christ that we kissed on Good Friday, the priest's vestments, the lovely mysterious language of certain prayers. Some had phrases like magical spells:

> *Turris davidica*
> *Turris eburnea*
> *Domus aurea*
> *Foederis arca*
> *Ianua coeli . . .*

> Tower of David
> Tower of ivory
> House of gold
> Ark of the covenant
> Gate of heaven . . .

The things of this religion were connected to other things of life: misty autumn, winter's chill at Christmas, summer drought. The bells told us, beyond the hour of the day, the hour to wash your eyes at the pump in the courtyard to ward off blindness, the hour to drink a finger of white wine against viper bites in spring, and the hour to come together in Grandmother's kitchen to pray for the dead.

The grown-ups sat in a circle, the lights were low, the pan of roasting chestnuts smoked over the fire. We children, kneeling on the straw seats (which stamped violet twine marks on our knees), exaggerated the strange endings in *s* that the women pronounced more like a z as the seminarians did, imitating them to make surreal sound effects: *Ora-pro No-bizz. Ora-pro No-bizzzz!* until the women noticed and gave us a slap.

The magical alternated with the entertaining, especially in the worship of the saints with their different personalities and talents. Saint Anthony, an orderly soul with a good memory who helped those who lost things find them, was very powerful among us. But to get him to act you needed an intermediary who was familiar with the necessary spell. It was called *i sequèri,* and my Aunt Lena knew it by heart: she would pace around the room reciting *Secuèri miràcula . . .* and so on with great concentration, and the second or third time Saint Anthony was compelled to cough up the thimble or the needle, the earring or the coin purse.

San Luigi Gonzaga had middle-level powers; his toes were never revealed, and he was considered a symbol of Purity. Doubtless, a task like that for an entire lifetime, however brief, demanded great Constancy, but what did Purity have to do with it, when toes were so far away? Some of us were inclined to believe that in the past there were impure acts involving the toes that have been forgotten, and can no longer be practiced. The way in old paintings you see ancient breeds of dogs that no longer exist.

Aunt Nina had her Registry of Saints, and was on good terms with some, cool toward others, and in outright conflict with others still; they alternated. Saint Peter was a mighty saint, in part because of the magnificent fair on his behalf at Schio, as well as the celebrations at home for his namesake Grandfather Piero. Saint John interested me particularly because the chamomile flowers are ready to pick just at the time of his birthday (or rather, his name day) and something simple and mysterious seems to happen in that brief, perfumed night, the heavens seem to stop for a moment and then turn and spin the other way.

Saint Paul resembled the Professor: a walking encyclopedia, the same beard, much the same way of looking at you; he also had a big sword that we envied and tried to copy in wood. Saint John's head had been cut off with this sword, but I wasn't sure whether he was the one connected with the chamomile, because there was more than one. John must have been a common name because this one had the tag "the Baptist" attached—in any case Herod had cut off his head with this sword. Before he became a Christian, Saint Paul was a Mohammaden, and he was a good friend of Herod and of the Thief of Bagdà (who then ended up crucified on Jesus's left-hand side), and Herod had given him this sword to remember him by, because they were good friends; and then when Saint Paul converted he kept it and used it to cut off the heads of unbelievers.

This sword of his was straight, while the one down under the stairs was curved, and you couldn't pry it from its sheath because it would get stuck halfway out. For years we would go down every day to try: two of us, three, four. We were forbidden to unsheathe it, and so we didn't turn on the light down there, we just pulled for four or five minutes in the dark.

All this part, the most conspicuous and least significant of our religion, corresponded on the moral and dogmatic plane to an interest in venial sins, and thus in the virtues, vices, and sins described in our Doctrine manual.

Here one sees the importance of the child in the system I am describing, for while respect for religion—in a general sense, as an underlying attitude—is primarily transmitted by women, its theological content and official set of rules is almost entirely absorbed during childhood, in catechism. What you learn, you learn as a child, and this accounts for the fantastic side of certain interpretations, interpretations that often survive right into adulthood.

Unlike other fields of learning, in which an adult, critical phase later sweeps away the childish, fantastic one, here adults do not restudy these matters, and even if they did, they wouldn't necessarily discover a new critical theology to replace the other, but merely a more complex version of the same unique theology.

Our childhood indoctrination gave us a fairly solid theological grounding (because it was based on learning *definitions*), a fact I've noted more than once when dealing with young people trained in Protestantism, who definitely know—all else being equal—fewer definitions than we do. On the other hand there was a whole series of incomprehensible matters, incomprehensible in part because of the language in which they were transmitted, in part because the matters referred to were remote or archaic.

What was *Accidia,* sloth? The best explanations seemed to point to a kind of laziness, and so why not call it that? *Accidia:* it was almost impossible not to think of a little, brown fish, rolled up and highly salted. *Anchovy.* This seventh mortal sin struck monks and hermits especially; they would wake up in the morning with countless *accidie* stuck on their bodies, and those who succumbed to the devil's temptation would pick them off like fruit and eat them.

Fortitude, the fourth of the Seven Gifts of the Holy Spirit, was clear to us. The Holy Spirit confers Fortitude (might) and allows the strongman at the circus to break his chains with unnatural force. But what was the third gift, called Counsel? Perhaps advice that the Holy Spirit advances, or maybe a certain Grand Council reserved for a very few of the fortunate?

The third of the Theological Virtues, Charity, was practiced above all on Tuesday, market day, when the poor turned up in great numbers. But what could Hope be? Apparently, it was meritorious to hope, and although it seemed so simple, it was a virtue, in fact it was a Theological Virtue. What did that really mean, Theological Virtues? They said it meant divine virtues. And what were divine virtues? It could mean that God also has them, but how could that be true, because God can't have Faith in himself, that would be silly; and it also can't mean that these virtues make us "like God" because one cannot be like God, that's heresy; nor can it be that God gives them to us, because then who gives us the other virtues? What is certain is that these are important virtues, because one of them is Faith, which seems to be the most important of all—it seems to be, but it is not, because it is written that the most important is Charity.

The Cardinal Virtues are not those practiced by cardinals, but "are called thus because they are the *cardini*," the hinges, of right living. I imagined them in the shape of wooden doors painted in floral patterns, oscillating slowly on their hinges, and I struggled to translate each name into moral advice. You must always be Prudent, stick close to the walls along the road and not expose yourself to risks. Justice must have something to do judges in the courts; we had no idea how to practice it. Fortitude, as we've seen, is a Gift of the Holy Spirit. Temperance—putting aside the crazy idea that it had something to do with *temperare*, or sharpening our pencils—was associated with excessive drinking at the tavern. Whatever *were* these hinges? They were quite important, okay, but how were we to think that hinges were the basis of right living?

And even when these and other fantastic ideas had been laid to rest and we began to glimpse something of the Thomistic and classical psychology underlying the names of those virtues, the question frankly remained: what were those hinges?

This happened a lot; in time we would find written explanations for each of these disconcerting concepts, but these were even more disconcerting, in part because they stripped the virtues of any personality so that they all came to mean the same thing (Hope meaning the hope to go to Heaven, Prudence meaning taking care not to sin—it was all the same old stuff), in part because they introduced new difficulties.

"*What is Charity?* That supernatural virtue by which we love God above all things, and our neighbors as ourselves because we love God."

"*How do we show our love to God?* Especially by observing his commandments."

"*How should we love our neighbor?* By doing works of spiritual and corporal mercy."

In practice, Charity, as well as meaning (with all the other virtues) that you must not sin, also means you must do these works of mercy of which fortunately we have the complete list.

There are fourteen of these works: seven of them works of corporal mercy, nearly all difficult to carry out.

Give drink to the thirsty: it sounded simple, but we could never find any thirsty. What to do: make the rounds of the workshops, walk around town, striking up conversations with the workmen and the passersby, trying to move the conversation onto the subject of heat? Fall back on our brothers and cousins overheated after their games, wait for them by the spigot with the copper dipper in hand? *Clothe the naked:* we never saw even one naked person. We had everything ready in the hay shed *to shelter the homeless,* but none came. *Bury the dead* was the family business of my friend Emilio, and Emilio himself lent a hand at the cemetery, but every time we proposed to go along too, our parents said no. The fourth commandment enjoins us to obey our parents "in all that is not sin." Is it a sin to omit the seventh work of corporal mercy?

And even where one could understand, there was a sort of imbalance between the small and easy things and the large and difficult things, which were listed all together. The first work of spiritual mercy (counsel the doubtful), how could that be compared with the fifth (forgive offenses willingly), when one is a trifle and even a source of pleasure, while the other is practically the sum total of goodness itself and obviously very, very difficult? Were they obligatory or optional, these works? Could one choose one or two at will and neglect the others? If it were not a sin not to instruct the ignorant, might it also not be a sin not to forgive offenses willingly?

Of the six Sins against the Holy Spirit, I won't even try to explain what we thought the first might mean ("despair of wholeness and salvation") where you didn't know if it applied only to the incurably sick, or also to the healthy, who might find themselves at risk too. Or the third ("impugning the known truth"), so ambiguous with that hint of the *pugno,* the fist, which is used both to strike and to grab. All I can recall is that in our supplementary lessons in the bosom of the family we learned that these six sins could be summed up in one: Sinning against the Holy Spirit, which our mothers defined as the stubborn habit of eating too much sauce and not enough bread, especially in wartime.

The four Sins That Cry Out to Heaven interested us because of that stupendous name and we pondered, vaguely scandalized, what the sin against nature might be. Nature was that secret place where Dr. Rossi's female patient hurt; there must be a kind of impure act one does *against* it, perhaps with a knife or a hunting rifle. This was the second Sin That Cried Out to Heaven.

The third was the Oppression of the Poor, which I personally thought consisted in a physical act against paupers captured one by one and packed into a room. The rich came in, sat down on the poor, and oppressed them at length with their rear ends. The poor cried out to Heaven.

Defrauding laborers of their Wages was also the work of the rich: they would tiptoe into the miserable rooms of the workers and defraud them. The Wages were silent but the women coming back from the silk mill saw immediately what had happened, and they stood at their windows to cry out to Heaven.

This childish nonsense was not without importance; some of these ideas disappeared by themselves with the imaginative life of childhood; others lay concealed underground in the thoughts and beliefs of adolescence and adulthood; some remained crystallized forever.

The explanations were not an invitation to reflect, but to "learn."

Read this book, learn it all from the first to the last syllable . . . When I shall visit your parishes, I hope . . . you will recite from memory the text of the Catechism . . .

And when we didn't understand what we had memorized? The explanations (written) didn't consist in "helping us to understand," but supplied more definitions, these too to be memorized. And if we didn't understand the written explanation? And if the verbal explanation of the written explanation still left us in doubt?

Finally, the important thing was not to understand, but to know. Doubts were discouraged, and if necessary, prohibited. Doubts were supposed to become less childish and foolish as we grew, like Jesus, in wisdom and age—but age, rather than assist in resolving doubt, seemed to make it more difficult. With time, you ended up falling back on the position taken by nearly all adult males: now that you were no longer a child, these things were best left to children and devout women. To children who recited the Sins That Cried Out to Heaven, to women who muttered prayers in incomprehensible jargon. Such things must mean something, but what they meant was no business of ours, it was church business. There was no connection between these abstruse lists of Vices and Virtues and everyday real life.

The prosperous body of religion was abandoned for the bare bones: there is God, there are mortal sins, there is Hell, and confession, which permits you to avoid it. The rest is just frills.

✦

I'd be sorry if there were no Heaven: the one that Aunt Nina imagined in her humble hopes, and Grandmother Esterina and Aunt Lena (although she wasn't that much of a Church person) and maybe Aunt Rose, and many other women relatives and fellow townspeople. It would be a consolation to know it was really up there, above the toil and trouble they so patiently bore on earth.

I know that up there they are all thirty-three years old, and so will their bodies be on the day of the resurrection of the flesh—and yet I believe they also resemble themselves as they were in the last years before they died. If their reward corresponds to hope, they will be there, some standing, some kneeling, reading from their missals prayers and litanies for all eternity, and once in a while they will lift their eyes timidly behind their veils to rejoice not only in that sweet and clear reflection that is God's presence, but also the nearby, familiar, yet amazing presence of the great angels and archangels, Michael, Gabriel, and Raphael, and all the great saints, recognizable one by one.

I don't know what sense it would make for my Grandfather Piero to find himself in the midst of all this, and to have to sit through the interminable ceremony. *Eh, can dal Passio!* he'd probably say like he used to say here on earth: "Oh, you dog of a Passion!" as Christ's Passion seemed to stretch on and on, lengthening the mass beyond any reasonable expectation. I think he's probably gone out to discuss the matter with Saint Peter at the gate.

Heaven didn't interest men; it was Hell that counted. And so we made our circle in Hell, next to the excruciating fire, the clasp and the seal of town religion. Santa Libera, preserve us from those flames!

Chapter 26

THE SUNDAY SERVICES MARKED the confine between "Church" people, who attended regularly, and the others. No matter how crowded the church, the others were the majority, and among the townspeople per se, they were actually the great majority.

To be "Church" was not in itself an entirely positive thing, and the expression was even sometimes used as a sort of generic warning: "Careful, they're Church." Not that they really seemed to be more wicked than the others, only a bit too sure they were not, and sometimes a little severe and impatient about things having to do with morality and faith, as if these matters belonged to them.

"Remember that I come before God, understand?" says an unusually devout, a belligerently devout, father to one of his many children, and it doesn't even occur to him to laugh after the words have slipped out. He urges them frequently to live Christian lives, relying, however, on a strange maxim:

"And remember that Jesus Christ said that first of all you must shave your own beards, understand?"

From the way he says this, it's apparent that not only does he believe this is a wise maxim, but that it was truly Jesus Christ who preached it.

"And a scribe stood up and said: *Domine quid me oportet facere ut salvus fiam?* And Jesus answered him: *Barbam.*" Beard.

What part did the priests play in Malo religious life? Their special position vis à vis things of the other world was universally recognized. Priests really were the representatives of God, and really did possess the sacramental powers they said they possessed, especially that supreme one of absolving our sins. All that they said in terms of doctrine was also true (I report town sentiment here), except perhaps for one thing: that it was a sin to speak ill of a priest. We often spoke ill of them, we talked about them without any special regard, ascribing to them many of the faults we all have, but always in their role as men; and even when we criticized "priests" as a group, we always meant the category in its purely earthbound sense.

Maybe the reason we often said bad things about priests was because there wasn't much to say about good, well-behaved priests. It was the least worthy of them, the least worthy aspects of their personalities, that impressed us—ours was almost an indirect form of homage both to the supernatural side of the priest and to the standard of propriety that perhaps even without being aware of it we had come to expect from him. Most likely our daily gossip, which tended to focus on the most unusual events, didn't take much account of the model priest, devoted to his work, essentially faithful to a code of conduct far more rigorous than the average, modest in his standard of living, and closer to the poor and the rural folk than any other figure among the *signori*.

A priest who drank, a "scandalous" priest, struck us as something enormous. I've often compared notes with peers of mine about my impression that certain priests remembered in town were stunningly, amazingly transgressive. We all had that same impression, but then, when you went to look at the facts, the amazement disappeared, and there was merely an alcoholic old priest, or a young, errant one.

One evening at the cafè Mino said:

"Today I was over at Campi-piani. I spoke to Fabretto, remember him? He's now the priest at Campi-piani."

He was the other Luigi in our class, dark-eyed, dark-haired,
pale, and sad. He wore the black socks and the worn-out clothes
country children had. He did just about as well in school as
I did, but for him, doing well meant entering the seminary.
If we'd each been born in the other's family, maybe I'd have
gone to seminary, and Mino would be meeting up with me at
Campi-piani.

Mechanically, I said to Mino: "How's he doing? I'd like to
go and see him." But I was thinking: It's pointless; I can't go
see him, he wouldn't understand my motives at all, and he's
so shy, so reserved.

"You know how Fabretto is," said Mino, "he's shy; he's reserved. However, this time he opened up a little. He says he
feels discouraged, the interests there are so limited; they come
to talk to him about their field, their goat, their barbed wire.
He's tried to move the discussion to other things, and for a
while they listen respectfully, but then it's back to the goat, the
field, the barbed wire. He says there are times when he doesn't
even feel . . . you know? He feels, well, alone."

I suppose Fabretto was sent to Campi-piani for health reasons; it's a peaceful place, outside of civilization, more or less
what Feo was a generation ago when Don Emanuele was sent
there. My first encounter with Don Emanuele, in fact, took
place up there. We went for a ride in the car, to try out the
Uno, and stopped by to see him. We sat on straw-backed chairs
in the kitchen; the door was open and a mild sun shone in,
brightening up the tiled floor—it must have been late autumn.
The priest showed us little cages and boxes full of snail shells,

sealed up and with the animal inside, and this was a great novelty for me.

"Papà, what does the priest do with the snails?" He ate them, I was told. That was how I understood the vague air of dishonor, of sleepy scandal that seemed to me to surround both the house and the man. No kidding! With a vice like snails!

Only many years later did I know Don Emanuele for what he was: the most drunken priest in the whole province of Vicenza. He had been a chaplain or a parish priest in another town, and then they'd sent him up there to purge himself like his snails in their cages. But he drank even up there on the mountain top, and every once in a while he also came down to drink on the plain, in the town he'd had to leave. My father would take the car on these expeditions, which lasted all day; on the way back the drunken, stinking priest would slump all over him and my father would have to push him away. "Lean on the window, there you go—if you can't manage to sit up," he'd tell him, but Don Emanuele no longer understood a word.

He was ten years older than my father, and had been a friend of my grandfather's. He came from a farming family that was said to be prosperous; there were ten brothers and sisters. Why did he drink? My father did not even understand such a question. He'd reply, depending on his mood, "He was the only one," or more often, "Oh, they all drank," and if he thought maybe we didn't get the point, he'd sometimes add, "Even the women." There was a time when the question *why* was not asked, and certainly the drinking habits were not the ones we see in urbanized society. My father says Don Emanuele was fairly rigorous in matters of the faith: he wouldn't hear of obscene language, and it wasn't true that he cursed when he was drunk, he merely called everyone *tu,* and said *putàna,* slut, to the women.

His exile up in Feo ended before the war, when he came to live here in town, and said mass at the hospital. Guido also remembers him at the evening Exposition of the Host in church: when he managed to grab onto the ostensorium, he would lean against the altar, rotating his back slowly so as not to lose his balance, until he had finally turned around to face the faithful, the Blessed Sacrament in hand. He would spend most of his days in the taverns, moving from one to another and shifting his itinerary from season to season when they stopped letting him pay on credit. He lived up in Capovilla and on his way home at night would pass in front of our house.

In his later years he was bent over and stiff, and you had the feeling he was coming to pieces: he spoke with difficulty and moved very slowly, his hands behind his back, his head down, shuffling along. He moved forward in a wavy motion along the Count's wall, hitting it with one shoulder, then with the other. His falls were ruinous, and by then he always had the marks of his injuries on his face. When there was someone around, they'd help him up and point him in the direction of home again, but sometimes he would lie on the pavement for hours, bloody and grumbling. Near the end of his path he would stop frequently to empty his bladder, there in front of the last houses.

From inside my cousins' front room you would suddenly hear showers. "What's that? It's raining?" the guest would ask, interrupting the conversation. My cousins tried desperately to put a polite face on the absurd reality.

Cossa ze sta? What was that?

> *I am the angel of reality,*
> *Seen for a moment standing in the door.*

✦

A shy, young, sweet-smelling priest passed through Malo, one I already knew and liked. He enjoyed the sound of our bells ringing (he read us something he'd written, full of naive rhetoric), and he loved music passionately. Directing a chorus, a small orchestra, he was transfigured: from his thin frame, his face suddenly flushed with color, came a vehemence that one time even carried me away, when the chorus rang out: *Vespere autem facto, venit cum duodecim / Et discumbentibus et manducantibus eis* . . . It was epic drama in Palestine.

✦

"Did you hear what Don Giocondo did at mass? It was disgraceful! He came up to the rail as if he were about to preach, and instead he lifted his cassock, right in front of all the women, and exposed himself!"

What was there to say to the crazy woman, poor thing, who was indignantly spreading this news? Maybe, "Oh, well, what can you do, we have to be understanding . . ."

Don Giocondo came from a faraway town and was with us only briefly, ad interim. He also acted as the censor, and saw all the films first in a private showing. Gaetano and Totò sneaked up the stairs and crawled into the dark hall, as they often did to see the movies free and uncensored. Don Giocondo usually sat in the second row and didn't notice anything. But unfortunately this time the censor was not alone, there was also another member of the audience, and she was at that moment sitting on the priest's knee.

Here, Gaetano and Totò lost their nerve: although the scenes on the screen were marvelous, the risk was too great, and so they went backward on all fours to the exit, craning their necks to see the scandalous things on the screen, and came back out.

It seems that during Don Giocondo's brief stay among us, he was destined to cross Gaetano's path. It was he who Gaetano—when he one day came suddenly into the kitchen—found racing around our table, arms out to grab Lina, who was also running around the table.

He was a hale and hearty priest with a tough beard: a peasant in a habit. In earlier times he would have served as the hammer to beat the unbelievers, or rather as the anvil on which to pound them, no excuses accepted, like you do with *baccalà*. In our effeminate times, he needed another outlet for some of his energy. There was a partisan here—big, fair-haired, and irascible—and when the war was over and the fun of the "actions" with it, he used to complain that whenever Don Giocondo saw him he was too warm and friendly, he always wanted to hug him with great pastoral zeal and kiss him on the cheek. Finally the partisan lost his patience, and one evening, climbing the stairs to the cinema with his friends and meeting the usual display of affection, he grabbed the priest brutally, like a woman to be subdued, and kissed him at length on the lips. How would my English friends put it? *Well, well, well . . .*

✦

The procession came up from Via Listón and turned on Contrà Barbè in front of a group of spectators at the crossroads. There were altar boys and standards flying, girls in white, the women of Catholic Action, the friars and all the rest, but when the baldachin arrived, swaying back and forth, and under the canopy sat our Monsignor in sumptuous garb with the Blessed, you could feel the air turn electric. Ten meters from us, Monsignor came to a halt and, skewering us with his eyes and clutching the Blessed, began to bellow in a wonderful dramatic voice:

"On your knees!"

The spectators fell to their knees, the procession started up again, and Monsignor and the Blessed passed by. But Ulderico Teodoro, watching the scene from afar as he came out his gate amid the pious prayers and exclamations being uttered by the processionaires, added some of his own that I'd never heard before.

Monsignor, our senior priest, had an activist and combative side, but was well liked. With his cap pushed back like an Ardito, his face grooved with deep, strong lines (thus the affectionate title by which he was known among us) he had the bearing of those dynamic captains who gave us our martial training, cursing and reprimanding us, playing the roles of themselves to perfection. When he would order silence, or command us to pray, or to fall to our knees, there was something military about him—more parade-style than battlefield. When he preached and in the important ceremonies, his gestures were vehement and somewhat extravagant, it was thought. A portrait of him ("Sunday morning,") survives in the voice of an anonymous fellow townsman:

> . . . *e su par le scalete*
> *co quei oci da gato*
> *ghe ze zà l'Arziprete*
> *che fa i sèsti da mato.*
>
> . . . up the stairs he goes
> with those cat's eyes of his
> that's our priest
> acting like a crazy man.

In the privacy of his parish house, the senior priest was quite different, a man of the world and a fine diplomat. During the war, I had occasion to go and speak to him on official business, and I found myself dealing with a shrewd, refined, and courageous man.

I listened to his rhythms of speech ("Now let me put it this way . . ."), looked at the books in his studio, ran my finger over the volumes of the *Lexicon Totius Latinitatis*. The job of a town priest, it seemed to me, had a note of sweet melancholy, and I was as sorry as I could be that it was practically impossible to become friends. When Katia and I were married, not in church and far from Malo so as not to offend anyone, we later went to see him privately. My aunts were making their novenas; he made conversation. Then he blessed us just as we were: two unbelievers and Katia, Jewish.

When the Pilgrim Virgin came to Malo, they then carried her to Marano in a night procession. It is all countryside between here and Marano, with narrow, winding roads that run down to the creeks—Proa, Timonchio, Jólgora. All around, the fields seem to go on forever, and only a hundred meters off the road you feel you're in an archaic, unexplored place, far from the world of maps and paved roads. The procession moved forward by candle light, and the peasants sang:

> *Parce Domine! Parce popolo tuo!*

> Spare us, Lord! Spare your people!

It was as if the Roàn family, the Rana, Maria Scusèle's people and Gegia Càne's, were actually supplicating the Good Lord to spare *them*.

> *Parce popolo tuo! Ne in aeternum irascaris nobis!*

> Spare your people! Be not forever angry with us!

Do not be angry with Sgualdo, with Vacaretto, with Pométi Bèi! Spare your little people of Malo in procession toward Marano, in the middle of the dark countryside!

✦

After the war we encountered the face and the actions of an aggressive new religious dynamism, in the person of a townsman who from time to time returned among us from city life.

He belonged to a typical Church family, with strict morals and members in the priesthood.

It was not an attractive face: the eyes were dark and velvety, secretly sensual, the features regular but vaguely unappealing, there was a modernizing fervor crossed with that particular sort of priggishness called, for short, "seminarian." A singular lack of charity shone through.

The actions were even less attractive. The man wanted to be urbane, worldly: he dressed with great care, although with a certain subconscious inclination for the funereal and the ecclesiastical; he wanted to show us how the things of this world and the things of the faith could be reconciled in a modern way. And so, in the middle of a normal procession, he would suddenly burst into flamboyant prayers and encourage the crowd in other such demonstrations, and at crucial points, fall to his knees dramatically in the middle of the road, getting his trousers all dusty.

You knew that this was not town religion, but merely that of Church families—escaped from the family, however, and trying to become the rule. But the pitiful little avalanche our townsman was hoping to ride, the avalanche of genuflection on the road, didn't carry anyone away.

✦

"No, no, you're wrong. It's not *ten, ten, tententèn, ten, tentèn, tentèn*—that's the second. The third goes: *tentèn, tentèn, tententèn, ten, ten, ten.*"

Serious study of the bells that announce the masses dates back to Gigio-Fiore, who trained the delivery boy from the bakery to reproduce the sound of the third mass on a hand bell, and sent him over to the churchyard one Sunday to announce the mass between two and three in the morning.

As the peals rang out they sounded huge in the night air, and the final *ten ten ten* was magnificent. The delivery boy went back to the bakery to light the oven, and Gigio-Fiore went to hide himself behind the bell tower. After a while, some of the old ladies who were habitués of the early mass began to arrive, grumbling, "It's so dark! So cold!"

Gigio-Fiore was hoping to see Toni Ruaro, who was in charge of the music in church, and who was the special target of the operation, but big Toni, awakened in his bed by the bells, didn't get rattled. "The sacristan's lost his marbles," he said to himself and went back to sleep, and after a while Gigio-Fiore went home. The old ladies shivering in their black shawls were still waiting in front of the church's main door, inexplicably locked.

Chapter 27

THE WAR YEARS DIVIDE the town's ancient history from the modern. My friends in the Compagnia dispersed, and the war played tricks on all of them.

Mino and Sandro, after attempting to escape from forced labor in a Todt camp, were tried and condemned to death. They were put in the same cell, and the hour of their execution was fixed. When they came to get them, the two were there staring at one another with their mouths open; they were made to march one behind the other down a long empty corridor and up to a door at the end. The guard knocked, announced, "the condemned," and pushed them forward. Before a table sat the commandant, looking furious.

"You are two traitors," he said, "and now you will get what you deserve, a volley of lead. But before I sign the execution order, I will give you another chance: return to your cell and write up an account of your miserable lives. And then we'll see."

Mino always hated writing essays in class. Back in his school days, while the others wrote, he liked to build up saliva behind his half-closed lips, and then blow it into a bubble. They were handsome bubbles, multicolored and ephemeral. This time, however, he understood he had to make an effort. He wrote the best essay of his life, pages and pages of it, concluding with the phrase "Long Live Il Duce" in capital letters, followed by three exclamation marks.

And Sandro, poor fellow? Sandro, too, detested writing essays in class. He sat there at a corner of the same table, chewing his pencil, and Mino, carried away by furious composition, paid him no attention. But at a certain point, Sandro made a movement and Mino looked up. Sandro was stretching his neck, shading his eyes with the palm of his hand—in short, he was copying Mino's essay!

It seemed to Mino that all was lost, and so he let him copy. Sandro copied every word, down to the final slogan and the exclamation points.

"Well, I can see you're no rebel," said the captain to Sandro, sticking out his chin, "and out of consideration for you, I won't have your buddy shot either."

✦

In the final weeks of the war, I came home three or four times on my bicycle, during that brief interval between the end of daylight and the start of curfew. I would ride through the piazza and up Via Listón to my grandmother's house, all wrapped up, in the hopes no one would recognize me. One evening I too didn't recognize someone: he was standing very still under the balcony at the corner of the piazzetta, not wearing his overcoat. The person I didn't recognize was one of my peers who'd been hanged from the balcony that afternoon; when he didn't die right away, Kurz had run him through a couple of times with his knife. They had called a group of kids in town, including my brother Gaetano who was fourteen, to watch. He couldn't eat anything for a couple of days.

Of my visits back to town, the most emotional was the first one. I'd been away quite a while, and the strange and various life I'd been leading made it seem an eternity. And then much had happened in my absence, and while I was familiar with other places at night, both in the mountains and on the plain, I didn't know much about the situation in our own town.

My brother Bruno came to get me at Santomìo in the evening and we walked along the track at the bottom of the mountain. Before we got to the Ponte Galline I began to feel uneasy. Bruno, too, had a gun over his shoulder, but he carried it negligently and with the safety on. He was wearing shorts and a shirt of blue cloth, the uniform of his group, for they even had uniforms down here on the plain. Because they were accustomed to circulate mostly at night, and always locally, I knew I could trust my brother—but wasn't he being a little reckless?

"Hey, just a minute," I whispered to him, with the excuse I had to stop and urinate on the terraced hillside—not really even an excuse.

"Now, around here," I said, "are there patrols?"

"Yes, sure there are," said Bruno.

"Well, let's see then . . ." said I, who after all, was the eldest. "Why don't you take your safety catch off? Or, supposing we run into a patrol . . ." I wanted to see whether he had an elementary grasp of what to do.

"Oh, you'll see, we won't run into any," said my brother.

We turned up the path behind Castello. The noise was terrible. I stopped again at the spring, against the wall of the priest's garden. Bruno began to laugh. "So we're feeling emotional, eh?"

Effectively, it was an emotional moment. I could feel two, or three, dimensions intersecting each other: over here you went toward the Fontanella, over there toward Paraìso, this is Castello, that's Montesèlo, the town is down below. It was difficult to superimpose the image of an expedition in time of war on all of this. How absurd it would be to have to shoot on these paths, and against strangers, too: here where we used to play at shooting only with our best friends. I sensed something

I wasn't expecting in my brother's behavior, as when you live abroad, and on returning, feel out of phase with those who stayed behind.

We climbed down to the creek, then up the road past the slaughterhouse to the piazza in front of the church. Here, my brother was good enough to remove his safety catch, and standing at the corner, we looked carefully up and down, although we couldn't see anything at all. And so we crossed the street and the churchyard in total opacity, and arrived at the red gate behind which Aunt Nina was sitting, waiting for us.

"Oh, my dear things," said my Aunt. "Did you meet the Germans?"

No, and obviously if we had met them, my brother in his blue uniform would have seen them off with a couple of big kicks, while I took advantage of another little piss behind the bell tower.

✦

No man seemed more solitary to me than the Man with the Beard, marching up the sidewalk in front of Grandmother's house, at the end of 1944. They tell me he never missed a day; at a certain hour of the afternoon he'd come up from the piazza, along the other sidewalk that coasted the wall of the spinning mill. He walked very, very slowly, gazing ahead sadly. He was pale and thin, maybe twenty-eight years old: a lieutenant of the Guardia Nazionale Repubblicana, he was the chief of the carabinieri station. He wore a small, thin, tired, blond beard.

He did not look like a protagonist of the civil war, more like a victim. Perhaps he hadn't understood anything, like someone who finds himself assigned to one team rather than another in a parlor game that hasn't been explained to him, and then perhaps, at the end, he has to pay a penalty. Or maybe this wasn't the Beard's case. Maybe he had understood everything, and was just resigned to it.

That afternoon walk had a motive; the Beard was courting, silently and with some dignity, a big, strong girl named Radetta who lived over that way. Most likely flattered, but certainly prudent, Radetta didn't even show her hand so much as to appear at the window. The Beard passed by, rigid and discouraged, on his daily procession. I felt I'd like to go out on the street and comfort him.

"I wonder where the Beard is now?" I said to my brother after the war. "You know, the lieutenant of the Guardia Repubblicana, the one who was courting Radetta."

"You didn't know?" said Bruno. "They gave him the big send-off right away, over there, on the road to Schio."

He reminded me of my own lieutenant, first platoon of the first company in my army training course. My lieutenant was much the same: pale, fragile, with a wavy little beard. *String up your officers with the guts of the chaplains:* well, yes, but maybe they should be the officers of the Command company.

✦

We come into town, there's the house, the truck brakes. Home. Rifle goes down on the doorstep, you run inside, embrace Mamma. They're all alive, whole. They laugh, we laugh. The new world begins.

It begins with a hunt for the Germans, who on their way out of town shot Martin, the one who used to wrestle with Bruno, and Esca, who was at school with me, and various others right here on these streets.

Bruno comes in; he's just captured another three not long ago.

"Did you kill them?"

"No."

"Good thing."

We were both ashamed.

The Liberation came to Malo when the partisan leader Tar officially came down from our hills. Tar rode in on a plumed white horse and went straight to the barracks. For three or four days the right-thinking middle class believed that the Revolution they had feared so much after the First War had now really come. There were machine guns and red kerchiefs in the streets; Tar, down at the barracks, sent for the town notables considered suspects, and interrogated his prisoners strumming a guitar.

His shirt open at the neck, a big leather belt, cavalry trousers, boots. He sat sideways on the chair, nicely shaved, hair combed, fresh, relaxed. The guitar lay in his lap; he tried out a chord. From time to time the door opened and two bailiffs dragged in a prisoner. Tar heard the case, played an arpeggio, didn't say a word. Did the music lull his passions, calm his judgment? Or was it just one of his tricks?

This was not in fact Tar; Tar had died that winter in a murky palace conspiracy up in the hills. The news brought immense relief as well as immense consternation. Then in the spring he was resuscitated: it was him in flesh and blood, but juridically he was a reincarnation of himself, and from then on he insisted on being called Tar II.

On the whole, there were few "excesses during the transition period," just a few days of revenge exacted on the *marescialli*, the *brigadieri*, on the big, bony knuckles of innumerable simple carabinieri.

When they came to tell me, "Hey, Tar has put up gallows in the piazzetta," (I was reading a grammar; by now the war had been over for a while) I went with Ulderico Teodoro, then a tall, skinny young man, to take it down, because we felt hanging was, by then, quite inopportune.

The piazzetta was deserted under the sun; from behind the shutters, anxious bourgeois eyes surveyed the bleak symbol in front of Davide's tavern. When we got there, Ulderico Teodoro and I saw immediately that our privileged, pampered hands were never going to be able to knock down a structure that had been sunk into the ground by Tar and his men of the people. How idiotic, to go forth alone and unarmed to take down the gallows, and not be able to take them down for technical reasons.

Luckily, Tar had ordered that the gallows be provided with a rope, and this had been tossed over the top in haste. This gave us the opportunity to do something. Standing on tiptoe we grabbed one end of the rope and pulled it down, then to make ourselves look professional, we wound it up carefully and deposited the coil on the ground by Davide's wall, in front of the weigh station. Then we carried out a table and two chairs and ordered a quarter-liter to drink under the gallows. We were Tar's friends, and acting brave wasn't all that difficult; but to be honest, we felt rather heroic.

Tar was famous for two qualities: his speed and his aim. The aim was remarkable: Tar could hit anything at which he pointed his gun, still or moving, near or far. The speed was even more remarkable.

Once when they arrested him—this was back in peace time—and took him down to the station, Tar, like a powerful spring suddenly released, flew up and grabbed the pistol of the carabiniere on his right, knocked that of the carabiniere on his left to the floor, jumped out the open window (they were on the first floor) and landed in the orchard behind the station. He took off between the fruit trees, shooting at the ripe cherries for fun.

In peacetime he wore a fur cap; during the war, a pith helmet, with long sideburns. After the war he took up beekeeping but continued to have trouble with the carabinieri. From time to time he'd come home on his motorbike and find one waiting for him. Once he persuaded the man to get on the bike behind him, but needless to say he lost him on the road over to the station.

Tar's rapidity when he took aim was beyond the scope of the normal human eye. It happened in some ultraviolet range of motion, his velvety Gypsy eye surveying from on high those sorts of timing we call quick, or speeded-up, or slow motion. I suspect that Tar would shoot and then—while the bullet, kicking off its inertia, lazily moved up the barrel—would begin to point at his target, letting the bullet get halfway out the barrel before giving it an infallible little assist on its tail.

✦

Marzotto's Hangman didn't come from Malo, but he was well known among us here because as a child he had come here on his holidays. There were two Paolos, both out-of-towners, called blond-Paolo and dark-Paolo to distinguish them. The other one, dark-Paolo, also came here in the summer and was the only member of the comfortable classes I knew who could throw a stone as far as the farm boys of Cantarane could. Marzotto's Hangman was blond, shy, and dreamy.

For a few days after the Liberation he had the destiny of Marzotto and his company town in his hands—Paolo and just a few others. In theory it was in their hands for some time after that, but he knew that really, the time to act or not would be brief: a matter of hours, if not minutes.

He watched the minutes go by, and the hours, trying to decide what to do. He went around deeply absorbed among his busy, happy comrades. When the right thing came to him (he looked gloomily at the clock), it was already late, and nothing was done. A few days later, and Count Marzotto was already in a position to hang *them* without consulting any clocks.

Postwar days: an American jeep arrives in the piazza, a G.I. in a helmet gets out and says, "Aahm Sega-toh." And in fact it was my schoolmate Segato, who had emigrated a dozen years previously. It was almost easier to speak to him in English than in *dialec-toh,* but several excited locals began to chatter with him right away. He went to visit the house up in the hills where he was born; had he stayed here, he would have been collecting firewood for a job, and picking up manure on overtime. And instead here he was, full of chewing gum and dollars in his pockets.

With two or three henchmen oohing and aahing, he showed off samples of the civilization across the Atlantic: some were utterly monstrous, like the camera that produced instant prints with which Segato took a picture of Ruaro. You pushed a button, and when you pulled out the already-printed photo you saw a swelling in the mist, and that was Ruaro.

Segato came back a few years later to hand out sales jobs to the henchmen, and to choose, with their assistance, a girlfriend whom he married in a flash. Then he went away—without out the wife—and never came back *again-oh.*

Other postwar days: Faustino turned up one Sunday. He had been a prisoner of the British in Africa, and in fact he spoke English brilliantly, and even taught me some. He said he'd gone lion hunting with a spear, but obviously we didn't believe him. He now lived in Milan, and had come over on a scooter, which he said was his. Two months later he was back on a new scooter, and the third time, in a car, a Topolino. We thought he was renting them, but Faustino casually pulled out the car papers and you could see his name on them perfectly well. The following year he appeared in an Aprilia; this time we asked to see the papers, but the Aprilia was also his. That evening Mino said, "One day he'll show up with a Maserati."

One Sunday in the piazza, there it was: a brand-new Maserati race car. Faustino insisted on showing us the papers, but nobody wanted to look. The rule was simple: whatever Faustino said was true. In Kenya, he had killed lions with a spear, a spear no bigger than a fork.

The postwar period also brought us the novelty of elections. Because the political situation was what, in the Veneto, is considered *normal*, the electoral battle focused on marginal matters, and especially on the problem of the retarded and their escorts.

They come in on wheelchairs, pushed by their escorts. Their heads loll, their lips are twisted, and they make "ih . . . ih . . . ih . . ." sounds. The head of the voting station (let's say he's a relative of mine), sighs, asks the retarded person if he or she wishes to vote, and whether he or she knows how to write and is physically capable of writing. The retarded person continues on making "ih . . . ih . . . ih . . ." sounds, and thus face is saved. The head of the polling station authorizes the retarded person to enter the voting booth, but the escort is determined to go in too.

"I'm sorry, but what do you have to do with it?"

The escort begins to make surreptitious gestures, touches his head with his index finger, winks, begs, by means of grimaces, merciful complicity. Finally he explains himself in words:

"But he can't, come on, he doesn't understand anything, poor thing!"

The retarded person continues on making "ih . . . ih . . . ih . . ." sounds.

The least expert among normal voters are patiently tutored in advance; they practice and practice, and some take the model ballot right into the voting booth with them and copy it slowly, sweating; some bite the pencil violently and give it back in a pitiful condition. Many suck it with vehemence and come out of the booth with violet-colored lips and long mustaches running down their cheeks. *Malo periculosam libertatem:* yes, even in Malo, freedom has it dangers, but at least there's no one shouting from the balcony, "All present for roll call!" and the Stakhanovites of the vote don't fear the punishment of their direct superiors, but do what they do out of a sort of conviction. And then there's always the recreational side; Cencio from the hospital probably enjoyed voting, and from the electoral point of view he is not classed as a voter with diminished mental powers, but as a cheerful biped with a prognathic jaw and a big grin.

And then, for those not comfortable with the printed page, comes the terrible toil of counting up the votes. Once, when at five in the morning no results had come in from an outlying voting station, the town official in charge of the vote went out to see what had happened. He found a pale and messy-haired little crew stammering incoherently, with ballots strewn across the floor and carabinieri stunned with exhaustion. They were informally urged to clear up and get out.

As morning approached in another station in the mountains, they all said "enough!" and stuffed everything into a pillow slip: armfuls of ballots both opened and closed, official statements and scribbled notes. They carried the pillow down to the magistrate in Schio and said to him: "You take care of it."

But as I write, I see that this is electoral folklore from before our new prosperity, and that perhaps it is already ancient history.

Chapter 28

AMID THE GENERAL RENOVATION that has taken place among the taverns in town, Nastasio's, near our house, is one of the very few to hold out. Nastasio, the innkeeper and a hunter, wears a handsome Assyrian beard. When you order a quarter-liter from him, he still goes down to the cellar each time to draw it off fresh.

The Professor—who also had a beard, a great, big Leonardo da Vinci beard, and dark, round, fearsome eyes—patronized Nastasio's tavern. As far back as I can remember he walked hunched over, as if broken into two pieces, moving very slowly but energetically in short, uncertain, wide-footed, choleric paces. His head was briskly pushed forward, as if brandished in front of his body. He sometimes wore a wide-brimmed hat, quite antiquated in style, and his clothes also had something antique about them, traces of lordly nonchalance and refinement, alpaca, raw silk, linen.

Seen on the street on his way to Nastasio's, he could seem a grotesque human object, a gouty knot, from which, however, there emerged a dignity and a force that incited awe. The walk from home to the tavern was tremendously long, a real expedition, although it consisted of a mere fifty meters: two houses and a gate. In his last years the outgoing part of the trip took the better half of a morning, and the same for the return in the late afternoon. When you met him you shouted out, "Good day, Professor!" and it was if you had switched off the electric

current to a complicated machine in motion. That busy traf-
ficking of limbs (occupying a minuscule space but energetic,
acute, and honed, as with certain huge machines that carry
out minute precision work) would suddenly come to a halt
in midstream. The Professor would stop, lift his head sharply,
point his predatory eyes—he never wore glasses—and give you
a vigorous hello.

He spoke slowly, with gnomic diligence and in distinct,
sonorous phrases. His rhythms were different from ours, his
ideas certain and well defined.

"Anyone who doesn't like them"—he was referring to radicchio with bacon—"is in no way a man." He said this to a
visitor in town, who had declined radicchio with bacon at the
tavern.

The Professor drank, on a scale that seemed to us superhuman.

"Before supper—I went to Nastasio—And I drank—Five-
six liters of wine." One day Gaetano and Leopoldo Evaristo
went to find him at Nastasio's in the middle of the afternoon;
he was alone at his table with an empty glass before him, and
on the table there were also—empty—nineteen quarter-liter
pitchers. The boys counted them, and then they helped the
Professor home.

He must have felt lonely; he had broken off all cultural relations with his children. And so he discussed and debated
with the other denizens of Nastasio's—artisans, farmers, and
laborers.

"Because dear Bepi," he would say, "as Ammianus Marcellinus says—in book XXXI of his History—*Carnem inter femora
sua*—you understand, by Gad—*Equorumque terga subsertam*—
Fotu calefaciunt brevi—can you believe that?" It seemed the
Huns "put the flesh between their thighs and the backs of
their horses and thus warm it a little." Meat warmed up like
that, said the Professor, wasn't worth a damn.

The conversation often turned quite lively over the *vino clinto* brought up fresh from the cellar.

"According to Velleius Paterculus . . ."

"Toni Vacareto says . . ."

"Aulus Gellius . . ."

"Checo Schèo . . ."

"Macrobius . . ."

"Onto . . ." "Mucky" instead says . . .

From what I know, the most frequently cited of these foreign personages had long become well-known figures to the denizens of Nastasio's; they probably imagined they were people the Professor had known in his youth in Germany, some Bavarian friends of his. The crowd at Nastasio's knew all about the Professor's friends' ideas and could even quote their most memorable sayings to their workmates. Older mason to his apprentice:

"Up yours, Toni, go to hell. You know what Tertullian said? *Ficùlnea enim prurìjine* . . . You know German don't you? They covered their *itching parts with fig leaves*."

But the Professor's chosen language was not the Latin of the Middles Ages, Church Latin, but classical Greek. He told me so, in what was all but a personal confession, when I was thirteen or fourteen. School had just started up and I had broken a leg trying out a triple jump at the athletics field, and so I spent a month at home. It was one of the most pleasant months of my youth. I had all the new school books, the first "real" French anthology, the first Greek grammar. It was autumn (which I've always liked), and I read and learned as if in a dream, my leg straight out on a chair in the kitchen. It was then that I went limping to the Professor to ask for a hand with the Greek. He listened as I recited the couple of things I'd learned, and then he said to me pensively:

"Greek—Is the most beautiful language—In the world."

As he knew just about all of them, that seemed to me not just a verifiable affirmation, but a true one, and I decided that

I would one day adopt that supreme language, never mind the problem of finding any interlocutors.

They asked the children, "And what does your *papà* do?" mostly to get them to talk, and each responded in turn; he's a doctor, he has a shop, he works in the fields. Last to reply was Cicci, also known as Leopoldo Evaristo, the Professor's second son, who already employed a childish version of the weighty paternal idiom.

"Cicci, and what does your father do?"

"My *papà*—He sits in his study—He smokes—His pipe."

It was a profession exercised with astonishing severity. Nothing came into the life of the Professor that might interfere with his absolute *otium,* his state of perfect ease and leisure— not that which others called work, nor family obligations, nor ambitions. He was a pure humanist, and his study was the rock around which the entire house, its entryway always closed (you rang a bell), the spacious kitchen, the sitting rooms, the big bedrooms, the peaceful courtyard, the sheds, the garden, formed the bastions.

This neighbor of ours was very much the most learned person we had ever known, and he seemed to us even more: a perfect example of *studia humanitatis* cultivated without profit, without purpose, for pure pleasure, and with unlimited scholarly endeavor. Certainly, that library of his was of its time and place; his classical culture, that German academic training, could be dated and seen in perspective. But the man was so much out of history that it's better he remain that way.

✦

With his sons, both of them good boys, the Professor had only rare and brusque cultural exchanges. Here is how things went for Ulderico Teodoro: already several years into the *ginnasio,* he still hadn't gotten up his courage to ask his father for help.

Finally, faced with a nasty big passage from the Greek, he decided that there was no shame in asking, and so he asked. The Professor was understanding, and he fixed an appointment with him in the study.

Ulderico Teodoro appeared promptly and laid the book on the table. The Professor began to read in a neutral voice, and then slowly began to emphasize the phrases, until finally he was declaiming them. "Beautiful prose," he said.

Ulderico Teodoro waited. The Professor, too, waited, but finally he grew impatient. "Well, and so?"

"What do you mean—and so?" said Ulderico Teodoro.

"What is the difficulty here? What do you want from me?"

"I, well . . . I would like to know what it means," said Ulderico Teodoro.

"What?" said the Professor, "you don't understand what it means?"

"Well, no," said Ulderico Teodoro.

"You don't even understand this limpid little passage from Thucydides?"

Ulderico Teodoro shook his head no.

The Professor was enraged. "And what are they teaching you in school then?" he shouted. "Out that door. Get out!"

✦

Leopoldo Evaristo, younger brother of Ulderico Teodoro, also once tried to get his father to help him. It was Latin, a passage that began decently enough, but you couldn't understand where it was going or how it ended.

Leopoldo Evaristo knocked on the door of the study.

"Papà, if you have time, could you help me with a page of my Latin?"

The Professor was in good spirits. "Come in, come in, Cicci. What is it?"

"Livy," said Leopoldo Evaristo. "I can't understand anything, there must be a mistake."

"Livy never makes mistakes," said the Professor.

He began to read loudly, frowned, slowly finished the sentence, and stopping to light his pipe, said: "Quite clear, quite clear." Then he went on reading sentence after sentence, page after page, and every once in a while he stopped and muttered, "Magnificent, magnificent." He read all morning, so absorbed that Leopoldo Evaristo didn't have the nerve to say a word. When the time for the noon meal arrived, the signora called and they went to eat. Eating: it was a key word in that household.

✦

The Professor had literally eaten up his estate, converting his lands, his money, and his house into legendary lunches and dinners with a lofty nonchalance about the future. The gaudy marks of gout seemed to be the direct result of a marvelous youth, during which the Professor spent his days taking prodigious walks on our hills (with his *al-pis-toc*) and his evenings eating chickens.

On rainy days he kept company in his study with Curtius Rufus, the German philologists, a few Anglo-Saxon historians, and the incomparable Greeks. His study was full of magnificent books, well furnished with pipes and matches and with those Attorney brand steel pens the stocks of which had finished during the last war, and which he later asked me to bring him from England.

He had decided he would go in eating and studying like a gentleman, thinking he would be gone before his means were, but instead his means expired. "He must have got his numbers wrong," people said, and in fact, he had gotten them wrong by a couple of decades. Just before the war there was a period when he had to teach for a while in a middle school. The Professor in a school! It was a sacrilege.

"How long has the Professor been drinking like that, Papà?"

"Oh, as long as I can remember; that much, it must be twenty years."

"I wonder why he drinks like that?"

"I'd say he wants to die."

If the mere *reason why* means nothing to my father in such matters, the underlying *purpose* evidently does. The Professor, like the Sibyl of yore, was unable to die, however. His life span was unending and incredible, and unending and incredible were his excesses. It was like a duel with death in reverse, a duel with "that baleful witch," as he himself once called her during a speech at a friend's funeral. He was determined to die in possession of all his faculties, without eyeglasses, with his mind fully lucid: as a man, not as a drooling beast. It took him many, many years, but when his hour came, he did essentially die his way.

Not of lucid mind and with spectacles: that was how the Professor's friend Tenin died, he, too, a reader of the classics, but only in the evening. He lived at La Lòdola, the red villa above Case, and during his last days he lay in bed groaning, seeking more light, and to see better he had a slice of salami placed upon each eye, and thus he received his friends.

✦

"What's become of Count Marietto?" I asked.

"We hardly ever see him," said Bruno. We had three counts: two live across from our house, the third at Santomìo, and this last was Marietto. He was small and lean, a bachelor, with boots and a reedy voice, not much different from that of Bertrand Russell. His secular spirit was private and reserved, marked with provincial echoes of nineteenth-century controversies.

"No, no, I'm not an atheist; I'm an agnostic."

Marietto was not a man of passions: he was sober, peaceful, wise, punctilious, and concrete. He knew about almost everything: mineralogy, anthropology, physics, botany, mathematics, physiology. He was the very incarnation of positivism. He cultivated science; he amused himself, as once upon a time in the country, men cultivated letters. Compare him to a specialist in any of these fields and most likely he would look like a mere dilettante, learned and curious, but a bit old-fashioned. That was the point: compared with the specialist, Marietto was an all-round cultural specimen. All of modern science came (somewhat tardily) to Santomìo, passed through his positivist filter, and became the stuff that nurtured his small person.

His opinions and inclinations were obviously liberal, but his liberalism coexisted with an extreme (and amused) pessimism, an almost naive cynicism about the ignorance of the ignorant, the bad instincts of the lower classes, the bad faith of professional politicians, the reduced cranial cavities of the peasants and hill folk, and in general the scarce reliability of human emotions.

Marietto could make you feel ashamed to read a book of poetry, or to admire the French Revolution. One of the last times I saw him, he was reading a tract on the sensations, including the most tenuous ones, that accompany the main bodily functions. "What are the actual sensations, describable in scientific terms, that one experiences when one is very sleepy, for example, or when one eats with appetite, or with all due respect, when one uses the . . . ah . . . urinal."

He completed his studies with ingenious personal experiments (I found this rather moving), in which he would scrupulously and impartially record the faintest messages that arrived from his fibers and tissues when he "used the urinal."

There was a single concept among us to account for learning and intelligence: *intili-jènsa*, which meant both understanding and knowledge, and in particular to have done one's studies, that is, to have—or to be—*studied,* affected. All young people who had studied without great mishaps were presumed to possess this *intili-jènsa.* Even today there are people (no longer young) on the streets and in the taverns who, when they see someone who has studied, doff their hats and begin the conversation with, "You, who are so very *intili-jènte.*"

Admiration for learning was almost universal, and it was especially marked in those who felt they had an inclination for it which had then been drowned in manual labor—in wine, say, or in oil. Negroponte, who was an oil merchant, adored *intili-jènsa,* and though he considered himself only an imperfect participant, a mere catechism student, he had bought himself an encyclopedia and worked through the contents on his own, in modest bouts of thought.

His reflections would explode in bitter maxims. One morning he stopped Bruno Erminietto in the piazza and in lieu of "hello," said to him:

"Man is a cannibal."

He tempered these severe, discouraging studies of his with an open-hearted love of music (he played the cymbals in the band), and with embroidery, a skill no one knew how he had learned. In a world of brutal devourers of their fellow creatures, he went forth serenely, meditating and embroidering. He sought out the company of beings simpler than man, like his dog Lillo, who had a glass eye and a sweet nature, and like his motorbike (not by chance a Cerbiatto, named after a fawn) on which you'd see him from time to time along the road to San Vito, standing and talking. "Poor thing," he'd say, stroking the bike, "you must be tired too, have a rest."

One evening—this was after the war—the Compagnia (including friends who were quite intelligent and even university educated) went for a stroll down to where the streets and roads intersect behind Castello, and at a loss for how to pass the evening, climbed the branches of a mulberry tree and settled on it like a flock of birds with the idea of using it as an aerial toilet, more for fun than out of necessity. Ampelio, who didn't like the idea, hunkered down under the tree instead. Along came Negroponte with his dog, and he stopped to enjoy the starry night, whistling. He probably wouldn't have noticed anything, but Lillo, the dog with the glass eye, sensed something, saw Ampelio with the other eye, and ran to make a fuss over him.

Ampelio tried to get rid of the dog with some acrobatic kicks, but silently. "What is it Lillo?" asked Negroponte gently, "What's the matter?" Then he went to look and found Ampelio crouched under the tree, and said to him, "my humble respects," with all the regard due to the *intili-jènsa*. The mulberry branches shook.

✦

"There he is!" Felice's neighbor lady shouted, pointing a finger. "There he is! The one who writes up the phony wills!" Felice was watching from his shop.

On the other sidewalk coming up from the piazza, returning from his late morning walk with his umbrella clutched in both hands behind his back, emaciated, bent, and austere, was Count Giustino the notary—a man who had always lived in the irreprehensible isolation of a country gentleman, in the palazzo at the top of town along with the elderly, devout, and distinguished countesses.

When he became aware of the shouting and gesticulations Count Giustino stopped and gazed for a long time, without understanding but also without losing his composure, and then asked very courteously from a distance, "Are you referring to me?"

"Yessir!" said the neighbor lady.

Shaking his head the Count crossed the street and said, somewhat embarrassed, "But madam I—do you know?—I am Count Giustino."

"Precisely," shouted Felice's neighbor. "The one who writes up the phony wills!" And she tacked on a further message to "those four whores" the counterfeiter kept at home.

It was not surprising, if quite unprecedented, that at this point Count Giustino hit her over the head with his umbrella. That she was crazy he only learned later, when he got home.

When the crazy woman got going, she could go on for hours. From time to time Damiano, exasperated by her rhymes and riddles in the courtyard, would wrap himself in a sheet and put on the cap he had worn up in the hills. When he was ready he'd fling open the window, raise his trumpet, and play the authoritarian notes of the second roll call. Unsettled, the crazy woman would remain silent for a couple of hours, and Damiano would finish another chapter of his studies in peace.

There was also another notary, a fellow from Valdagno who came to town on market days. The most notable thing about him was the way he drove his car practically supine on the seat, so that you could just barely see the brim of his hat standing up vertically. What he could see from inside the vehicle one can only guess: clouds, blue air, tree tops, the faraway ridge of the Pasubio.

He arrived in the morning and parked his car in the piazza among the market stalls. Around noon he would depart using a technique that was much admired: lying down in his usual way, he would put the car in reverse and move backward, judging his position by the crunching sound of broken pottery; then he'd go forward, overturning a certain number of stalls, but not more than necessary. His moves were rapid and precise, and after another couple of maneuvers by ear he was ready to leave for Valdagno. Out the window he would say to a broker friend of his, "Close the deal," and then he was off, observing the marvelous clouds on high.

Once upon a time the town professional was a figure largely associated with leisure, his actual business being a mere appendix. When today we see a professional completely taken up by his work, with no time at all for the classics, it still seems very strange to us. *Che fannullone!* say my friends (in Italian, not dialect): "what a deadbeat," a sign of bewildered respect for his industriousness. In the evening he passes in front of the bar, coming from work and on the way to supper, probably ready to return to the office after the meal. We greet him with a touch of unease (for stealing his time and energy for something ultimately so frivolous as a hello) and the brief response that plays on his lips, inaudible, almost comes as a surprise.

There's not much left of the old professional mode. "Diziano!" shouts the substitute doctor from out of town gaily as he comes into the room where ancient Tiziano—old Titian, we would call him in English—the oldest man in town, sits in a corner with his leg shattered, uttering little yelps of pain. "Diziano! A great bbainter!"

The cultural input from other parts of Italy can at times be heard in tiny things. In a Roman accent, you hear the abyss behind an ordinary word that normally goes unnoticed. "When the boar is being chased and can't get away, she turns toward the dogs and lies down. *E aspètta.*" She *waits.* It's like a jump into the void, far from our own landscapes.

The veterinarian who came from Turin many years ago brought a new style with him. Aside from reading Sallust for fun, I think he did just about everything there was to do. He was a model of absolute extroversion: his life was crammed with hobbies, and thus with gadgets and instruments, but these hobbies didn't stem from a passion for something—underwater fishing, skiing, go-karting, photography, ice-skating, ping-pong—but rather the contrary. First the hobby was born and then the enthusiasm for it, which largely involved the external form and the practical organization of the thing.

He was full of zest and threw himself into each new activity with childish enthusiasm, but with all the technical and organizational skills of an adult. The camera quickly gave birth to thick and thin lenses, long-range lenses, filters, time meters, projectors, and screens. The veterinarian made tumultuous use of everything, invented experiments, ran to photograph road signs, doorbell name plates, from a distance of two meters, one meter, with a yellow filter, a blue filter, with a tripod, without a tripod—and then he dropped the entire thing and moved on to target shooting.

He would hold forth on all of this with great joy: the record of the cotter pins he'd changed, the discounts on brake pads, the lens-grinding certificates. You sensed a new social model in him, at least a decade ahead of the rest of town. I wonder if our young people will be like him?

I'm reminded of the Jewish refugee who was here in war time, a small man, very distinguished, Viennese, who read the Greeks, and said over and over:

"All is problematic."

He knew that we appreciated the ontological basis of his great preoccupation, and I hope this brought him some consolation. When he came out of his house he would give three kicks to the sidewalk, spin around, and move off in irregular jumps to avoid the cracks between the paving stones.

Experience in Malo is reflected upon and processed through the spoken word and mimicry, and thus by its nature is fleeting and written on air, but that does not mean it is crude. The genre is almost universally that of laughter—life as comic theater—but expressed so effectively, with such pliancy and richness, that it could make many similar sides of contemporary literature seem dull and labored.

The mimed and spoken performance is rigorously outward; it exhibits words and gestures, doesn't comment or analyze feelings. There's nothing elementary about it; it's rather sophisticated, in fact. The narrator or mime chooses, composes, constructs. That the performance be based in "reality" is essential, but as it gradually departs from pure factual details, there is often a tension between the material truth of the facts, and the elegance of the tale, the purity of the line. In the end, fable and chronicle become indistinguishable; some of our most important personages (often still alive and among us) are by now classic dramatis personae with whom it is almost embarrassing to have a conversation in the tavern.

We also have our artists and creators: Felice in the older generation, and a few decades younger, Mino and Damiano, and perhaps others who are even younger. The relationships linking artist, public, and material are particularly felicitous; we all know the context, the prelude, the characters, the circumstances, the shadings of character, the intonations of the language. Comedy explodes as the form of things themselves, but it is a form that obviously cannot be reproduced in writing, nor preserved except as oral storytelling shaped for a selected audience.

This modest spoken art is dying rapidly, and in recent years, more rapidly than ever. All that one can do is testify that it once existed, and say that a good night at Felice's tavern was at the level of an evening at the Establishment Club in London.

When Felice would "do" Il Duce, it was as if for the brief duration of his performance, Il Duce was really among us. The show was mute and without hand gestures. Employing minute, imperious contractions of his face muscles, the Founder of the Empire arrived in Malo, came into the bar wearing a sweater, sat down at the table next to ours, and painlessly electrocuted us with his predatory eyes.

Felice's head was very well suited to such a part, but the top head in town in terms of pure dimensions was that of the fellow called, just for that reason, Suca, pumpkin. When he went out on the street he looked like he was carrying it in a procession, his pride tempered with prudence, for an incautious movement could easily have sent it to the ground, and then who would have picked it up? Others had large heads, but Suca's blocked the view of the landscape, it altered environmental conditions. If they were all to go out together on a blinding July day, we often thought—Felice in his undervest, Gabriele, two or three others, and if the Maia were also to arrive at that moment from Bassano where he now lives—the town would be cast in shadow, but if at this point in our misfortune Suca were also to leave his house and come outside, we would be groping around in the dark.

✦

Felice also played Count Giustino the notary, in the act of reading a long document that had to do with a townsman nicknamed Pométi Bèi, which was a curious nickname in truth, suggesting red, ripe apples that were however quite small.

We watched the old gentleman prepare himself for the reading nodding and bobbing about; we heard him intone the sentences of the text, aristocratically muddling up the vowels and consonants, coming back time and time again to pronounce the client's nickname. In this solemn context, the sounds of the words so nobly deformed, the name of our fellow townsman rang out, precise and preposterous:

> Ao ao ao ao—also known as Pométi Bèi . . .
> Eo eo eo eo—also known as Pométi Bèi . . .

The branch with its dwarf apples moved back and forth in the shadowy light of the notary's office; a brigade of *r*'s chased the nasal stops, stabbed them with sharp swords and made them explode in the air.

But such things have a form that cannot be described on paper; it's useless to try.

✦

Felice loves his art so that at times he himself has trouble distinguishing between art and life, and happily plays the part, now of the man who's terribly overworked, now of the loving father whose children are indifferent, now of the hardworking, pious citizen. I like to talk to him in the intervals, when he's relaxing backstage. But sometimes practical circumstances can take the upper hand. We all remember, for example, the visit of the three bishops.

Three bishops all at once! Felice had made a special trip to Vicenza to buy colored paper lamps with lights inside, and had hung them in festoons over the tables outdoors. The three bishops were supposed to spend the entire day with us; it was sunny, and we expected a great conclave of visitors from the countryside as well.

Felice was up at dawn to supervise the preparations, one ear out for the arrival of the cars, which were supposed to go straight to the parish house. All of a sudden, there they were! Felice ran outside with a child on each arm, and all three fell to their knees on the sidewalk.

He was dressed (not by chance) in a white apron and an undershirt, the picture of a devout working man surprised by grace in the midst of his honest labors. The dignity of his work, the simplicity of his manners, the spontaneity of his faith: it all shone on his face. His words and gestures prompted reverence in his children, and when the blessed automobiles appeared in front of his shop, he bowed his head and gave a jubilant little smile.

The storm burst out suddenly in the afternoon. Felice, now wearing his Sunday best, didn't even have time to get to the door and look up at the heavens before drops began falling from the black clouds, and in seconds, the rain was pouring down.

"Hurry! Let's get these things inside! Quick!"

Sons and daughters overturned the tables, chased the napkins, trundled in piles of chairs. Felice was standing on a table trying to save the lanterns, but the battle was already lost.

Mino, in the doorway of the bar across the street, caught sight of Felice just then, and it is to him that we owe the story. The table was wobbling and Felice, standing on his toes, was trying to take down the last lantern that still seemed to be intact, round and firm—he could barely reach it. Just then the lantern, which was full of water, tipped sideways, and in a single gush, water poured all over him.

It was too much for Felice. In that moment of legitimate exasperation, the image of the three bishops must have leaped to his mind as the first and basic cause of the disaster. He raised his arms to the heavens and repeated as if he were praying:

"Up yours, Three Bishops!"

And when he had finished blowing off steam, he stepped down from the table and added firmly: "And the whore that had them." They were like brothers to him.

Jokers, the legendary inventors of hoaxes (often spurious or old as the hills, you can find some of them in dusty old collections), the professionally original—all were appreciated in Malo. One branch of this innate theatrical streak found its outlet during Carnival (when we had floats in costume) and during the festival of Mid-Lent, with the trial and the burning at the stake of the Vecia-fila, the witch supposed to be responsible for all the town's misfortunes. The prosecution and the defense spoke from the balconies in the piazza, and made people laugh. Another outlet for these humors of ours were speeches at weddings, baptisms, school graduations. At times, other humors came to the fore.

"Who would ever have thought that our Sante, so skinny, so bashful, so ugly, with those dirty teeth and foul-smelling breath, would have succeeded in getting this sought-after diploma? But, my friends, here he is . . ."

What did the orators in the square denouncing the Vecia-fila in their derby hats and spectacles, have to say? What did the crowd in the piazza laugh at? At times, the comedy was no more than puns and hackneyed jokes, some of which have been passed down an entire generation. With Gastone-Fiore today, I heard one of Righella's today:

"Woe is me! Woe is you! Woe is Bò! Woe is Cow! Woe is Lapo's bull!

Lapo didn't like that last crack at all, that public exposure of his bull, and he stopped speaking to Righella. Lapo's bull was a stupendous animal. Once while they were weighing him on the scales at Piazzetta, he glanced at a heifer standing nearby. No more than a single glance, but the heifer became unhinged, hurled herself at a gallop toward the shop that now belongs to Gastone-Fiore, and went right in through the window.

✦

How wonderful it is when the event collapses, the festival falls apart, when the gusts of chance hit town and everything whirls around.

A game of *tombola* in the piazza, with the novelty of loud-speakers so that the voice of the announcer could be heard all the way to the piazzetta. Feverish repairs at the last minute, a short circuit when the game was already underway, grunts and explosions, numbers sounded now in a whisper, now re-verberating like cannonballs. Then the loudspeakers were struck with a heart attack, there was silence on high and men-acing waves from the crowd. Now there appeared a Man with a Megaphone on the corner balcony, from where he could see the game board and shout out the numbers toward the piazzetta.

"Sixty-seven!" howled the Man with the Megaphone.

"*Cinquina!*" howled a peasant. Bingo!

A huge wave, followed by a black undertow. The peasant reached the balcony and was pulled up, card in hand. Inspection, rejection, semaphore signals. Now the Man with the Megaphone was starting up again:

Not Seventy-six! Sixty-seven! Six-seven!"

"Bingo!" howled another peasant who had a line of four.

Now everyone was howling; there was a great shrieking, rumbling noise, and no one could hear a thing. Everything was confused, all the numbers seemed to have come up at the same time, and for every number that hadn't, another two or three had; everyone was shouting "bingo" and none of the scores were valid. Dismayed, the announcers took ever more incomprehensible initiatives, some gave up and sat on one side of the platform, then some reprobate hid behind the game board laughing and splattering huge tears around, until finally the lights in the piazza went out, and the fireworks started up as if by themselves. The Catherine wheels spun around, and the tumult of the event dissipated into the air.

When the fireworks were over and the lights came back on, the bingo platform was deserted. The crowd, as if roused from a dream, headed home grumbling.

✦

Gigio-Fiore has a little shop devoted to the fanciful. In the summer he likes to fill the window with bed warmers; in the winter, with paper fans; a sign announces "we buy eggshells." Inside he has toys, picture postcards, and all kinds of contraptions.

To the child who comes in asking for a fishhook, Gigio-Fiore says obligingly:

"Simple, double, barbed, or spiral? Number one, number two, number three? Copper-plated, chrome, or zinc? For tench, for trout, or for mullet?"

Then he puts out his hand, takes down the only kind of hook he's ever carried in his shop, and the client feels relieved. But now Gigio-Fiore gives him the price. He goes through all the options: unfinished metal, type of point, chrome plate, surtax, parish duties, authors' rights, jotting down fearful numbers and totting them up. Three, four, six hundred, four and seven, three thousand, four thousand three hundred . . . And looking up at the terrorized child, he says, "five lire."

Chapter 29

BERTO PREPARED THE FIRST skewer of the year, and because he kept on quenching his thirst with wine while he was fussing with the birds, he was a bit drunk this evening. Birds, he says, are almost too easy to sell these last few years. Toss them out the window, and people will eat them on the wing, he says. This is his idea of affluence. As a matter of fact, a skewer of birds is something you prepare more out of professional pride than to make a profit. In normal times, the risk you wouldn't sell them was great.

On skewer Sundays, when Berto was small, at about five in the afternoon his mother would send him out to church with half a lira for Saint Anthony, so that the saint would make sure the birds were sold. Her prayers were not always answered, though, and it would fall to Berto to eat the leftover birds for days and days. Sometimes right up to Friday, and then Berto would get a special dispensation from the Friday fast for compelling family reasons. He says that once while gnawing the bones he broke a tooth on a starling, and he shows us the stump.

It was all a bit like that. Abundance, even merely of food and wine, was something unknown, something the very oldest would attribute to brief, long ago, mythical epochs in which "they watered the cabbages with wine."

Bruno, Guido, and I were engaged in a three-man duel in the courtyard. My mother came to the door of the kitchen; "come here," she said. "Come here all three of you. I have something I want you to see." We went into the kitchen, and Mamma had a piece of colored paper in hand—rectangular, huge—and she said:

"You see? This is a one thousand lire note."

We admired it for quite some time, and then we went back to our duel.

It's almost unbelievable how much poverty there was in town, not only for the sizeable families of ordinary people—it was impossible to understand how they managed to survive—but in just about all classes. The large families of the most indigent have disappeared. There were the virtuous large families and the no-account large families, and the people had opposite opinions about the two, but the practical consequences were nearly identical.

The last ones I know of, the Borboni family, have now left town and set up somewhere else connected to their children's jobs. The sacristy at San Bernardino is empty, the church is going to be restored, the little monument—the pissoir—outside, after all due art historical consideration, was demolished by the same restoration experts who came from the city.

The Borbonis lived in the sacristy, that is, in a single room, but they also occupied, covertly, a piece of the church, where they spent the night. There was a curtain between the altar and the wall, and that's where they slept. Their quarters were very clean, and he in particular cared a great deal about cleanliness, and even tried to keep the street, which was made of packed earth, clean. If a child passing by tossed a piece of paper on the road, he would go outside to shout and run after him. When one of the Borboni children had to write an essay at school on "A happy occasion in our family," he told the story of that evening when his father invited a friend to dinner. It was clear from the text that the other Borbonis—the wife and the innumerable children—merely watched from the side while the two men ate an abundant meal, with wine on the table.

Let us hope that is the last time a child in town considers it a memorable spectacle to see his father eat as much as he wants. Our current prosperity has shifted the perspective.

Essay: "Your family."

"Both my Parents work. My *papà* stays in the shop making Riparazioni; my *mamma* goes around in the car paying Le Tratte." *Riparazioni:* repairs/amends. *Le tratte:* the bank drafts/ the hookers.

✦

In villa Malado fit mercatum in die martis. At Malo they do the market on Tuesday. There was an old man from a town nearby who'd been in the shelter at Schio for years, and he also came to "do" the market. Markets were his great passion: he'd done some markets in his days, when markets were a serious thing! He had laid out his merchandise and sold it with his own words, his sales pitch!

Even after he entered the shelter, his sons, to keep him happy, had gotten permission for him to come down to Malo every Tuesday. He came down on the coach, and without a doubt the cost of the ticket exceeded his profits, and maybe even the day's earnings. He had a little box with one hundred lire worth of buttons, one hundred lire worth of hooks, a handful of shoelaces, a few boxes of matches, and in the proper season, the new year's almanacs.

He invariably set up on the corner next to Mino's shop, and to get people's attention would sing the final verse of the song. "È arivato l'ambasciator" adding a unique falsetto shriek:

Àio-óo! Èio-óo!

The shriek obviously expressed his joie de vivre, his joy at doing business in the world, at doing the market. Yes, but what did it actually mean? Mino asked himself that question for many years. Finally he decided to ask the old man, for as a matter of fact, they were friends.

"Do tell me," he said (we addressed, or were supposed to address, our old as *Voi*), "what is it that you say after you finish your song? *È arivato l'ambasciator*—Here comes the match maker—and then?"

"I say, *àio-óo, èio-óo*, no?"

"How's that again?"

"*Àio-óo, èio-óo*," said the old man.

Mino thanked him and went back to his stall. One Tuesday the old man didn't show up at the market, and later, Mino learned he had died at the shelter. And then one day he suddenly understood: it was about the almanacs, obviously. The old man had been saying:

Lu-nà-rio nó-vo! Quelo vè-cio sul fó-go!

Get your new almanacs here! Toss the old one on the fire!

So that was the message of the "ambassador": "Live it up! Burn what you are no more! Look to the future!" And the old man was the ambassador, the merchant of new times.

Mino also used to receive a well-behaved mendicant, who not only never openly requested money, but each time insisted on playing the part of an old friend of the family who had just happened to stop by. He would come into the shop, inform himself about how "life" was going, and he never failed to ask, his voice whining and shrill:

"And how are things going with your *papà*?"

Because he was deaf he didn't pay much attention to the letter of the reply, only to the spirit, and he'd say:

"Pleased to hear it . . . pleased to hear it . . ."

And then Mino would give him some money. At times when Mino was busy, he found the whole thing somewhat irritating, but he couldn't bring himself to offend the old fellow. So when the usual question came up, he began replying with a cordial smile:

"He's dead, Giovanni, he's dead."
The old fellow nodded contentedly and said,
"Pleased to hear it . . . pleased to hear it . . ."
And Mino's annoyance would pass.

✦

Giacomo Zanella, in his sonnet cycle *Astichello,* explains to the Virgin that our humble people pray to her in the name of that tramp "in whose countenance they see the face of your divine Son." Quite frankly I've never heard of anyone who saw Jesus in a tramp's face. On the contrary, a tramp once made a rude remark at the door and received quite a few slaps on *his* face. He staggered back, and the man who was slapping him followed him step for step; they emerged from the entryway and crossed the street and the sidewalk, until the tramp was backed up against the facing wall, where he took two more slaps, one on this side and one on that.

We almost never see mendicants anymore; the last one of any importance was the fellow who used to come, even fairly recently, to count his money at Franco's. He would sit at a table and build up piles of fives and piles of tens, his week's earnings. And Franco would change them with hundreds and five hundreds, and give him a small percentage. In the past, these "poor things" were very numerous: there was almost a procession coming to the door, men and women, young and old. There were the regulars, who came on a certain day of the week, and the occasionals; there were the ones who got five and the ones who got ten (cents of the time, or *schèi*). You would hear someone saying "Alms!" and you would go and get one of the coins that were lined up on the credenza. When it was a woman or an old man, he or she would be intoning a prayer, and some would repeat it after getting the coin, while others would stop short and mutter rapidly, "May God bless you." As if we deserved a blessing. Some asked for a piece of bread in place of the coin, but we didn't always have permission to give bread.

A beggar collected alms in nearby towns, not in his own, as a rule, but we did have a few real hardened derelicts right here in town, and above all there was the king of the mendicant paupers, Giacomo Golo.

He didn't, as I recall, station himself in one place or another; his station was the entire town. His real activity, it seemed to me, was as unknowable as it was indubitable: a sort of majestic Thing-In-Itself. On the phenomenological level, he carried a stick that he used to threaten children who bothered him, but with the polite ones he would try to speak through his gums, incomprehensibly however, because he had no teeth. His clothes, in shreds, had lost all color; over them he wore a military cape and his feet were wrapped in rags.

One time Guido actually understood one of his remarks, the finale to what must have been an invective against the poor food he had to eat:

> *Sempre ròcoli*
> *stechetoni*
> *cago verde*
> *come rughe.*

> Cabbage, broccoli
> stems like wood
> my shit's as green
> as caterpillars.

The mirth of the drowning. Giacomo Golo was always drunk and had many times been found in the morning asleep in the snow in front of the milk shop. They had to wake him up in order to take the milk canisters in.

There are still some chronic drunks in town, certainly right up to my generation and even somewhat younger, but once there were many more. Gaetano says he became aware of how the town was in this respect only quite late, when he had already begun to go back and forth to Padua. And of course that's how it works: the matter was right before our eyes, but we didn't notice it until we shifted perspective.

Besides the major drunks, perhaps about a dozen of them, there were many normal alcoholics, and many more who would get drunk occasionally on work days, and regularly only on Sundays. The numbers of those officially dead of cirrhosis of the liver were not large, but there were many considered to have "drunk themselves to death." Of course some quit drinking near the end, usually quite late.

Sopèlo, still alive and in the shelter, was drunk for many, many years before he was admitted. Intelligent, unemployed, and lame, he drank practically without interruption. There was an almost ascetic discipline to his drunkenness. An excellent weaver, unlucky with his wife (those were his words), he decided one day to leave his job forever so as to be able to get drunk more freely, albeit with fewer means. It was a way of life, a vocation openly chosen. Sopèlo withdrew to the cloister of wine, happily rejecting the world and its pomp and circumstance, patiently accepting the hardships, and with great good humor, the arrests and prison. Deaf both to blandishments and threats, incorruptible, he lived his own way, immediately drinking up any money he managed to scrape together. When he wasn't in prison he would fall asleep wherever sleep came to him. Sometimes it came to him in the piazza, and before putting his head down he would sing at length.

Below the drunken cheer, there was a note of perfect and almost painful joy in his voice, especially toward evening, when he could savor the satisfaction of having brought another day to a near close. Of course, when he had been chased out of a bar, or couldn't find an old friend, if only for a silly game of billiards, or when Zac-zac put a hand on his shoulder and said "Okay, let's get going!" life must have been hard for him too. Zac-zac was our *maresciallo,* and when people went awry, *zac-zac!* he'd toss them in jail. There was also a carabiniere first class down there who was always grinning and saying things like, "Nossir—it's my beard and I shave it myself."

When Zac-zac wasn't around, Sopèlo lay in the middle of the piazza at midnight, innocently airing the jubilation in his heart, his arms and legs sprawled out. A woman came by to protest, but Sopèlo, sparkling with glee, shouted, "You cow! Whore!" and the woman went away.

Of course there were times when he wanted to die, but mostly for technical reasons, such as the fact it was impossible to procure a quarter-liter early in the morning while in prison (he used to say it wasn't so bad in prison, the carabinieri were kind to him, but the torture of that quarter-liter in the morning was like dying every day)—that and the trouble with his overcoat. This overcoat was almost indispensible in winter so that he could sleep under the bridge at Proa, but some *tùsi* had taken it away from him, and so he was forced to sleep in haylofts, and the owners bothered him because they feared he would steal something. He was terribly disconsolate in the mornings at times; you would find him there on the town hall steps quite early. He'd sit there rubbing his eyes, saying, "I've had it, I'm really fed up."

✦

The landscape of the piazza can never be the same now that Ranarolo is no longer with us. It's strange to think that for the very young, he's probably only a vague memory. He would hunker down on one side of the piazza or the other, changing position morning and afternoon, depending on where the sun was. He had short, bristly hair and his skin was yellowish and wrinkled. What did he think about, hunkered down by the wall hour after hour? His face, like that of a redskin, was strangely not without its beauty; it suited this creature who heard all and said nothing, this sort of mummy of the mind. He was probably ashamed of being imperfect, of not being a man (because he was a *nuco,* a eunuch) and preferred a life without comment.

Remo, the other ancient caryatid of the piazza, is still with us, his pipe and cap; it's been years now since he had a bout of Saint Valentine's fire, otherwise he's the same.

There were two Ranarolos; they had a shop in which they sold various things, and on Friday, fish. This fish seemed to be the same each week, and the buyers anyone can remember were few. Just by a hair, Katia was not among their small number, for when she was new in town one Friday she approached the stall with the thought of buying something, but watching the continuous drip that fell from the nose of one of the brothers handling the fish, she changed her mind.

The Ranarolos were, however, clean people, and they swept their shop and kitchen very punctiliously. Pushing the heap of dust toward the door that opened on the stairway to the cellar, they would open it and sweep the rubbish down the stairs. In time the steps leveled out and became a ramp, and according to Mino you could slide down it, or as he says, *rissigare. Rissigare!* How different that is for us from merely sliding: it means the dark strip of ice in front of the fountain, the sprinkling of snow crystals, the danger, the flying clogs.

Flora once, wanting to be kind, went to buy some butter from the Ranarolos. It was chilled, and Flora wondered why that was. She later learned: inside the cylindrical hole on the floor that was the toilet, an arm's length down, there was a little niche in the plaster, and if you left the butter there it stayed cool.

Chapter 30

WHAT BECOMES OF A GENERATION organized in Compagnie, as the years go by? Some of us leave town, others get absorbed by work and family, the nucleus loses its magnetic force, the meaning of everything changes without us even noticing.

You can see, though, how strong the ties of the past were by the way we continue to seek each other out. Few pleasures are as great as that you feel seeing such friends when you return to town, be it every Sunday, or once a month, or in summertime, or just every once in a while. You find that you still think these friends are the most pleasant you've ever known, that they are the people you'd most like to spend your time with—and yet you also sense it's all close to being a habit. Sometimes it seems we are friends because we *were* friends; often we don't have much to say to one another except to talk about when we were friends. The events of the past become a real cult, and when we're together in the evening, we never tire of repeating tales and anecdotes from a repertory that by now even our wives know by heart.

At times you sense the glimmer of a thought springing up in the minds of those wives, especially those who didn't grow up around the Compagnia. You almost fear that one of them, distracted, will open her mouth and say, "Oh, I'll tell you this one." That would be a disaster, for our stories are not just amusing tales, they are "true stories," history-fable. You sense they're part of a repertory, inevitably, but you also sense the thing-that-happened, and that is the secret basis of our little world, a form of memory a priori that is the basic convention of even the most extravagant stories. "I was there" is always the underlying presupposition, or at least, "He told me so himself," which is very different from "I've heard it said." This the wives know very well, and they hear us out with great self-discipline. They must also know something more, I'm not sure what, for the smiles on their faces are peculiar.

The interest we continue to have in such old friends even touches the real person somewhat. These men growing old in a dry goods shop, a tavern, or an office are still in part projections of a Mino, a Sandro, or a Guido of yore. At the heart of these remnants is Mino, my old desk mate at school. Year by year he's watched just about all of his closest friends leave town one by one, and watched the others disband. He lives right in the center of town, and all the departures seem to depart from him; he feels he's in the middle of something that's breaking apart, and complains that every year he is more alone. Mino is the great chronicler of our generation, a man with an irresistible feel for the comic, and when we go back we spontaneously gather around him.

We meet at Davide's Place (now Franco's) in the morning. In the evening we usually go to Berto's (he took over from his father quite a few years ago). Quite a few of our peers now occupy—at least in name—the position of their fathers; the houses, shops, taverns, bars, and small businesses have become ours. You could say that what once seemed to us to be the *town* is now ours. But there's less to it: that authority brought to bear inside a household, in the space of a shop, in a shop window or a warehouse, seemed far more interesting before one had it.

Some find this state of affairs distressing, and their pallid faces, the bags under their eyes, launch accusations against the strictures of town society. The tavern keeper perhaps dreams of a more refined occupation: in an office, for example (in our day that was the height of refinement). The one selling dry goods, it seems, had only one wish in life—to fly. Some continue to dabble in ambitions they've long abandoned; once they'd dreamed of being a real painter, musician, or singer. Perhaps it has always been this way. From the cupboards, from the cracks of the wall behind the shop counter, old sheets of paper with a few bygone verses or an ancient piece of prose periodically emerge. We recognize the handwriting of some strange great uncle or second cousin long dead, and underneath a date—July 17, 1924—we see a faraway effort to give shape to something witnessed from a shop doorway, while we were still infants:

> Now a violet tempest
> comes whistling in from Schio.

But wait, is this really the original verse, or something I wrote myself, thirty years later? I, too, have seen these tempests arrive, and they really are like that: violet and whistling. So many things are made and remade through the generations, at times better, at times worse.

Things get exchanged, decanted: "I was there," no longer means "I was there," but "Here, there was . . ." The doings of a toothless uncle are similar to those of a nephew who still has a mouthful of teeth, sometimes even identical, so that at a certain point we no longer know if we are speaking of the uncle or the nephew, where one ends and the other begins. Some of us have the habit of saying *What's-his-name,* and for the most part we know who we mean, although sometimes we don't. Does it matter? Yes, for some things it matters a great deal, but in those cases we don't say *What's-his-name.*

Our friends who have stayed in town are all distinct individuals, but would it make any difference from my present point of view if they were to exchange roles? And if we all exchanged roles? Is it Berto who flatters his clients, or is it Gastone-Fiore? However you look at it, one of them treats the clients badly.

"*What's-your-name,* give me a coffee."

"Coffee, no way. Grappa for you today."

Silence.

To ennoble a job you haven't really chosen you can try to emphasize the artistic side. The perfect innkeeper is a figure that doesn't exist in town, but he can try at least to suggest the outlines, working with the muscles of his face and widening his eyes. One of the tavern owners in our fathers' generation also played to the artistic side, but not in the same way. To amuse the company at a nuptial banquet he stuffed a towel soaked in blood between his legs and with his voice, imitated either the bride who'd been broached, or a Female in a more universal sense, the ridiculous Bleeding Woman.

Some friends withdraw into their particular forms of recreation; people here do not yet make a net distinction between life and entertainment, as they do elsewhere. One repeats sweetly his brief maxim, "Women, women" (but using a figure of speech), making it clear by his very tone of voice that what matters is quantity, the multiplication of coitus, the sum total of women, and you sense in him the austere pragmatic pessimism of the man who has understood that all the rest is vanity.

Another is a hunter, one of the three or four hundred in town, about whom I keep trying to explain to Katia that she must absolutely not wish them good luck on Saturday night. Someone once thought to say "Good hunting," to Tano who was roaming around with his rifle the night before the season opened, and Tano opened the season—shooting low, however, only at the legs. The hunters in town are terribly nervous. They have scarcely hit a thing in years; only three or four birds circulate in the area annually, and these are regularly pulped under heavy fire in the first hour of hunting. For the rest of the season, even a sparrow is cause for excitement. The hunters gather in their confraternities. "We could use another war," they say moodily, "in two or three years we'd have some game once again."

The hunting instinct runs deep in Gastone-Fiore. In childhood he could communicate mysteriously with the sewer rats, he'd call them with a kind of bird whistle and they'd come. His friends would say, "Gastone, call them," and the frightened rat on top of the wall would run down the other side. But Gastone-Fiore would lift his hand to impose silence, and begin to whistle softly. Slowly, at the top of the wall, there emerged the paws, the pink snout, and then the whole rat; it would hesitate, seeing so many people, and then following the thin, tuneless whistle would come down the wall like a sleepwalker, cross the street, and come to a docile death under the quick feet of Gastone-Fiore's friends.

✦

Something like the collegiality of the past is temporarily recreated during our outings, the summer excursions to the swimming pool, to the mountains or the sea. Last year Nino walked out into the water off Sottomarina, between the second and third sandbars. He doesn't know how to swim, so he does his bathing upright. After a while he wanted to go back to shore, but high tide had arrived, and he could no longer touch bottom between the sandbars, although he is quite tall. He didn't like the idea of calling for help, and so he decided to return by walking underwater, on the Adriatic bottom, bouncing up every once in a while to take a breath, until he arrived at the second sandbar, and then went down again. Of my friends, he's the only one to have crossed the sea on foot. Nino has always been quite reserved, and when he drinks he becomes taciturn, and does various impossible things in silence: uproots trees, climbs up the marble capitals on our Via Crucis. You lose sight of him for a moment, and then you see him up there, in a trance.

Our fastest excursionist (and a superb consumer of pastries) is Sandro. He leaves early in the morning, keyed up by the prospect of the long trip, riding fast, his eyes trained on the asphalt. Schio, Valli, la Streva, Rovereto; there's the lake, there's Torbole. Sandro stops in front of a pasticceria, looks at his watch. One hour and ten minutes. An average of sixty-three. Pastries. He races out, heads toward Desenzano, toward Brescia (his average rises), he arrives in some really faraway place, perhaps in Lombardy or Emilia. Another pasticceria, another stop. Average: seventy-two. Pastries. He pays with his mouth still full and begins the return trip, speeding so as not to lower his average, riding with his eyes on the asphalt thinking about the pastries he'll eat tonight in the piazza.

He's the most ingenious man in the province of Vicenza. When you need to repair, to nail, to sharpen, to thread, to prime, to couple, to drill—if there's something to twist, to split, to sharpen, to partition, to extract, to shake, to reduce, you only need call him. He has two or three small tools in his pockets, like miracle lock-pickers, and when he needs something specialized, they do the job in a flash. You sit down at the bar and talk for a moment, then ask, jokingly, "Well then, Sandro, have you finished?" and Sandro says, "Here you go," and hands you back a beautiful piece of work.

✦

Those who have gone away come back at irregular intervals. Guido, who works in an office at Bassano, loses his touch when he's far from town; he'll just tell jokes, if you let him. He knows every joke in the world; they come to him from distant places in a matter of hours. It's a shame to fritter away time with jokes, though; we want to hear the story of Greta Garbo, who when she disappeared into the icy water at the Cinema San Faustino *faceva le lune,* "made moons," as Guido was the first to notice. Everyone makes moons in the water, but the best were those Gelindo made when he sank with the pig's slaughter board in the Livargón: the board tipped over and Gelindo fell in and there were these graphic *lune.* Dino told us about them many times (the expression is his invention and the town is in his debt for it) along with Gelindo's other friends: we'd never seen *lune* that fine, at any rate until Guido noticed those of Greta Garbo, which were excellent.

Bruno Erminietto teaches in Bologna, and from time to time goes to Karakorum or to Abyssinia, but he always comes back here to tell us how it went. From the time he was just a boy, he'd meet girls on a beach or on a train, and they'd become quite famous. Before he got married, they would even give him their photographs, and only later did he identify them with public personalities—from the Eleonoras of yore, right down to the latest Monicas. Everybody likes him; he's discreet and fortune shines on him.

A few, we hardly see anymore. There's one fellow in Schio who they say lives for word games, or rather syllable games, and when he bids you good-bye he says, "Bless Gesino Bambù" instead of "Gesu Bambino," the Christ Child. He says he hates the Communists because they'd like to fire him. "And why should they fire you?" It seems he does nothing all day long.

The lorry drivers, the van runners, the three-wheel men, and even the cyclists bring news to us of another fellow who lives not far away. They ring the bell when he's not at home, and his wife lets them in. The first had gone to deliver a package, and the word spread, and by now just about everyone who has a means of transportation in town has visited. Her husband's the one who in his time "ruined" a couple of girls here in Malo, and people say it serves him right.

Piareto passed through town briefly some time back, after many, many years; we hadn't seen him since he was a boy, in fact. Mino saw and spoke to him, and he tells the story. One day he met Berto in the piaza, and Berto said, "Piareto's come to town; he's over at my place, at the tavern, why don't you come and say hello?" Mino went right off. When he entered the tavern, however, the room was empty; there was no one but little Stefania who was pulling the cat's tail, and in one corner, an old man eating.

Mino was silent. And so, was it Piareto?

"Yes, it was."

O my chevalier! Good Lord.

We get together and perfect our stories, observe what happens. We all bring Mino news of the world. Bruno Erminietto tells us, laughing, the latest developments in the great contest between the Migmatists and the Magmatists, in other words, the key to understanding many things about Italy's current scientific culture. I no longer remember which side Bruno's on, but I do know that many play double agents, pretending to be a Mig but in their hearts working for the Mags, or vice versa. We've been following this battle for years, and the university where our friend teaches is one of the strongholds on the Italian front. In one of the halls, they found the scrawled words, "No Pasdaran." But who was holding the line against whom?

Then my brother Bruno the judge tells a story about one confounded witness who remained sitting in the courtroom through a long hearing. There was no more need for him to be heard, and Bruno, who was presiding, said to him, "You may go; yes you, who so rudely didn't stand up when you were called on. You may leave." The witness let himself down the legs of the chair and went off crawling on his chest, using his elbows as oars. Lacking any legs, it was the natural way for him to depart, and for a moment it seemed also natural to those present, they were all paralyzed and it took a while before

Bruno shouted out, and the ushers, released from their spell rushed to lift up the witness and carry him out.

And the negotiations to get Sonny Liston to fight somebody-or-other in Milan? Faustino is in charge of these, and he tells us where they stand. We wouldn't be surprised if he himself were to face the black heavyweight, maybe in Piazza Duomo or in his living room. A black man also showed up at the woolen mill where Gaetano works, but he was from South Africa, however, inside a bale of pressed raw wool. Imagine the scene as they were packing the wool: great haste, confusion, a man falls into the packing machine. "Holy shit! Oh, well, never mind. Come on, hurry, wrap it up." That evening a black man was missing, but no one took any notice; there are many of them. And so this fellow showed up here among us, whole but badly flattened. When they opened the bale eleven workers fainted and the wool was pretty much unusable.

We bring Mino small bits of news from the world. I talk about how you return from Sicily at night, in a car. You drive and drive, always in a northerly direction, toward the high plains just visible in the first glimmers of dawn. What high plains? The *high* plains. The roads are empty, and all the rest is just about invisible: hidden hills and dales, ups and downs, curves, everything comes in waves. We kept on going, faster and faster in the black MG, toward the north, toward home, passing Campania, then Lazio, then Abruzzo, sawing off the knots of the valleys. The dawn twilight went on for hours, it didn't seem to want to change, and it was still half-light when we reached the high plains and saw, in the distance, not the flatlands of Emilia, but the ashy cone of Mt. Etna. What now? It's thus that you return from Sicily by car.

Mino collects our news, and then we ask for news ourselves.

Our elders continue to die; the most we can do is tell stories about how they died. Last year Mino's uncle Erminio was in the hospital; it was clear he wouldn't come out alive, and Mino went to visit him every evening. Erminio had arranged to lie where he could see, from the window, the roof of his house beyond the garden. He was despondent, and they were trying to cheer him up. The man in the bed next to him, a peasant, now on the mend, was telling stories about World War I on the Carso: he'd lost his helmet, he was standing in the trench, and all around him the air seemed to be buzzing with darts, with arrows. He could feel them passing through his hair, lifting tufts of hair from his head, but he had come back without a scratch. You could see it was an effort for Erminio to smile. The peasant, sitting on the edge of his bed, explained he was very satisfied indeed. That morning he had received a letter from his son in America, full of good news. "I'm very satisfied," he said, "I feel fine. There's just this tiny pain, right here, in my head . . ." He put his hand on his forehead and keeled over dead.

All forms of life die, and so it is natural (if hard to believe) that it also happens in Malo. There's no escaping the fact that something new is being born here; at first it seems merely inane, freakish, and then we see that it occupies the streets, the taverns, and the houses, it has become the foundation of the town—and the freak is us. We laugh to hear the girl in the piazza, mocked by Dino on account of her boyfriend, rail against "that old guy, Meneghello!" But really, there's not much to laugh about.

"The babies," as they will always be for us, are now quite grown up. The male generation under thirty is mostly tall and reedy, like Balocchetto, or my cousin Roberto. When they gather in front of the bar, they look like the children of a new race that must have taken over the town after the war.

One can't help but feel sympathy for these young giants: they look better and are better at getting things done than we were. In competitive sports (when they play) and in games, they are negligently unbeatable. They don't wear themselves out the way we did, with bike trips, competitions, expeditions, rows; they are more languorous, more restrained. The new mayor is one of them: he has an open, appealing face, and I don't think he'll do a bad job administering town affairs.

✦

New things arrive and become second nature in the interval between one year and the next. One year when we came down from England, Lina, who did the cleaning, wanted to know whether I preferred *bongiorno* or *tortora*. I didn't have the courage to tell her that I had never tasted either (I imagined she was talking about new products that had come out in our absence) and so as not to offend, I told her to prepare both. Two TV show hosts, they were.

The girls have adapted to modernity; many of them work, and you can see they are more capable than their parents. Businesses are changing too, and for the moment, prosperity is the mother of invention. New forms of enterprise emerge in which all is rapid, smooth, and practical. There's great confusion too: at times the new elegance and cultivation are mixed with the old plebian ways. It's not change as we might have imagined it; it takes its own course.

"What do you think of Cardinale?" yells the hairdresser (the daughter), who's lovely to look at but has a grating voice. Under the hood, Katia, not knowing what kind of cardinal this might be, makes vague negative gestures. The hairdresser (daughter) turns to the other hood and asks, screaming:

"What do you think of Gauguin?"

From under the other hood comes a shout in two beats:

"The landscapes yes! The figures, no!"

The hairdresser (mother), whispering, you can just make out the words reading her fine melancholic lips: "I like the figures as well."

The girls of Malo were always quite beautiful. Now they've become elegant as well, and they paint, and study languages (usually not Italian, however; people ought to be warned, while there's still time, that Italian is not a spoken language). We watch the new conscripts come up every year.

A friend says to me as we pass Marta on the street, "Last night I sucked her titties." You could dream about worse things: Marta is spectacular this year, and her little sister is also worth dreaming on. What sort of dream? Connected with the fluty overhang of her lips, the way they form a crooked point.

At noon the most beautiful girl in town comes forth regally, accompanied not by a page, but by a younger girl I haven't seen before. They stroll along, the princess and the child, without speaking; there's something like tension in the air; they stop, turn, and go back a few steps; it's like a ceremony. The perfect beauty of the most beautiful girl in town is unusually vivacious; she's manifestly excited somehow, almost vehement. What's happening?

My father smiles. "Oh, look at that, the sisters are quarreling," he says, and he calls them by the comical nickname by which their father was known. The old verities, growing pallid under the bright summer light, are turning upside down. The piazza circles around once, twice, as if the world were spinning.

✦

And then there are the children coming up. I watch them play the American Civil War. A Northerner, leaving his companions behind, gallops toward the enemy front. There's a moment of reciprocal embarrassment, then they confer rapidly:

"Are you all by yourself?"

"Yes."

"We're going to slaughter you!"

"Try."

They try, boisterously and confusedly, but it ends up in a massacre: a pile of dead Southerners belly-up among their horses. The Northerner trots off slowly on his plastic mount.

This was the first time I had heard Enrico, aged five, speak Italian. This language of the movies was quite appropriate to the occasion: you saw those wily scoundrels trying to get information from the enemy ("Are you all by yourself?"), the ingenuous hero giving them his candid reply, and that premature, lowdown shout of triumph. That "Try" like a line out of a Western, cool-handedly lighting the fuse.

The children are exposed to mass communications like all the rest, but these influences, I suspect, are processed through translation. "Look, look," says Enrico the first time they take him to the cinema with his elders. *Si bèccano!* They're pecking each other! And in fact the actor was ardently kissing the actress. A good cinema critic would not merely mock celluloid kisses as an involuntary parody of hens pecking, but would try to probe the depths of things flattened on the screen, showing how the human kiss is like all those things that peck and sting: the snake, the nettle, the tarantula's dark bite.

Enrico's linguistic problems are similar to those I had at his age. He had gone to Vicenza with his mother, Annamaria, and he was listening enchantedly to two ladies speaking Italian in front of a shop window. "Hey," he said to his mother, "what language is that those two there are talking?" Annamaria was very embarrassed and decided she would give him lessons in Italian that very evening. She explained her plan to him carefully, and then she said, *Siediti,* "sit down." *Diciassette,* replied Enrico grinning, "seventeen." Comes after s*edici,* sixteen.

Annamaria just gave up.

I've heard Enrico recite *Le campane de Masón,* which I had almost forgotten.

Din dòn dòn
le campane de Masón.

Le sonava tanto forte
le bateva zó le porte.

Ma le porte ze de fero
volta la carta ghe ze un capèlo.

Un capèlo pien de pióva
volta la carta ghe ze na rosa.

Una rosa che sa da bòn
volta la carta ghe ze el limón.

El limón bòn da magnare
volta la carta ghe ze el mare.

El mare e la marina
volta la carta ghe ze na galina.

Na galina che fa cocodè
volta la carta ghe ze un Re.

Un Re con due sergenti
volta la carta ghe ze du denti.

Du denti e un masselaro
volta la carta ghe ze un peraro.

Un peraro che fa bei piri
volta la carta ghe ze i sbiri.

I sbiri che ciapa tuti . . .

Ding dang dong,
the bells of Masón.

When they ring, they ring so loud
Bim, bam, they knock the doors down.

But the doors are made of iron
turn the card and there's a hat.

Yes, a hat that's full of rain
turn the card and there's a rose.

Yes, a rose that smells so sweet
turn the card and there's a lemon.

Yes, a lemon that's good to eat
turn the card and there's the sea.

Yes, the sea and with it the shore
turn the card and there's a hen.

Yes, a hen that goes cluck-cluck
turn the card and there's the King.

Yes, the King with two sergeants
turn the card and there are two teeth.

Yes, two teeth and one molar
turn the card and there's a pear tree.

Yes, a pear tree that makes nice pears
turn the card and there's the police.

Yes, the police who grab us all . . .

It pleases me greatly that Enrico, who's Nino's son, knows these things. They come to him through Annamaria, from my Aunt Lena who was his grandmother (his grandfather was my Uncle Checco, and Mino, who married Flora, is his uncle). His lives on Via Chiesa, and this year he'll go to school, like all the good *putèi,* the good children. *Putèi:* could be *puti* in a poem.

> *I puti che zuga la bala*
> *volta la carta ghe ze na cavala.*

Na cavala che trà de culo
volta la carta ghe ze un mulo.

Un mulo che tra de cao
volta la carta ghe ze un pao.

Un pao col bèco rosso
volta la carta ghe ze un pósso.

Un pósso pien de aqua
volta la carta ghe ze na gata.

Na gata che fa i gatèi
volta la carta ghe ze du putèi.

Due putèi che fa ostaria
volta la carta la ze finia.

Yes, some kids that are playing ball
turn the card and there's a mare.

Yes, a mare that hauls from behind
turn the card and there's a mule.

Yes, a mule that hauls from the head,
turn the card and there's a turkey.

Yes, a turkey with a big red beak
turn the card and there's a well.

Yes, a well that's full of water
turn the card and there's a cat.

Yes, a cat that's having kittens
turn the card and there are two kids.

Yes, two kids playing *ostaria*
turn the card, and the game is done.

Ostaria is also a game of course: it was already rare in my day and I don't think anyone in town plays it anymore. It's still with us as a word in a nursery rhyme.

✦

There are times in the evenings when all of a sudden we don't know what to do with ourselves. Ciùcia, born in 1922 and now drunk, would like us to understand that Tito is not the real Marshal Tito—they kept him in Russia and sent back a fellow who looks like him. He explains this theory three, five, eight times. The women are over there in the dark watching the *telly;* the men are getting bored under the neon lights. At the table in front of us a friend gulps down another thick sandwich and tries to flirt with a young woman. After a while the girl begins playing solitaire and she's evidently thinking, "Go to hell old man." The old man is winking at her; you can hear his patter, and it's not very clever.

Even the pleasure of being together has vanished. One or two play a tired game of table football or ping-pong. What are we doing here?

Chapter 31

A STRANGE EVENING AFTER our football game yesterday. We went for a walk up to the top of town, Mino and Nino, Katia and I, talking about this and that. The town was half-empty, the temperature was in the fifties, and after the rain a beautiful clear sky had come out. There was tall grass growing along the sidewalk that leads up to the Count's house. Brunoro used to have it removed but this year he died and nothing has been done. We stopped along the wall in front of our house. While we talked, we began to rip down advertising posters. Katia and Mino were absorbed in the job, the way one is when one is feeling dissatisfied. You could see it especially in Katia: the haste, the silence, the suspended judgment, as when one wants to press on a boil, or use a fingernail to lift the scab on a cut. Nino realized that there was a corner of a poster unattached at the top, where only he could reach, and that if he pulled it down carefully, off would come two, three, four posters side by side, a whole wall of posters, a neighborhoodful of posters. He pulled down the edge, and together we all began to detach posters. There was a crack and we had a wall of colored paper in hand, and we put it down on the street, and then, somewhat regretting what we'd done, we crumpled it up in pieces and threw them over the Count's wall.

In the cool of evening we walked down to the piazza, not saying much. Beyond the Castello bridge, along the deserted boulevard lit up by new streetlights, we sat down on a bench.

Mino told us how one evening recently he had come here to enjoy the cool, and had heard the distant rumbling of two motorbikes, surely those of the kids who live up in the hills. They all have motorbikes now. One of them was coming down from Monte Piàn at racing track speed; the other was coming up from town, at the same speed. Mino calculated that they would hit each other right in front of the bench. And in fact they hit each other in front of the bench. There was a pool of gasoline and blood in equal parts. Mino also pointed out to us the hole in the cement on the other side of the creek, which Guido had bet he could hit with a stone inside one year exactly. They came here daily after their meal, and Guido threw his stone, one per day. They began on January 1 and kept going through late autumn. On the third of December, Guido hit the hole in the cement, and the bet was decided.

We didn't know what to say to each other anymore. Above us was an old-style streetlamp, the only one left with its plate on top among all the new ones. "We must give it a fair chance," I said, "just one small stone for each of us, and sitting down." I threw my stone, a bit to the right, then Mino, a bit to the left. Then it was Nino's turn and there was a little bang, and it seemed that a globe full of darkness had exploded. We laughed for a long time in our embarrassment, and then we got up and left. *Volta la carta la ze finia.* Turn the page, and the game is done.

This book comes from inside a world where the language that is spoken is not written; it is a report by one person from Malo to those Italians interested in hearing it, and it is written, necessarily, in Italian. I haven't attempted either to translate or reproduce the dialect; rather I have transported some words and constructions from the dialect where it seemed necessary, and always guided by the criterion that these "transports," these leaps of mine, should be understandable to the Italian reader from the context.

Had I written only for my fellow townsmen (as for one moment I thought of doing), the book would have come out somewhat less ungainly perhaps, but only those of us from Malo would have been in a position to read it. It would have been pleasurable to work in complete freedom, following unfettered the inspiration of the only language I know well, and historically speaking it would have given me great satisfaction to compose the first literary document in the Malo vernacular. Besides the practical difficulties of addressing such a narrow audience, there was the greater problem that such a book would have seemed somewhat pointless to its readers, given that here in town we already express these things orally.

It would be quite a different book if it were addressed only to upper Vicenza province readers. Indeed, almost every sentence would be different in upper Vicentino. My method has been to consult a single source—what I know—and only on rare occasions have I verified my data with fellow townsmen. Often, I found that when asked to define our usage, even the clearest, most elegant speakers would fall into manifest error. I came to the conclusion that in terms of knowledge of the living language of Malo, I am no less authoritative than any other source. In some cases I've deliberately maintained forms that might appear philologically incorrect when these were the forms that I know, and which I therefore judge to be alive.

Possibly some fellow townsman will judge the authenticity of certain expressions and the legitimacy of certain transports to be inexact. As the transports are of my own doing, I consider that here, I'm the boss. In other cases, I must say that to all of us, including myself, the written transcriptions of words we are accustomed to hear and not see often seem strange and inauthentic. But I don't think it will be difficult to persuade any Maladense of the authenticity of every word I have written down, if I say it out aloud to him or her.

Subject	Cause of Death	Page
Anzoléti	God	9
Roberto	Gastroenteritis	9
Unnamed infants	Nasty little men	10
Little angel of Capovilla	Subdivision	11
The Author's unlucky double	Bad luck	13
Nursery school children I	Lost hearts	28
Nursery school children II	Broken hearts	28
Consumptives	TB	passim
An Pan	Malediction	56
Mino	The Author's bite	64
Moro Balào	Truck	74
Balài	Cancer	74
Human race	Lìpara, sioramàndola	80
Green grasshopper	Brown grasshopper	81
Brown grasshopper	Swimming meets	82
Brombóli I	Natural causes	82
Brombóli II	Soup	82
War dead	War	82
Soga	Fall from War Monument	83
Brombóli III	Saint Ubaldo	83
Ciupinàra	Knife	84
Viper	Drowning	85
The Author's enemy	Arrow with poison fang	85
Silkworms	Swallowing	86

Subject	Cause of Death	Page
Companion of the Author	Plane tree	89
The Maia	Gastone-Fiore	96
Kittens	Water holes	113
Upper Malo landscape	The Author's melancholy	117
Malo population	Explosion of "la Pisa"	121
Rabbits	Sharp blow	122
The Author's generation	Fall into manure pit	122
Kid from the mountains	Sàura	126
Parish priest	Meneghello, the priest	149
Neighbor	Scythe	150
Grandparents	Old age	154
Aunt Gègia's relatives	The usual	156
Pharmacist	Shotgun shot	157
Killer of pharmacist	Aftermath of prison	157
Carabiniere	Fender/radiator	176
Officer	Austrian artillery	176
Pèrin	Rope	179
Bruno	Uphill, bicycle	193
Pompeo	Spring	199
Giovanni, son of Cattinella	Roundup	217
Signora Orsolina's son	Electric current	226
Lice	Pickax	243
John the Baptist	Big sword	256
Thief of Bagdà	Crucifixion on the left	256
Unbelievers	Saint Paul	256
Mino and Sandro	Execution, rifle	276
Peer of the Author	Kurz	276
Man with the Beard	Aftermath, Liberation	279
Three Germans	Brother of the Author	279
Right-thinking middle class	Gallows	281
Marzotto, Count G.	Blond-Paolo	282

Subject	Cause of Death	Page
The Professor	Victory, duel	293
Tenin	Not enough light?	293
Rat	Bird whistle and feet	321
Greta Garbo	Insufficient buoyancy	323
Black man	Packing	325
Erminio's roommate	Tiny pain	326
Southerners	Northerners	329
First motorcyclist	Second motorcyclist	336
Second motorcyclist	First motorcyclist	336

In a book like this one it is often assumed that the author has "thrown in" various people known to him, perhaps disguising them somewhat. In this book there are no real people, apart from those to whom I've given their real names. Every other person is entirely fictitious. Obviously even fictitious people have occupations, children, shops, habits, nicknames, etc. Distributing these and other characteristics among my nonexistent fellow townspeople, I've taken pains to avoid involuntary coincidences that could cause displeasure. My subject is the things of Malo, and among the individuals, only those who are dear to me or whom I find sympathetic. It would be pointless to search for any others in these pages; they are not here.

I am one of you and being one of you
Is being and knowing what I am and know.
—Wallace Stevens, "Angel Surrounded by Paysans"

Chapter 1

3   The "Inno dei Fascisti," as posted on several websites devoted to Fascist songs, opened with the words *all'armi,* ("take up your guns") and not *alarmi* ("beware, watch out"):

> *All'armi! All'Armi! All'armi! Siam Fascisti,*
> *Terror dei comunisti.*
> *Noi del Fascio siamo i componenti . . .*

> Your guns! Take up your guns! We are the Fascists,
> Terror of the Communists.
> We are the Members, the Members of the Fascio . . .

4   The Arditi ("the bold") were Italy's World War I storm troopers. After the war, Fascist extremists were so known.

5   *Vibralani:* As a child, LM imagined that this verse of the Fascist song "Fischia il sasso" spoke of a valiant race of men, the "Vibralani." In fact, as he explains, the actual words were *Vibra l'anima*—"the soul throbs," and the *freni* (brakes) should have been *freme,* "flutter."

> *Vibra l'anima nel petto*
> *sitibonda di virtù;*
> *freme, Italia, il gagliardetto*
> *e nei fremiti sei tu.*

> The soul throbs in the breast
> avid for valor and for might;
> flutter, O Italy, your flag
> and in the fluttering there be you.

7   *Impueracts:* "Impure acts," the Catholic Church formula for sexual misdeeds. *Atti impure,* or in LM's childhood term, *Atinpùri.*

11   clay pit: In this courtyard, a local artisan made ceramic pots of the clay (*Jura* [Milan: RCS Libri, 2003], 214).

11–12   Bisa was another popular name given to cows in the time and place LM writes about.

12   *bai da tabacco:* In this case *bao* is a worm—or a weevil as the tobacco pest is called in English. More on the nature of *bao* in chapter 5.

12   Castello: In the part of Malo known as Castello, nothing remains of the town's ancient fortress. It may have been destroyed in a thirteenth-century Guelf-Ghibelline conflict, says the Wikipedia entry for "Malo"; no mention of it is found in any documents after the year 1311.

Chapter 3

27   *panaro:* The board on which cooked polenta was poured for serving; also, figuratively, "backside." In his dream the old lady's cheek (behind?) he has to kiss is tangled up with a lined and worn wooden polenta board.

28   artless infant souls: Italian *l'anima semplicetta,* a reference to Dante's *Purgatory,* Canto XVI. "The soul is simple, unaware" in Allen Mandelbaum's translation, line 88 (London: Everyman's Library, 1995).

28   *Schiti:* Of this dialect word for bird droppings, LM wrote that he loved the way "it expresses the acid, oily, yellow and greenish, meager and caustic" nature of those excretions (*Jura,* 195).

29   "you could see all the way to Venice": Something you didn't ordinarily get to see (in this case, all the way up their skirts). *Fiori italiani* (Milan: Rizzoli, 1976).

31   *Orca miseria:* A euphemistic variation on the oath *porca miseria,* "pig-poverty" or "swine-poverty" that perhaps carries with it the faint memory of the impoverished damning their state of destitution. *Orca miseria* does not have the hard edge of a curse, and as LM explains in *Maredè, maredè* (Milan: RCS Rizzoli, 1991), the expression merely means "gosh!" or "bad luck!" or "can you imagine?"

31   *broda, brosa:* A skin affliction that looks like a scab. Although LM does not give the medical name, he is evidently referring to impetigo (*Pomo pero* [Milan: Rizzoli, 1974–2006], 161n).

Chapter 4

38   Nick: The dialect word *guzzare* literally means to turn on a grindstone; it also refers to sex.

Chapter 5

41   Arquà Petrarca is the town where the poet Petrarch died.

44   *Infuria sale o grandine?* From Eugenio Montale's "Motet XIV."

45   "man-locked set": The phrase is from Wallace Stevens, "Angel Surrounded by Paysans."

Chapter 6

50   Edmondo de Amicis's popular, sentimental nineteenth-century novel *Cuore* (Heart) had a chapter called "From the Apennines to the Andes" about a lad who emigrates to Argentina to save his ailing mother.

50   *balilla:* A boy aged eight to fourteen in the Fascist youth organization.

54   *dugare, zugare:* Italian *giocare,* to play.

54   "salt in the milk": According to LM, grandmothers mixed salt and sugar in equal parts for the treat "milk and sugar."

55   *Bando bandìa . . . :* Lines one and two are nonsense words.

55   *schinca:* In *La materia di Reading* (Milan: RCS Libri, 1997), LM says this could also be called a "body-swerve."

56   *Aliolèche . . . :* nonsense rhyme.

57   *All hits pay:* In Borèla, a game of marbles, LM explains in *Maredè, maredè,* players would vie to call out how the shot would be scored. If the shooter yelled *Boni capi,* he had the right to another turn if he made a hit; if his opponent beat him to the punch and hollered out *Gninte boni capi* first, it meant no rights to extra turns. Theirs was thus a rule of law based on who hollered first.

57   Santa Libera: The parish church of Malo was dedicated to the Virgin, there known as Santa Maria Liberatrice.

57   "losing your turn": *Brusa* is the expression in dialect, and it refers to a state of play when a player's stone lands on the lines traced on the ground, and "the player is grounded for one or two rounds, as if in purgatory," says LM. Kan-Pa-Nón, is "a lovely, dreamy game, especially when the little girl proceeding up the squares pushing the stone with her foot, bends down to pick it up and puts it on her shoulder or her head, moving along with her little load through a gentle land of signs and symbols."

Chapter 7

61   *Ostia:* Commonly used oath on the "host," the Communion wafer.

61   *Piccola Italiana:* Girl's Fascist youth organization member, the feminine equivalent of the *balilla.*

62   The Befana is the Twelfth Night witch who dispenses gifts to good children.

Chapter 8

63   *dans d'immenses efforts:* From Baudelaire's "La Cloche Fêlée," where the poem speaks of a soldier under a heap of the dead "striving fearfully" to die. Thanks to Giulio Lepschy for this point.

63   *lìpara, sioramàndola:* Mythical beasts in the peasant/childhood imagination, closely related to the viper and the salamander.

66   *Pa-fiò-san-sìa:* LM says of this expression: "in cases of urgent need to go out to play while praying, or faced with a rush of fear before great danger, the Sign of the Cross was abbreviated in a rapid counterclockwise circular motion of about 195 degrees and the words, 'In the Name of the Father' etc. were shortened thus." An abbreviation of *In nome del Padre, del Figlio e dello Santo Spirito.*

67   *pande, pandere:* Dialect, to confess.

Chapter 9

70   the *salto a pesce,* the "fish dive": Extreme, like a fish out of water (Francesca Caputo, in *Luigi Meneghello, Opere scelte* [Milan: Mondadori-I Meridiani, 2006], 1635).

73   "Innertube": LM uses the term *Càmera Dària* (*una camera d'aria* is the inner tube of a car tire), which he explains in a note means the rubbery substance from which the inner tube is made.

76   "And the French are Chickens": For "chickens" LM writes *pandòli,* which means "stupid, good for nothing."

Chapter 10

82   *brombólo:* The name of this insect, a beetle, varied greatly from town to town around Vicenza, LM notes.

82 War Monument: The names were inscribed in alphabetical order in two columns, thus Zanella and Vanzo at the bottom right; Agosti at the top left.

83 il Dente del Pasubio: A mountain peak on the Austrian-Italian border in northeast Italy, site of pitched battles in World War I.

88 *Dio-Dio:* "God of a God," the ultimate taking in vain of God's name.

Chapter 11

90 Achaean-Finnish: Here, perhaps a reference to the great Finnish runners of the 1920s and 1930s such as Paavo Nurmi.

95 Maia: In *Pomo pero* LM refers to Il Duce's great defect, *la maia pelata,* his big, bald cranium.

Chapter 12

102 Pietro Badoglio: What if any relationship LM intended between this name and Marshal Pietro Badoglio (who signed an armistice with the Allies in 1943, then fled the country leaving Italy in turmoil) he doesn't say.

103 *sul campo da lor,* "on their own field": This may have been a corruption of *sul campo d'alor,* "on the field of laurels," says LM.

106 *Tinfo,* a deformation of *tifo,* means typhoid, but also the activity of supporting or rooting for a sports team.

Chapter 13

110 *Sacramèn:* On this oath LM explains (*Maredè, maredè*) that there were even nicknames for the act of cursing itself. "He let out a stream of curses": A stream of *ostie* (blessed hosts), *pòrchi* (pigs), or *sacraménti* (sacraments).

112 *Val di Là* literally means "that valley over there," "yonder valley." It perhaps brings to mind the Italian word *aldilà,* which means "the next world," the hereafter.

117 Eugenio Montale, "Gerti": "Do you ask to hold back the silver bells / above the town and the hoarse sound / of the doves?"

119 *Pelagroso,* a diet overwhelmingly based on cornmeal polenta meant that pellagra, caused by a niacin deficiency, was widespread in northern Italy. In a late nineteenth-century survey by

the Direzione di Agricoltura del Regno d'Italia, 30 percent of peasants in the Veneto region had pellagra.

120 *La Pisa,* a local name for the nearby Villa Muzani, a Palladian mansion destroyed by an exploding powder house on March 25, 1919.

123 *Libera nos amaluàmen:* A corruption of the Lord's Prayer, "Deliver us from evil, amen."

123 "police-search": LM uses the term *rastrellamento* (*rastrellare*—to rake, to comb), which is imbued with the memory of the methodically deadly Nazi roundups in Italy between 1943 and 1945.

125 Cardinal Gaetano De Lai, born 1853 in Malo.

125 Basadonne: The name, which does not seem to refer to any historical figure, literally means "lady-kisser."

125 About Giacomo Golo, see below, p. 312.

Chapter 14

133 LM (*Maredè, maredè,* 75–76) professes his ignorance about these fabled, now extinct occupations that he heard of as a child. He wonders what the *scoattìne* did with the *scoato,* the broom? And how the *ingroppìne* made *gròpi,* or knots? Francesca Caputo (in *Opere scelte*) and other sources confirm that the *scoattìne* immersed their hands in boiling water and used a small heather brush (broom) to clean away incrustations on the cocoons and find the end of the thread. The *ingroppìne* were charged with retying the silk thread when it broke.

134 "went to pot": *Andare a vacca,* the Italian expression, means to slack off, become indolent; also the terminology for silkworms that failed to thrive.

134 *Filò:* A wake, a vigil, or nighttime gathering, usually in a stable.

135 *vino clinto:* Veneto wine made from an American variety, the naturally occurring hybrid known as "Clinton." After the devastating phylloxera blight of the late nineteenth century, resistant American varieties were introduced in northern Italy.

135 Hannah Arendt, *The Human Condition* (Chicago: University of Chicago Press, 1958) distinguishes among labor, work, and action.

142 but always *ji* ("yee"): Thus, Meneghello's own nickname Gigi (Gigio in dialect) became Jijio. (Giulio Lepschy, personal communication.)

Chapter 15

147   "Of the seven, the most welcome of days!" Here LM takes a line from Giacomo Leopardi's pensive "Saturday in the Village" (*Questo di sette è il più gradito giorno*) and layers it with sharp irony.

Chapter 16

159   Hermes Trismegistus: A Hellenistic Egyptian deity, hence the concept of "hermeticism."

160   Catholics were taught that they should despise the Protestant emphasis on the word of the Bible. Even reading the holy book was a sin.

161   "Beni, you dirty dog, you": LM reports that the expression *can de l'ostia* suggests: "So, you're still hanging in there. I'm happy for you but don't forget that I know very well what a raunchy type you are," where "raunchy" meant both dodgy and sympathetic.

Chapter 17

168   *E la pace del mondo, o gelatina!:* LM explains that the real verse from the Fascist "Hymn to Rome" was "e la pace del mondo oggi è latina" (And world's peace today is Latin), but *oggi è latina* was heard as *o gelatina*, "O Jelly!" (The "Hymn to Rome," lyrics by Fausto Salvatori, music by Giacomo Puccini, was composed in 1919 and later adopted by the Fascists.)

171   *turnichè:* Italian pronunciation for a "tourniquet" curve, a hairpin turn.

172   "Wuthering-Heights": In the original these are *orridi-della-frica,* a local name for "horrible" plunging gorges, from the real gorges named Orridi della Fricca northwest of Malo.

172   The British company Standard and the French (Clement-)Bajard were two early twentieth-century car makers. I owe this information to Giulio Lepschy.

Chapter 18

176   *Orcocàn:* A euphemistic variation on the curse *Porco-cane,* "swine-dog," it means "Holy Cow!" or "Heavens!"

176   "Wait here for me": LM is playing on the reputation of Gabriele
      D'Annunzio, poet, dramatist, adventurer, a man of verbal extrav-
      agance not known for being laconic.
177   Count Francesco Baracca was Italy's foremost military pilot dur-
      ing World War I.
178   promoted *littore:* Between 1934 and 1940, the Fascists held com-
      petitions among promising young intellectuals and artists, the
      Littoriali della Cultura e dell'Arte. LM won the award in the cat-
      egory of "Fascist Doctrine" in 1940. Years later, he used to joke
      that he was still the title holder, having never been superseded.
      (Personal communication, Giulio Lepschy.)
179   "a squadrista of the first hour": An early supporter of the Fascists.

Chapter 19

184   *Voi:* The polite form of address *Voi* (as distinct from the informal
      tu) was imposed by Mussolini in preference to the formal *Lei,*
      which had been popular in northern Italy, and which is nearly
      universal in Italy today.
185   *lo stilo:* A pike or spear; literally "the stylus." Derives from Latin
      stilus, stake or pale; also, a pointed instrument for writing on wax
      tablets. A term in the bellicose spirit of D'Annunzio, likening
      stabbing and writing.
188   wood-burning engine: During World War II when gasoline was
      scarce, some vehicles were converted to burn charcoal.

Chapter 20

197   Catholic Action: Association of lay Catholics, under the watch
      of the Italian bishops, seeking to increase Catholic influence in
      Italian society.
197   *metoikoi:* In ancient Greek cities, these were resident aliens.
200   *Io-porco/porco-io:* Colloquial pronunciation of *Dio-porco* or *porco-
      Dio,* an oath on God's name, literally "pig of a God."
204   "The light of evening, Lissadell": From William Butler Yeats, "In
      Memory of Eva Gore-Booth and Con Markiewicz."

Chapter 22

215   Between 1870 and 1929, women married in church had no legal
      matrimonial rights. The Lateran Treaty and Concordat of 1929,

signed by Mussolini and Pius XI, gave church marriage legal status.

216   *Alfa-Beta-Gamba-Svelta:* The recitation of the Greek alphabet (*alfa beta gamma delta . . .*) as an Italian might hear it. *Gamba svelta* means "fast leg," a speedy runner.

218   "Whore! Sow! Pig!": In dialect, all these curses are words for "sow." LM (*Maredè, maredè,* 180–81) tells us there are five different dialect swearwords devoted to the female pig, considered the most shameless of feminine creatures.

219   The Latin word *fornix,* meaning vault or arch, is the root of fornication.

221   Luana: A Polynesian maiden played by Dolores del Rio in King Vidor's 1932 film *Bird of Paradise.*

221   *Manu turbare* is sometimes held to be the root of the word "masturbation."

223   The concept of "ideal eternal history" from Giambattista Vico's *New Science.*

223   Coupling: In his *New Science,* Vico writes of *concubiti incerti* or *vaghi,* which could be translated as "erratic coupling" meaning unregulated intercourse, versus the development of human marriage, defined as *concubiti certi,* "certain coupling" from which "certain" fatherhood could be inferred.

225   "The madhouse . . .": From William Empson's poem "Let It Go."

Chapter 23

231   "We must love . . .": From W. H. Auden's poem, "September 1, 1939."

Chapter 25

244   *puìna:* Veneto dialect for ricotta.

247   Virgin in heaven "body and soul": The Assumption of the Virgin (her bodily ascent to heaven) was declared Catholic doctrine by Pope Pius XII in 1950.

249   *Sa tulì su na manà de sàbia:* In the Italian edition, LM expressed in Malo dialect what the townspeople knew about hell from their catechism lessons.

253   San Gaetano (Saint Cajetan), born 1480 at Vicenza.

255   *i sequèri:* From the Latin *si quaeris miracula,* "if thou seekest miracles."

255   San Luigi Gonzaga (Saint Aloysius Gonzaga), born near Mantua in 1568.

257   Grand Council: The Grand Council of Fascism was Mussolini's governing body.

258   *cardini* means "hinges" but also "fundamental principles."

Chapter 26

268   "naive rhetoric": In the Italian text, LM compares the priest's naive rhetoric to that of the *Astichello,* a sonnet cycle by a nineteenth-century abbot and poet from Vicenza, Giacomo Zanella.

270   "thus the affectionate title by which he was known": Probably Battilana, or "Wool-Carder." In the Italian *donde si feo il soprannome* alludes to Dante's *Paradiso,* Canto XV, where the poet explains the origin of his own surname. (Thanks to Giulio Lepschy for this second point.)

270   This verse, LM tells us, begins: "Sunday morning / the cock crows—the hen shits."

Chapter 27

278   The Guardia Nazionale Repubblicana was a military police corps created in 1943 by the Fascist government of the Repubblica Sociale Italiana. While fighting the anti-Fascist partisans, they also murdered civilians.

279   "They gave him the big send-off": That is, they shot him.

280   "Tar" was the nom de guerre of Ferruccio Manea, commander of a partisan brigade active in the Italian Resistance around Vicenza. A natural anarchist "born and raised among the wretched of the earth . . . his real enemy was the Law," says LM in *Bau-sète!* (Milan: Rizzoli, 1988). There is also a fondly ironic portrait of Tar in LM's *Piccoli maestri* (Milan: Feltrinelli, 1964) (*The Outlaws,* trans. Raleigh Trevelyan [London: Michael Joseph, 1967]).

280   "Tar II": After he spread rumors of his death and then reappeared, he called himself Tar the Second. Thanks to Giulio Lepschy for clarifying this point.

280 In the Carabinieri, the Italian gendarmerie, the rank of *maresciallo* is roughly equivalent to warrant officer, and *brigadiere* to sergeant.

282 Count Gaetano Marzotto, the wealthy, all-powerful owner of the woolen mill at Valdagno, and later, an important Italian industrialist. The town revolutionaries of the time dreamed of overthrowing him.

284 "the political situation" considered "normal" in the Veneto: The region voted overwhelmingly for the Christian Democratic party (DC). In the early postwar period, the DC swelled its vote by recruiting in hospitals, mental asylums, and convents. Italo Calvino wrote a celebrated story, "The Watcher," about a poll watcher at a voting station in a mental asylum.

Chapter 28

288 Latin author Ammianus Marcellinus in his *History*, wrote of the Huns that "they eat the roots of plants and the half-raw flesh of any kind of animal whatever, which they put between their thighs and the backs of their horses, and thus warm it a little." Trans. J. C. Rolfe (Boston: Loeb Classical Library, Harvard University Press, 1939–50).

289 Onto: A name in dialect, meaning something like Mucky, Greasy, or Filthy.

289 *Ficùlnea enim prurìjine:* Tertullian writes that Adam and Eve covered their "sexual itching with fig leaves." LM uses the dialect pronunciation for the Latin *prurigine*. To an Italian ear *ficùlnea* brings to mind *fica* (dialect *figa*), the vulgar term for the female sex organ.

292 *al-pis-toc:* Alpenstock walking stick.

298 "the boar that waits": Here LM may be playing on the rather indolent way a Roman speaks, suggesting perhaps a wholly different kind of inactivity than that which the verb "wait" would connote in northeast Italy.

300 Establishment Club: A London nightclub famed for satirical shows.

304 The Italian game *tombola* (not the same as the British tombola) is much like bingo.

Chapter 29

310   *Lu-nà-rio nó-vo!* The same sort of almanac seller, same cry, is captured in Giacomo Leopardi's poem of 1827, "Dialogo di un venditore di almanacchi e di un passeggere."

314   *tùsi,* young people: According to LM, "No one ever understood who these *tùsi* were. People who went around at night?"

315   Saint Valentine's fire, *mal di San Valentino* in Italian: Epilepsy. I'm grateful to Francesca Caputo for this information.

Chapter 30

322   Malo has its own Via Crucis, leading to the church of Santa Libera.

323   *faceva le lune:* "Made moons," meaning, probably, that she produced bubbles when forced underwater. In the 1929 film *The Flesh and the Devil,* Garbo falls through the ice and drowns.

323   Gesino Bambù: The man's lame joke on Baby Jesus's name means something like Jesus Bamboo Junior.

324   "O my chevalier": From Gerard Manley Hopkins's "The Windhover," where the poet is addressing Christ.

324   Migmatists and Magmatists: Two schools of thought in early twentieth-century geology.

325   Liston: Sonny Liston became world heavyweight champion in 1962.

327   Mike Bongiorno ("good-day") and Enzo Tortora ("turtle-dove") were two popular TV show hosts. LM thought perhaps they were breakfast pastries.

327   Cardinale: The film star Claudia Cardinale.

330   The magic way "The bells of Masón" transforms one thing into another in each couplet cannot be fully appreciated without the end rhyme. But making the couplets rhyme in English means sacrificing the literal content of the poem, that mix of people, animals, and things dear to the rural world out of which the couplets come.